JOURNALISM ETHICS GOES TO THE MOVIES

JOURNALISM ETHICS GOES TO THE MOVIES

Edited by
Howard Good

ROWMAN & LITTLEFIELD PUBLISHERS, INC.
Lanham • Boulder • New York • Toronto • Plymouth, UK

ROWMAN & LITTLEFIELD PUBLISHERS, INC.

Published in the United States of America
by Rowman & Littlefield Publishers, Inc.
A wholly owned subsidary of The Rowman & Littlefield Publishing Group, Inc.
4501 Forbes Boulevard, Suite 200, Lanham, Maryland 20706
www.rowmanlittlefield.com

Estover Road, Plymouth PL6 7PY, United Kingdom

Copyright © 2008 by Rowman & Littlefield Publishers, Inc.

British Library Cataloguing in Publication Information Available

Library of Congress Cataloging-in-Publication Data

Journalism ethics goes to the movies / edited by Howard Good.
     p. cm.
   Includes bibliographical references and index.
   ISBN-13: 978-0-7425-5427-6 (cloth : alk. paper)
   ISBN-10: 0-7425-5427-9 (cloth : alk. paper)
   ISBN-13: 978-0-7425-5428-3 (pbk. : alk. paper)
   ISBN-10: 0-7425-5428-7 (pbk. : alk. paper)
  1. Journalists in motion pictures. 2. Journalistic ethics. I. Good, Howard, 1951–
   PN1995.9.J6J575 2008
   174'.90704—dc22

                                                                2007021581

Printed in the United States of America

∞™ The paper used in this publication meets the minimum requirements of American National Standard for Information Sciences—Permanence of Paper for Printed Library Materials, ANSI/NISO Z39.48-1992.

This book is dedicated
with gratitude, respect, and affection
to Joe Saltzman,
the very image of a colleague

CONTENTS

HOW TO USE THIS BOOK

One expects a set of instructions for a chain saw or another potentially life-threatening power tool, but instructions for a book? Well, it seemed to us that given this book's unique and innovative approach to journalism ethics, both in terms of tone (engagingly conversational) and primary sources (movies), a few words on how to maximize its usefulness in the classroom might not be amiss.

The twelve chapters of the book each deal with a major ethical issue as dramatized in a movie: *Absence of Malice*, *Shattered Glass*, *Wag the Dog*, and others that, though perhaps lesser known, are no less provocative. Even a quick glance at the table of contents will reveal the wide range of topics, from war coverage to reporter-source relations to crime news, that this book examines. What it can't reveal is the sensitivity with which they're examined. The contributors to the book, all of whom have experience teaching, not just studying, ethics, draw instructive parallels between the ethical predicaments of the movie characters and those of real-life journalists. They also specifically address many of their comments to journalism students, often sounding as if the students were sitting right there in front of them.

Although no traditional textbook, *Journalism Ethics Goes to the Movies* is intended for classroom use. A semester-long ethics course can easily be designed around it, or instructors in any journalism course—news writing, copyediting, the history of journalism—can pick and choose among the movies and chapters as best suits their needs. Want to give students a glimpse of what it's like to be an editor working under deadline pressure? Then show them *The Paper*. Looking for a way to convey the basement atmosphere of the founding era of network news? *Good Night, and Good Luck* fits the bill.

Class time may seem too limited to allow for watching a lot of movies, but it isn't necessary to watch all the movies in class itself or even all of a movie. It's perfectly feasible to select off the menu of a DVD just the specific scenes mentioned in a chapter. In fact, the Image of the Journalist in Popular Culture, a project of the Norman Lear Center at the Annenberg School for Communication, University of Southern California, is offering a free DVD compilation of movie clips to use in conjunction with the book. Visit its website at ijpc.org for details about the offer.

To make the book even more teachable, it includes questions for classroom discussion and/or reaction papers, as well as suggestions for further reading and ideas for class projects. There's also an annotated list of other movies that students, whether majoring in journalism or public relations or something in between, would benefit from analyzing.

Ethics courses have been prevalent in journalism and mass communication programs for a quarter-century now. Yet 69 percent of newspaper editors recently surveyed disagreed with the statement that "Today's journalism graduates have a better understanding of ethics than graduates had five years ago." If journalism ethics education must improve, and it must, then here is one place to start.

INTRODUCTION

When I got in checkout line 11 at Stop & Shop, a boy with blond hair was ringing up items while another with brown hair bagged them, but when I actually reached the counter with my cart, the bagger strolled off on break.

Uh-oh, I thought.

My wife, Barbara, usually does the bagging, but she wasn't there. She was at home, resting in bed with a broken foot ("From kicking you in the ass?" a "friend" had wondered out loud). It was now, unfortunately, my job to bag.

At first, I couldn't open the thin plastic bags hanging at the end of the counter; the tops seemed to have been maliciously glued shut by some disgruntled employee. Then, when I finally did get a bag open, I couldn't decide what to grab, the package of Windex Wipes or the cans of Campbell's Tomato Soup. As I hesitated, the conveyor belt kept conveying. The soup cans slammed against a box of Meow Mix, sending it skidding into the Thomas's English Muffins, which then knocked over a bottle of Hidden Valley Ranch dressing. I shook my head in despair.

"Are there any principles to doing this?" I asked the boy at the register.

"What?" My question had ambushed him. The look on his face when he turned around was a cross between alarm and annoyance.

"Are there any principles to bagging?" I repeated. "You know, guidelines for how to do it?"

His face cleared. "Yeah," he said, "there are. A full bag should be able to stand up on its own. And you should put similar things together. Like when you load a dishwasher."

Good analogy, I thought, not that it improved my bagging much. I was still so slow and fumbling that I'd only filled a couple of bags by the time he finished ringing me up.

"That's one-seventy-nine-o-three," he said.

Although stunned for a moment by the total, I gladly wrote out the check. Having a pen in my hand gave me an excuse to leave the rest of the bagging to him.

That day, I carried away from the supermarket, in addition to bags of groceries, two valuable insights: (1) if a thing as small and trivial as bagging groceries is governed by certain principles, so must more complex and significant activities; and (2) just because you know which principles apply in a situation doesn't guarantee you can follow them with alacrity or precision.

Both insights inform *Journalism Ethics Goes to the Movies*. Sometimes, in fact, the basic principles of journalism ethics don't seem very different to me from those of bagging. I mean, shouldn't journalists also be able to stand up on their own?

No doubt, but in the eyes of the public, most can't, or at least won't. Between 1985 and 2002, the number of Americans who thought news organizations were moral fell from 54 to 39 percent, while the number who thought news organizations tried to cover up their mistakes rose from 13 to 67 percent. Survey after survey has found that Americans increasingly think "the press as a whole is motivated by money and individual journalists by ambition."[1]

As the credibility of journalism has crashed, journalism ethics education has taken off. Since 1977, the number of journalism ethics courses at U.S. colleges and universities has tripled.[2] This raises a rather embarrassing question: why, despite the huge growth in journalism ethics education, are journalists still seen as—and often actually are—rude, pushy, inaccurate, sensational, and callous?

It must be that the education isn't too effective. But what accounts for its ineffectiveness? I have a couple of theories.

One is that journalism students can't take ethics seriously when journalists themselves don't. Mike Barnicle affords a perfect example. In 1998, Barnicle, then a popular columnist for the *Boston Globe*, was discovered to have plagiarized one-liners from comedian George Carlin's best-selling book *Brain Droppings*.

Carlin: Someday I wanna see the pope come out on that balcony and give the football scores.

Barnicle: Someday I'd love to see the pope appear on his balcony and announce the baseball scores.

Carlin: I read that a Detroit man and his friend were arrested because they forced the man's five-year-old son to smoke cigarettes, drink alcohol, and perform oral sex on them. Can you imagine? Cigarettes!

Barnicle: When liberals are told that a couple has been sentenced to jail for forcing a seven-year-old to smoke cigarettes, drink liquor, and have sex with an adult for money, they say, "Cigarettes? That's awful."[3]

The *Globe* suspended Barnicle for two months, during which time other ethical lapses of his were exposed, including his fabrication of a tear-jerking story about two children, one black and one white, who became friends when both were hospitalized with cancer. In the midst of the new revelations, he resigned.

You'd think that a journalist who defaced truth, who betrayed the trust of readers, who lied and plagiarized and cheated, would become a journalistic pariah, a figure of ridicule and scorn. He didn't. Barnicle became a bigger media star than ever.

Today, he's a columnist for the *Boston Herald* and a commentator on local and national news programs; he also hosts his own radio talk show. When the *Herald* hired him in 2004—he'd been at the *New York Daily News* for the previous five years—the paper crowed, "We Got Mike!"[4] Instead of an industrywide occasion for shame, Barnicle's return to Boston journalism was treated as a cause for celebration.

The Society of Professional Journalists Code of Ethics states unequivocally that journalists should "seek truth and report it." I say the same thing in class. There's no place in journalism, I lecture my students, for people who don't respect truth or consider truth-telling their first responsibility. Then the press undercuts me by sheltering a liar like Barnicle because he's a circulation draw. I can talk all I want to students about the importance of journalism ethics, but they can see for themselves what the press actually respects, and it isn't truth—it's dollars.

My other theory as to why journalism ethics education is ineffective concerns pedagogy. According to a survey by Gary Hanson of Kent State University, students in journalism ethics courses, as well as news managers, think that journalism ethics can best be learned on the job. Ironically, however, few students who served internships or held media-related jobs during college reported any firsthand exposure to ethical issues. Two-thirds said they didn't receive a written ethics policy, 70 percent said they hadn't taken part in a discussion of ethics while at work, and almost 60 percent said they never witnessed anyone making what the survey termed "a tough ethical decision."[5] Not surprisingly, Hanson concludes that the "enthusiasm for on-the-job ethics instruction may be misplaced."[6] If students are to learn journalism ethics, they have to go where it's actually being taught—the classroom.

Most journalism ethics courses, including mine, use the case study approach (probably because most of the textbooks available for the courses are structured around case studies). As Hanson explains, "Case studies place students in situations in which they must decide how to resolve an ethical issue, often by looking at accepted or current industry norms."[7] But there can be a problem with basing ethical decisions on industry norms; those norms—remember the delight with which Barnicle was welcomed back to Boston—aren't always exactly ethical.

I prefer, therefore, to have my students base their decision-making on classic ethical theories: Aristotle's golden mean, Kant's categorical imperative, Mill's principle of utility, and the like. Even so, I struggle with doubts about the efficacy of the course. It's not that students can't keep straight which philosopher goes with which principle; they can. Just because they pass my course, however, doesn't mean they'll pass their first real test.

Once my students move from the classroom into the workplace, will they be able to recognize when an ethical issue confronts them? Will they search out the best principle to apply in the situation? Will they actually have the courage to apply it? Or will they simply adopt, as studies indicate most entry-level employees do, the attitudes and practices of the workplace, whether ethical or not?

Oh, sure, some will act in concert with principle. But the rest? Harvard University researchers have confirmed that young journalists typically work in "chaotic settings with little supportive mentoring." The journalists told the researchers that they "were under the thumb of powerful editors whose desire to beat the competition all too often overshadowed the traditional journalistic values of fairness, objectivity, and responsibility to the audience." More than one-third said they were seriously thinking about leaving journalism for other careers, where they hoped to keep their integrity intact.[8]

It's this depressing state of affairs that led me to consider new ways to teach journalism ethics. *Journalism Ethics Goes to the Movies* is the result.

The book is founded on the assumption that stories matter. "They can offer us," child psychiatrist and author Robert S. Coles has pointed out, "kinsmen, kinswomen, comrades, advisers—offer us other eyes through which we might see, other ears with which we might make soundings."[9] Stories have the power to admonish us, console us, get inside our heads, and change us. Without stories, there'd be no testimony or record of "how real human beings can live through various crises and trials and remain human."[10] Without stories, there'd be no Homer, no Bible, no Shakespeare. What might seem even worse to many, without stories, there'd be no movies.

Case studies are stories, but, at a thousand words or so apiece, thin ones. Movies can tell longer, more complex stories of journalists who run up against ethical dilemmas—and do it with popular stars like Cate Blanchett and George Clooney in the lead roles.[11]

If movies are a source of ethics, however, it's not because they express a fully worked-out moral philosophy. Journalism movies tend to be much better at starting a dialog about ethics than finishing it. This isn't necessarily a bad thing. As Leigh Hafrey, who uses novels and movies to teach business ethics at the Massachusetts Institute of Technology, says, ". . . we can fill in the gaps in our knowledge of the events, our vision of the characters, our assessment of the action, with details drawn from our experience and inclinations."[12] In the process—and here's where students benefit greatly—we gain practice and confidence in answering ethical questions for ourselves.

Journalism has long been an attractive subject for moviemakers. A number of the earliest sound movies—*Big News, Gentlemen of the Press, The Front Page, Five Star Final*—were newspaper dramas, rowdy with scheming editors and hard-drinking reporters. Director Sam Fuller, whose *Park Row* re-creates the era of yellow journalism in gaslit New York, detected a natural affinity between journalism and movies. "Page One and the Screen are bed-mates," he says. "A headline has the impact of a headshot, pulp and rawstock fight lineage and footage, a news lead is the opening of a film."[13] Every year brings yet more journalists to the screen, sometimes to play the hero, sometimes the villain, and sometimes something of both.

Contributors to this book were given the task of analyzing movies that highlight the uncertain nature of journalism ethics. Some drew on classic movies like *The Pride of the Yankees* and *Mr. Deeds Goes to Town* to explore how far journalists should go in getting a story or befriending a source. Others turned to more recent movies like *Veronica Guerin* and *Welcome to Sarajevo* to investigate a specific virtue—courage in the former movie and empathy in the latter. But whether they examine print journalists (*Absence of Malice*) or TV journalists (*Broadcast News*), whether they discuss merely meddlesome reporters (*Die Hard*) or downright lying ones (*Shattered Glass*), the contributors all use the movies to teach lessons about truth and dedication and compassion that journalism students must learn now, before heading out into the work world, or they probably never will.

Today's press has broken through the last remaining ethical constraints, spreading a kind of capricious oppression, like the mad king of a tragic country. Gossip and rumor masquerade as news. Reporters run political errands for sources. Computer-enhanced images of dead bodies pander to the morbid curiosity of a jaded public. News organizations are sacked by barbarians in tailored suits. Where there should be depth and dignity, there's advertising and entertainment, convenient drugs to help us sleep.

Journalism Ethics Goes to the Movies won't reverse the trend; maybe nothing can. But, as the poet Robinson Jeffers writes, "corruption/Never has been compulsory/when the city lies at the/monster's feet there are left the mountains."[14] Ethics is the mountains. We've got to climb to reach them.

The movie characters described in the following pages can serve as our guides and companions. Some represent examples of how we should act, others of how we shouldn't. Either way, it's ultimately our choice whether to climb or not. Do we have the strength, the will? Do we have the necessary nerve?

Well, what do you think? Do we?

NOTES

1. Project for Excellence in Journalism, "The State of the News Media 2005," journalism.org (accessed 3 October 2005).

2. Andrea Tanner and Jennifer Wood Adams, "Journalism Ethics Education from the Students' Perspective," http://aastudents.unco.edu/students/AE-Extra/2005/6/Art-6.html (accessed 2 October 2005).

3. "Barnicle's Borrowings," Transparency, www.transparencynow.com/image/globebor.htm (accessed 12 October 2005).

4. "We Got Mike!" *Boston Herald*, http://bostonherald.com/local/Regional/view.bg?articleid=1333 (accessed 4 October 2005).

5. Gary Hanson, "Learning Ethics," *Insights* (Fall 2001): 5–7.

6. Hanson, "Learning Ethics," 7.

7. Hanson, "Learning Ethics," 5.

8. Wendy Fischman, Becca Solomon, Deborah Greenspan, and Howard Gardner, *Making Good: How Young People Cope with Moral Dilemmas at Work* (Cambridge: Harvard University Press, 2004), 56, 58.

9. Robert S. Coles, *The Call of Stories* (Boston: Houghton Mifflin, 1989), 159–60.

10. John Barton, *Ethics and the Old Testament* (Harrisburg, PA: Trinity Press, 1998), 31.

11. For a discussion of the comparative merits of movies versus traditional case studies, see Lee Wilkins, "Film Ethics Text," *Journal of Media Ethics* (Spring–Summer 1987): 109–13.

12. Leigh Hafrey, *The Story of Success: Five Steps to Mastering Ethics in Business* (New York: Other Press, 2005), 48.

13. Sam Fuller, "News That's Fit to Film," *American Film* 5 (October 1975): 20.

14. Robinson Jeffers, "Shine, Perishing Republic," in *Selected Poems* (New York: Random House, 1963), 9.

I

RESPONSIBLE JOURNALISTIC INQUIRY

The Paper

Sandra L. Borden

For every newspaper reporter who has dreamed of stopping the presses and slugging his penny-pinching managing editor, the 1994 Ron Howard film *The Paper* offers a golden moment. *New York Sun* editor Henry Hackett (Michael Keaton) strikes his boss, Alicia Clark (Glenn Close), so that he can get to the key that will bring the presses to a halt, even though ninety thousand copies of the paper are already being delivered. The tabloid's front page plays up the day's lead story with a huge headline and photograph: the police have arrested two young black men as suspects in a crime that has the city up in arms. However, Hackett has just turned up evidence that the police have framed the teenagers for public relations purposes. Clark adds it all up and decides to let the erroneous story go to press.

> Clark: We run what we've got.
> Hackett: It's wrong!
> Clark: Given the information we had at the time, the story's right.
> Hackett: Yeah. But it's not right. I got a cop. I got a quote. It's wrong.
> Clark: Not for today, it's not. Tomorrow, it's wrong. We only have to be right for a day.
> Hackett: This shouldn't be semantics. This shouldn't be money. People will read this, Alicia, and they'll believe us.

This chapter considers the responsibilities of Hackett and Clark as participants in an intellectual practice. Intellectual practices, such as journalism, science, and teaching, are defined by the goals of generating and disseminating authoritative accounts of the "truth." Among the ideas to be explored are philosopher Lorraine Code's concept of *epistemic responsibility*,[1] which highlights the moral significance of the investigative processes journalists use to make sense of the world for citizens living in today's information society. What are the standards of inquiry and verification that should characterize excellent journalism? How is the achievement of these standards affected by deadlines, preconceived storylines, and other hazards of journalistic work? This chapter uses examples from *The Paper*, as well as the 2006 coverage of a West Virginia mining accident, to explore these questions.

INTELLECTUAL PRACTICES AND THE PURSUIT OF TRUTH

Ancient Greek philosophers believed we are all on a great quest as protagonists in our own life narratives. The object of our quest is human excellence. For people like scientists, teachers, and journalists, the good life is essentially an intellectual life, and the object of their quest is truth. They pursue this life with others on the same quest in cooperative activities called "practices."[2] The goal of intellectual practices is to seek and share truth using reliable processes of inquiry and verification. You might say journalism and other intellectual practices specialize in knowing how to know about the world, although each practice engages in this knowledge quest in its own way. Journalists believe in learning about the world by observing events. When they are not in a position to witness an event, they are supposed to inspect materials that document the event or to interview people in a position to know about the event. They pride themselves on obtaining details that thoroughly and accurately describe the event, especially those that can be checked by others. They convey these details in news stories that are written following prescribed formats. These accounts go through layers of editing to ensure that they are "news."

If all of this sounds awfully scientific, that's no accident. Science's emphasis on facts that can be reliably observed and recorded has influenced all intellectual practices since the nineteenth century, when the scientific mind-set came to be viewed as the apex of human sense-making about the world. Journalism developed norms and procedures for objective reporting at that time. In this regard, journalism is thoroughly "modern," believing that there is a reality "out there" just waiting to be sniffed out by people with a nose for news. But truth is tricky. Even from the standpoint of objectivity, any claim to know the truth is tentative and provisional, subject to

revision in light of new information. Some sociologists suggest, furthermore, that all knowledge is socially constructed; that is, facts as such don't
even exist independently of the historical, social, and personal context in
which they are perceived.

Philosopher Sissela Bok distinguishes between what she calls *absolute
truth*—arguably beyond human reach—and what she calls *truthfulness*,
which is anybody's game. Truthfulness simply requires that we do our best
to convey what we believe to be the truth.[3] Of course, even this relatively
modest standard implies that we will take reasonable care to ensure that we
are using appropriate procedures for finding out the truth. Code refers to
this as *epistemic responsibility*. She says the processes we use to make sense
of human reality are morally significant in themselves because how we
know affects what we know, and what we know affects what we do. Ethics
and knowing, in other words, are connected. And that means that some
ways of knowing are more responsible than others.

If anyone is called to exercise epistemic responsibility, it is journalists and
others who claim excellence in the pursuit of the truth. Given their role,
they are expected to meet "standards of intellectual achievement over and
above those expected of persons simply *as* persons."[4] Are journalism's procedures for seeking and verifying the truth up to the moral demands of
epistemic responsibility? The strengths and limitations of these procedures
become evident by the end of *The Paper*, but we can already glimpse their
moral implications during the fictional *Sun's* 3 p.m. budget meeting halfway
through the film. Hackett wants to sell his senior editor, Bernie White
(Robert Duvall), on a follow-up on the murder of two white bankers found
dead outside a New York restaurant with racist graffiti scrawled on their car.
The crime comes on the heels of a race riot prompted by the police shooting of a black man. Clark suggests "Gotcha!" as the front-page headline, to
be illustrated by a shot of the police leading the two black suspects to their
arraignment.

All Hackett has to go on are a couple of tantalizing tidbits. His somewhat
unstable columnist, Dan McDougal (Randy Quaid), says he heard some
buzz on the police scanner that the arrest was bogus, and a paper Hackett
saw lying on top of the *Sentinel* editor's desk earlier in the day said the victims were under federal investigation for losing millions of dollars in savings
and loan deposits. As the characters debate what to do, we learn about some
key assumptions underlying journalistic work: that sourcing is a reliable de-
vice for limiting individual bias, that truth claims should be tested against
intuitive notions of what makes for a believable "story," and that time con-
sciousness is inherent in journalistic knowing.

"You Got a Cop Quote?"

> White: You got a cop quote?
> Hackett: A what?
> White: A quote. You know. They talk. You write. We print.
> Hackett: Oh, oh. Cop quote [Hackett quickly sticks his head out the door to check with the police reporter, who has not had any luck getting a comment one way or the other. Hackett rejoins the budget meeting.] We're working on the quote.
> Clark: OK, fine. It's a great lead. We'll follow it up tomorrow. But without confirmation, we still run "Gotcha!"

Without a quote from an official source, Hackett's got nothing that can beat a shot of the suspects being led to an official court proceeding. Most of the movie from this point on chronicles Hackett's increasingly desperate efforts to nail the almighty cop quote. As the people in charge of making and enforcing public policy, official sources, such as police officers, elected officials, and public school administrators, carry extra weight in journalistic epistemology. Close behind are elite national media, such as the *New York Times*. The only thing that beats one official source is more than one official source. Reproducing their exact words, using quotations or sound bites, conveys a sense of immediacy and access to power. The position of official sources speaks for itself as a guarantor of reliability. Nonofficial sources usually require more explanation to prove that they are qualified to comment and that they can be trusted.

This lesson was reinforced in 2006, when several newspapers around the country incorrectly reported that twelve workers trapped in a West Virginia mine had survived their ordeal. The truth was that only one miner had survived. What went wrong with journalism's procedures of verification? No one was really in a position to know except the surviving miner (if he was conscious) and the rescue workers who had managed to get through to the accident scene. Reporters didn't have access to those sources, so they settled for the next best thing: the people "in charge" of the rescue operation and miners' families who had gathered at the mine. Around midnight on January 4, family members started reporting that the miners were alive. The good news was soon carried by the Associated Press and CNN and repeated by the governor himself. With this confirmation, a number of newspapers carried front-page stories hailing the miraculous rescue.

Several editors defended their papers' reporting on the basis of official and elite media sources, while apparently renouncing responsibility for checking the information independently or awaiting solid confirmation. "All the wire services were running the same thing and our people had no reason not to believe it was true," said the managing editor of the *Plain Dealer* in Cleveland. The *Boston Globe*'s editor explained, "There were officials commenting on this. As it turned out, wrong information was given out." The *Washington Post*'s executive editor was even more blunt: "The mistake was not ours."[5]

In *The Paper*, Hackett and McDougal use similar reasoning to pressure a reluctant police officer to talk. "We just run what you guys give us, and you gave us 'Gotcha!'" McDougal tells the cop. Horrified, the officer protests, "I didn't give you that bullshit. Downtown gave you that shit." Finally, the officer admits that the police framed the teens to put the public at ease and keep the tourists coming to New York City. Hackett pushes for a quote on the record. The cop's words are music to his ears: "These kids—they didn't do it."

What seems to be missing from these examples is an adequate measure of humility about the tentative nature of *any* knowledge claims, but especially claims that journalists make about inaccessible or rapidly changing events. Besides carefully describing the factual basis for their reports, the papers that ran the miracle rescue story out of West Virginia should have included a disclaimer about their inability to confirm the reports. As it turned out, these papers received few reader complaints. Even the readers seemed to understand the challenges involved in ascertaining the miners' status. But then, why didn't the papers just acknowledge this upfront? Similarly, Clark and Hackett could have exercised epistemic responsibility in *The Paper* by simply acknowledging their uncertainty.

"They Didn't Do It"

During the budget meeting, Hackett tries to convince his peers that these teenagers are not the villains; the real villains are still out there.

> Hackett: What if these aren't the guys? What if they're innocent?
> Clark: We taint them today. We make 'em look good on Saturday. Everybody's happy [There's approving laughter in the room. Someone says, "Makes sense to me," in the background].
> Hackett (incredulous): Wait a minute. This is a story that could permanently alter the public's perception of two teenagers who might be innocent and, as a weekend bonus, could ignite another race war. How about that? Whadya say we think about this?
> [The others ignore Hackett and get on with business. Hackett stands up and confronts White.]
> White (exasperated): So, whadya wanna run, then, Henry? What?

Hackett: Run? I dunno. What do I want to run? "They didn't do it."
Clark: "They didn't do it?"
Hackett: I don't know about these things!
Clark: You don't have that. You don't have close to that. You have unattrib-
uted cops, you have something you read upside down and—
Hackett: You don't have "Gotcha!" You don't have "Gotcha!" either, not
page one, not until you get a shot of the kids.

Words tell stories. Pictures tell stories. Which narrative framework will prevail at the *Sun* depends on the photographer's luck in getting a good shot of the suspects and Hackett's luck in scoring the elusive cop quote. These are the missing plot elements that will help Clark and Hackett piece together "what really happened" using their sense of *narrative fidelity*.[6] In other words, the story that will ring true will be the one that most closely fits with journalists' own experiences, including their familiarity with cultural myths about good guys and bad guys, about the authorities, about race, and about murder. These common experiences provide ready-made themes, plots, and characters that journalists can use as handy templates for writing news stories, even in the face of contradictory facts.[7] A good story, after all, has to hang together.

Hackett's problem is that he hasn't been able to latch onto a viable storyline to counter the familiar "cops catch black criminals" theme. His tidbit about the bankers' being under federal investigation appears to Clark and the others as an anomaly that can be left out without violating narrative fidelity. Not even Hackett is prepared to suggest a storyline with Wall Street suits as the villains; that just doesn't make sense. It's not until his wife finds out that the victims' largest investor is a mob boss that he can see how all the pieces fit together, narratively speaking. The story is not "cops catch black criminals"; it's "cops cover up mob hit." Police corruption. Now that's a theme Hackett and the others have seen before. The cast of characters is complete, the heroes and villains are known, and everyone knows what comes next.

Hackett's uphill battle illustrates the tendency of journalists to converge on "obvious" storylines that reinforce a culture's common sense, including its prejudices. This temptation may be greatest when the setting and the characters are foreign to a journalist's personal experience. Then, many journalists will slip into stereotypical representations and simplistic explanations. In a culture that stereotypes African Americans as violent and impulsive, it is not a stretch for the staffers at the *Sun* to believe that two black teens could retaliate for the police shooting of a black man by murdering two white businessmen.

Sometimes journalists' narrative choices are more benign, if equally inaccurate. The editor of the *Journal Times* in Racine, Wisconsin, suggested that he erred on the West Virginia mining accident because of wishful thinking. "Should I have hedged?" he said afterward. "In hindsight, probably yes. But contrary to popular belief, news people are as inclined to hope for the best as anybody else, so we hoped for the best, based on the best information available at the time."[8] To be epistemically responsible, however, journalists should be duly skeptical. Journalistic skepticism involves "continual testing" to avoid a rush to judgment.[9] Journalists should force themselves to examine the assumptions that are driving their coverage to make sure that there is at least reasonable correspondence between the facts that they are able to confirm and the storyline (or storylines) they choose to interpret those facts. They also should be mindful of racist, sexist, and other myths that have historically fueled social injustice. Journalists seek the truth to enlighten and empower citizens; they should not unwittingly lend their storytelling authority to oppress.

"We'll Stretch the Deadline to Eight"

A major reason journalists settle on conventional storylines is that they are narrators pressed for time. When Hackett challenges the newsroom's mind-set at the budget meeting, White plays the time card.

> White: So, what time do [the suspects] walk?
> Hackett: Seven-thirty.
> White: So, we stretch it a little?
> Clark: Are you going to pay for that?
> White (annoyed): Yes. We'll stretch the deadline to eight. If we get art of the kids on the walk of shame, it's "Gotcha!" If not, the subway is page one.
> Hackett: Ah, the subway is bullshit! Bernie, come on!
> White: Hey, hey! You don't have it, and you know it. You wanna run the story? You have five hours until eight o'clock. Go get the story.

The Paper chronicles exactly twenty-four hours in Hackett's life, underscoring the sheer time pressures inherent in the daily news cycle. Time for journalists, however, is so much more than a deadline. Time is money. Time is winning. Time is owning. Time is implied in the very notion of news itself.[10]

Time itself—particularly the present—seems to be a good in journalism. Journalists value the present in the sense of being present—wanting to be a witness, to be in the know—and in the sense of the current times—wanting to

record what is happening now, to get the word out now, to make sure that today is not forgotten. If historians hope to recapture the past for present times,
journalists hope to capture the present so that it may one day become a record
of the past; it is in this sense that journalists write the first draft of history.[11]

Time-consciousness also is inherent in the scoop mentality. Beating the competition means getting the story first. If you get the story first, you may be
able to negotiate exclusive access, which means you, and you alone, "own"
that story. The urgency and intensity of Hackett's campaign to prove the innocence of the arrested teens is motivated largely by his desire to make up
for the *Sun*'s failure to report the murder when the story first broke.

This competitive impulse is not just a personal trait of Hackett's; it is woven into journalistic culture, shaping news work beyond the economic demands of the marketplace. Competition is an especially prominent value
among journalists who work in markets where several local news organizations compete head to head for the same audience, as is the case with most
local TV markets and some newspaper markets, including New York City.[12]
Although competition can motivate journalists to persevere in difficult circumstances and to avoid following the pack, it also poses some challenges
to the practice's intellectual mission. Besides tempting journalists to rush a
story, competition has the unfortunate effect of pitting colleagues against
each other. Journalists need each other to pursue the truth responsibly.
They need checks and balances, moral support, and common standards of
excellence. When competition interferes with the essential cooperation required by participation in a practice, we have reason to suspect its virtue.

Competition in journalism is closely related to the definition of news as a
perishable commodity and to the organization of news production. Consumers have come to expect newscasts and newspapers to fill certain time
slots in their own lives, and they expect their news products to have the "lat-
est." To meet consumers' expectations, news organizations rely on deadlines
throughout the news day.[13] Stretching production deadlines, let alone stopping a press run, has implications for customer satisfaction as well as the
newspaper's bottom line. Indeed, by the time Clark and Hackett face off in
the pressroom, pushing the paper's deadline has already cost close to
$50,000 in overtime pay (and that's in 1994 dollars).

Several editors in the West Virginia mining case made the same call as
Clark. It wasn't until about 3 a.m. that rescue workers at the scene corrected the misinformation that had been distributed by the Associated
Press. TV and radio journalists simply updated their live reports as new information developed. Many newspapers likewise updated their websites

through the night, but newspapers' print editions were another matter. By then, most morning papers were well into their press runs or had even finished printing that day's editions. Some newspapers found out in time to change the story for their final editions. Some had to stop the final press run to make the correction. In many cases, a large number of papers had already been shipped, so some readers got the correct version, and other readers got the incorrect one.

Some papers published the incorrect story in all their editions. The Charleston (West Virginia) *Gazette*'s editor defended the faux pas in words reminiscent of Clark's: "That was the news at the time and we did the best we could."[14] In Philadelphia, both the *Inquirer* and the *Daily News* got the story wrong. Their editors expressed regret in words echoing Hackett's. At the *Inquirer*, editor Anne Gordon said she was sorry that editorial staffers had decided not to stop the presses, even though the *Inquirer* had printed almost all of its copies for that day. "Whether we have 300,000 or three copies of newspapers left to print, a story needs to be right and we weren't right," she said.[15] *Daily News* editor Mike Days apologized to readers even though he said he couldn't have changed the story because of a maintenance shutdown. "The paper is responsible for everything in the paper and if there is an inaccuracy, in this case a huge one, you have to take responsibility," he explained. "We are in the business of reporting truth, and we can't just ignore it."[16]

Because time is an inescapable and prominent feature of journalism, the practice's standards of excellence are partly defined by the hectic pace of news work. To be epistemically responsible as a journalist means to know "well enough" under the time constraints of the newsroom, rather than the more leisurely pace of the laboratory or the classroom. That being said, wise journalists do not let themselves become prisoners of time. Sometimes they have to acknowledge that they don't have the whole story or maybe that they don't have a story at all. Deadlines don't justify filling the news hole with stories that journalists know are misleading or incorrect.

EPILOGUE

With the presses rolling again, Hackett says disdainfully to Clark, "Congratulations. You've officially become everything you used to hate." Clark snaps back, "What the hell is that supposed to mean?" and stalks off. Clark doesn't get it until later, during a tête-à-tête with McDougal at a nearby bar. "As far as I can remember," he tells her, "we never, ever knowingly got a story wrong—until tonight. That's what Henry meant."

Clark becomes determined to set things right, even after she is acciden-
tally shot in the leg during a bar fight and rushed to the hospital. Before
she'll consent to surgery, she demands a cell phone. She makes the call. The
presses stop another time. The headline goes from "Gotcha!" to "They
Didn't Do It." Clark lies back in her hospital bed, closes her eyes, and
smiles. She's a real journalist again.

NOTES

1. Lorraine Code, *Epistemic Responsibility* (Hanover, NH: Brown University
Press, 1987), 3.

2. Alasdair MacIntyre, *After Virtue*, 2nd ed. (Notre Dame, IN.: University of
Notre Dame Press, 1984), 187.

3. Sissela Bok, *Lying: Moral Choice in Public and Private Life* (New York: Vintage, 1989), 13.

4. Code, *Epistemic Responsibility*, 62.

5. Joe Strupp, "Editors Explain Why They Announced 'Miracle Rescue,'" *Editor & Publisher*, 4 January 2006, editorandpublisher.com (accessed 6 January 2006).

6. Richard C. Vincent, Bryan K. Crow, and Dennis K. Davis, "When Technol-
ogy Fails: The Drama of Airline Crashes in Network Television News," in *Social
Meanings of News: A Text-Reader*, ed. Daniel A. Berkowitz (Thousand Oaks, CA:
Sage, 1997), 353.

7. S. Elizabeth Bird and Robert W. Dardenne, "Myth, Chronicle and Story: Exploring the Narrative Qualities of News," in Berkowitz, *Social Meanings of News*, 338.

8. Strupp, "Editors Explain," 27.

9. J. Herbert Altschull, *From Milton to McLuhan: The Ideas behind American
Journalism* (New York: Longman, 1990), 355.

10. Philip Schlesinger, "Newsmen and Their Time-Machine," *British Journal of
Sociology* 28 (1977): 336–50.

11. Sandra L. Borden, *Journalism as Practice: Virtue Ethics, MacIntyre, and the
Press* (Hampshire, UK: Ashgate Publishing, in press).

12. Matthew C. Ehrlich, "Competition in Local Television News: Ritual, Enact-
ment, and Ideology," *Mass Comm Review* 19 (1992): 21–26.

13. Schlesinger, "Time-Machine," 341.

14. Mackenzie Carpenter, "Changing Reports from W. Va. Made for Tough
Night at News Outlets," Post-Gazette.com, 2006, www.post-gazette.com (accessed
6 January 2006).

15. Carpenter, "Changing Reports," 10.

16. Strupp, "Editors Explain."

2

FABRICATION IN JOURNALISM

Shattered Glass

Matthew C. Ehrlich

Every year the American Dialect Society announces its "Word of the Year." In 2005, the winner was *truthiness*, or "the quality of preferring concepts or facts one wishes to be true, rather than concepts or facts known to be true." The person credited with coining the word was Stephen Colbert, host of the mock news program *The Colbert Report* on Comedy Central. "I don't trust books," Colbert once said on the TV show in the guise of his pompous pundit persona. "They're all fact, no heart."[1]

Some see truthiness as running rampant in America. "What matters most now is whether a story can be sold as truth," one observer says. "It's as if the country is living in a permanent state of suspension of disbelief."[2] Fudging the truth, if not blatant lying and cheating, is increasingly seen as necessary to get ahead. "When 'everybody does it,' or imagines that everybody does it, a cheating culture has emerged," writes David Callahan.[3] That culture has manifested itself in the news business through a host of incidents of plagiarism and fabrication, with Jack Kelley at *USA Today* and Jayson Blair at the *New York Times* being among the most notorious offenders.[4]

But Stephen Glass's deceptions at the *New Republic* magazine may have been the most outrageous of all. ("Compared to Glass, Jayson Blair was an amateur," one of Glass's former coworkers would say.)[5] Glass, a writer not long out of college, was fired in 1998 for fabricating more than two dozen articles for the magazine. His story is the basis of the 2003 movie *Shattered Glass*. In the film's climax, *New Republic* editor Chuck Lane fires Glass and then confronts the young reporter's closest friend on the staff, who still insists on defending him. "He handed us fiction after fiction, and we printed them all as fact," Lane tells her. "Just because we found him entertaining. It's indefensible. Don't you know that?"

In *Shattered Glass*, things seem relatively simple: a reporter is caught lying and is summarily banished. In real life, questions regarding what is and is not defensible in journalism are not always so clear-cut. "Everyone agrees journalists must tell the truth," write Bill Kovach and Tom Rosenstiel in *The Elements of Journalism*. "Yet people are befuddled about what 'the truth' means."[6] A critical look at *Shattered Glass* and the Stephen Glass case helps us confront not just lofty questions regarding the nature of truth but also more down-and-dirty questions: How do you maintain trust in the people you work with and still keep necessary tabs on them? How do you balance loyalty to your friends (especially those who seem most in need of your help) with loyalty to some ill-defined "public"? When does the desire to live up to expectations go too far? When is a good story not good enough, and when is it too good to be true?[7]

JOURNALISM, TRUTH TELLING, AND MOVIES

For real-life journalists, of course, the whole concept of *truthiness* is repellent. Even while acknowledging truth's confusing nature, Kovach and Rosenstiel assert that truth is the press's "first obligation." They add that journalism is a "discipline of verification" grounded in confirmed fact rather than emotion or hearsay.[8] Similarly, "Seek Truth and Report It" is the first principle of the Society of Professional Journalists Code of Ethics. "Test the accuracy of information from all sources and exercise care to avoid inadvertent error," says the code, and, not least importantly, "Never plagiarize."[9] It goes without saying that outright fabrication also is forbidden.

The idea that truth is at the heart of journalism's role in society dates back to classical libertarianism, the philosophy underpinning the First Amendment. Libertarianism assumed that freedom of speech and the press was key to a self-righting marketplace of ideas: "Let all with something to say be free to express themselves. The true and sound will survive; the false and the unsound will be vanquished."[10] The social responsibility model of journalism that evolved from libertarianism asserted that the press should present "truthful, comprehensive, and intelligent" news in a meaningful context. Press ethics came to embrace the belief not only that journalism had a professional obligation to seek and report truth but also that individual journalists and news organizations should independently decide what truth the public needed to know.[11]

That has come under challenge in recent years. It is not that truth is no longer seen as important; on the contrary, one media ethicist declares that truth always must be the press's guiding principle given that "human existence is impossible without an overriding commitment" to it. Rather, the concern is that "mass-media ethics has failed to develop persuasive critical reflection about journalism's collective culture and institutional structure."[12] Critics charge that journalists have been attuned more to their own professional privileges and pretensions than to the common good and that the press has been slow in addressing concerns that extend well beyond a few scoundrels who broke the rules. Chief among those concerns, according to the *American Journalism Review*, is "a 24-hour, multimedia news world of rampant downsizing" that "pushes reporters to dig up scoops and attention-getting stories, write it all like the great American novel, [and] do it faster than seems humanly possible."[13] In such a world, it is small wonder that there have been so many transgressions against the truth.

Even conscientious journalists differ regarding just how stringent the professional commitment to truth should be. One study based on in-depth interviews with reporters found that nearly three-quarters of them had engaged in some form of deception, taking into account such things as using hidden cameras, not identifying oneself as a journalist, and even insincerely flattering sources. The journalists asserted that some practices were clearly worse than others (insincere flattery does not equal fabricating news), and circumstances helped determine when deception was acceptable (e.g., the story's importance, the harm that deceptive means could help prevent). Still, the study's author observes that "method and effect are linked. What a journalist does to get the news affects the believability of news."[14] A utilitarian view justifying deception on the grounds that it does the greatest good for the greatest number may overlook the possibility that it also "fuels the public's concerns about the power and morality of today's news media."[15]

If truth has long been a subject of concern within journalism, it also has long been a subject of movies about journalism. Indeed, the films, and the real-life figures and events that inspired them, suggest that "truthiness" is not just a twenty-first-century phenomenon.[16] The prototypical journalism movie is *The Front Page* (1931), based on a play by ex-reporters Ben Hecht and Charles MacArthur.[17] A highlight of the film is a group of reporters calling in wildly exaggerated and contradictory accounts of an escaped convict's capture. Hecht went on to write *Nothing Sacred* (1937), in which New

York's leading citizens beseech a newspaper to keep alive a hoax about a young woman supposedly dying of radium poisoning so that everyone can keep cashing in on her story. So it has continued in the years since: media moguls promoting fakery and demagoguery in Frank Capra's *Mr. Smith Goes to Washington* (1939) and *Meet John Doe* (1941); a reporter lying about a man trapped in a cave for the sake of a scoop in *Ace in the Hole* (1951); a photojournalist staging a picture in *Under Fire* (1983); a magazine writer fabricating a story in *Street Smart* (1987); newscasters faking tears and covering up murder to advance their careers in *Broadcast News* (1987) and *To Die For* (1995), respectively; and television executives manipulating public opinion in *Network* (1976) and *The Insider* (1999).

At times, fakery has been played strictly for laughs (as in *Nothing Sacred*), or a journalist has otherwise "gotten away with it" (as in *Broadcast News*). More often than not, though, the lying villains get their comeuppance, or a journalist finally gets out the truth, albeit sometimes through less-than-responsible means. As Joe Saltzman writes, it seems permissible in the movies to "lie, cheat, distort, bribe, betray, or violate any ethical code as long as the journalist exposes corruption, solves a murder, catches a thief, or saves an innocent." On the other hand, if a journalist's actions serve only "his or her personal, political, or financial gain, if the end result is not *in the public interest* . . . evil has won out. The only possible salvation is resigning and leaving the profession—or death."[18] Such is the case in *Shattered Glass*, in which a wayward journalist suffers his professional, if not actual, demise, and a real-life case of journalistic treachery is transformed via Hollywood into a tale of responsibility and triumph.

STEPHEN GLASS IN LIFE AND ON SCREEN

Stephen Glass joined the *New Republic* soon after graduating in 1994 from the University of Pennsylvania, where he had edited the campus newspaper. By age twenty-five, he was "the most sought-after young reporter in the nation's capital,"[19] not only a star writer and associate editor at his own magazine but also a contributor to such publications as *Harper's* and *Rolling Stone*.

Glass specialized in what he later described in a lightly fictionalized memoir as "ironic-contrarian" journalism that engaged in "sophisticated, low-key takedowns" of its subjects.[20] His first big *New Republic* piece labeled the head of the Center for Science in the Public Interest, Michael Jacobson, "the closest thing we have to a national nag." When Jacobson challenged the story's veracity, *New Republic* editor Michael Kelly called him a liar. Glass continued in the same "snarky" vein with subsequent stories: "Spring Breakdown," about a gathering of "dejected, depressed, drunk and dumb" young conservatives; "Monica Sells," about sex novelties themed around the young woman implicated in an affair with then-president Bill Clinton; and "Hack Heaven," about a teenage computer hacker blackmailing a software firm by demanding a sports car and a lifetime subscription to *Playboy*.[21]

By 1998, Michael Kelly had been ousted as editor due to political and editorial differences with the publisher. His replacement, Charles "Chuck" Lane, was less popular with the staff, but he supported Glass to the point of contributing the titles to "Monica Sells" and "Hack Heaven." That ended after *Forbes* online reporter Adam Penenberg investigated the hacker story and found it to be completely fabricated, leading to Glass's dismissal.[22] It was then discovered that Glass had made up part or all of at least twenty-six other stories for the magazine, including the young conservatives and Monica Lewinsky pieces. He had avoided detection via faked notes and other deceptions that included a phony website for the nonexistent computer firm in his hacker story, even going so far as to put "fake mistakes into his fake stories so fact checkers would catch them and feel as if they were doing their jobs."[23]

The Glass case, and the Jayson Blair and Jack Kelley cases that followed, generated considerable media discussion. For some, the blame for the scandals fell squarely on the deceitful journalists themselves. In a note to its readers following Glass's firing, the *New Republic* said it had been victimized by "the systematic and intentional deceptions of someone who actually has no business practicing journalism," adding that it had "promptly removed the culprit" and "publicly acknowledged the problem."[24] Glass's former coworkers later said he was "a very confused soul" who lacked "any capacity for grappling with moral questions" and who failed "to get that truth is essential to journalism, or that journalism done the honest way serves a critical role in society."[25]

Others similarly declared that Glass and his fellow fabricators had "violated the First Commandment of journalism: Thou shalt not lie," that as such they represented individual "pathology," and that, furthermore, "no newsroom reforms will alter that mutated variety of human nature."[26] At the same time, it was asserted (much as the *New Republic* implied in its note to its readers) that the news business could police itself. One journalist noted that an "honest, blue-collar" reporter, Penenberg, had exposed Glass, whereas another wrote that "the press's continuing exposure of the press is the best protection the public has against bad journalism."[27]

However, some argued that the scandals signified broader problems. Even before Glass's deceptions were discovered, the *New Republic* was condemned for having "become smug and cynical—the embodiment of much that is wrong with political journalism today," with the young staff taught to "meticulously wrap a web of venomous words" around the magazine's selected targets.[28] After Glass's firing, critics again lambasted the *New Republic*'s cynicism and how the magazine exemplified a "youth-happy journalism industry" that "catapults reporters into the big leagues before they have learned the fundamentals of their craft."[29]

The criticism accelerated in light of the deceptions of the similarly youthful Jayson Blair at the *New York Times* a few years later. One observer wrote that the press could not simply blame a few "skillful liars" for such misdeeds when they pointed toward declining editorial oversight in a "buzz-and-bucks era of journalistic celebrityhood."[30] Another asserted that journalists were increasingly being "seduced by fashion, money and fame to use their talents to invent a good story," in turn contributing to the "vanishing borders between fact and fiction."[31] And some suggested that the press's hand-wringing over the likes of Glass and Blair deflected attention from more fundamental problems. For journalism educator James Carey, the highly publicized cases of deception exposed "a well-kept secret: The culture of journalism professes loyalty to truth, thoroughness, context and sobriety but actually rewards prominence, the unique take, standing out from the crowd and the riveting narrative."[32]

When writer-director Billy Ray first considered the Stephen Glass story as a potential film subject, he viewed it as a satire along the lines of *Network*.[33] However, he eventually came to see the movie as "an open tip of the cap" to the Watergate-era investigative journalism of *Washington Post* reporters Bob Woodward and Carl Bernstein. "I was always raised to believe that what they had done was heroic," Ray said. "I still think it is."[34] During the film's production, when a columnist charged that journalists' "willingness to manufacture fraud can only be encouraged by movies that put their bylines in lights," the filmmakers responded by saying "the real heroes of *Shattered Glass* are the editors, who, once they uncovered evidence of Glass's transgressions, acted immediately and decisively, defending their honorable profession."[35]

In short, the film shifts the focus away from Glass and toward the men who had supervised him. Michael Kelly and Chuck Lane both served as paid consultants and were given approval over the script (Glass himself did not cooperate with the making of the film). At first, Kelly had threatened to sue over how the movie might portray him; he was afraid that it "might forever immortalize him as the Editor who *didn't* catch Glass."[36] Instead, he is depicted as a beloved boss who had been as victimized by Glass as everyone else at the magazine had been. After Kelly died covering the Iraq war prior to *Shattered Glass's* premiere, the filmmakers dedicated the movie to his memory.

As for Lane, he too had regrets over his role in the Glass scandal, saying he had fully expected it to result in his firing. However, he comes off as the true hero of the film. Billy Ray involved Lane closely in the production, aiming toward producing "an accurate account of a complicated mess."[37] Much as Woodward and Bernstein said they had done in reporting Watergate, Ray "checked with two separate sources" to confirm that an event had occurred before including it in the movie. He and his cinematographer also viewed *All the President's Men* "dozens of times, to see how a story about journalism could be told in a visually compelling way."[38] Dissatisfied with a preliminary cut of the film that portrayed Lane and rest of the *New Republic's* staff as being glumly resigned over the Glass affair, Ray wrote and shot new scenes for the final version that opened in theaters in fall 2003.

Shattered Glass is narrated by Glass himself (played by Hayden Christensen). "There are so many show-offs in journalism, so many braggarts and jerks," he is heard saying in an opening voiceover. "The good news is, reporters like that make it easy to distinguish yourself. If you're even a little bit humble, a little self-effacing or solicitous, you stand out." He then is seen rising at the *New Republic* by flattering and flirting with his fellow staffers, most of whom are little older than he is. He also wows them with his fantastical stories that regularly find their way into print, defusing any potential questioning by plaintively asking (as the real-life Glass did), "Are you mad at me?"

The only staff member cool toward Glass is Chuck Lane (Peter Sarsgaard), with whom Glass is engaged in a running game of one-upmanship. Whenever Lane talks about working on a serious piece regarding Haiti or the Falklands, Glass upstages him with his own stories about felonious debauchery at the young conservatives convention or "human-on-human biting." After Glass's champion, Michael Kelly (Hank Azaria), is replaced by Lane, Glass subtly works to undermine Lane's already tenuous authority.

Matters come to a head when *Forbes's* Adam Penenberg (Steve Zahn) exposes the fabrications in Glass's computer hacker piece. Under Lane's relentless questioning regarding the story, Glass wavers but does not break. "If you want me to say that I made it up, I will," he tells Lane. "If that'll help you, I'll say it." "I just want you to tell me the truth, Steve," Lane replies. "Can you do that?" Glass cannot, and Lane fires him. When Glass's friend Caitlin (Chloë Sevigny) challenges the decision, Lane confronts her in one

of the newly written scenes added to the final cut of the film: "We're all going to have to answer for what we let happen here. We're all going to have
an apology to make . . . because we blew it, Caitlin!" He then blasts Glass's
"indefensible" actions.

At the end, the staff presents Lane with a written apology to the magazine's readers and then breaks into applause for their editor. As for Glass,
he appears still to be trapped in his make-believe world. The movie has
been framed with scenes of him triumphantly returning to his old high
school to speak to a journalism class, but the implication is that they have
occurred only in his imagination. Billy Ray visually underscored the shift
from fantasy to reality by shooting the early scenes inside the magazine offices with a handheld camera and the later scenes with a steadier tripod-
mounted one, "the suggestion being that truth as an idea was beginning to
take hold there, and that order was beginning to be restored."[39]

On balance, reviews of *Shattered Glass* and its portrayal of Stephen Glass
were positive. One said, "Glass wound up looking even worse in the movies
than he had in print," being "so smarmy and transparent in his obsequious
behavior, so nauseatingly disingenuous in his self-deprecation."[40] Others
wrote of "the immense satisfaction of seeing a smarmy, brown-nosing little
fake get what's coming to him" and of how the movie "makes us feel the way
our forefathers must have felt after a really good public stoning."[41] In contrast, Sarsgaard as Chuck Lane was praised for making "ethical conviction
tough and attractive" and for "metamorphosing his character's stiffness into
a moral indignation that's jolting and, finally, invigorating."[42] Another reviewer declared herself "heartened that someone still has enough faith in
the fourth estate to imagine this tawdry saga as an old-fashioned morality
play in which the good guys come up tops."[43]

The film's moralizing tone did irritate some reviewers, whose criticisms
recalled those aimed at the press in the wake of the Glass scandal. The *New
York Times's* Frank Rich wrote that there was "a gaping disconnect between
a Hollywood critique like *Shattered Glass* and the news media's more distressing ailments," including its role in perpetuating a "star-worshipping
celebrity culture."[44] Another critic said the film "might have delivered a
blow to the barking narcissism of our age" but instead gave journalism "a
big wet kiss at a time when the profession might benefit from a kick in the
ass."[45] The *New Yorker's* Anthony Lane was especially contemptuous, pro-
nouncing *Shattered Glass* "the most ridiculous movie I have seen this year"
in how it portrayed Glass as "a rotten apple in the barrel" while suggesting
that "the barrel itself, the noble calling of the reporter, is as sturdy and polished as ever." He added that it was silly to heap "wrath and lamentation on

dodgy reporting" instead of on "the strains of harm and negligence that genuinely corrode our lives."[46] Yet Lane's review prompted a rebuttal from another critic: "If truth isn't something worth making an issue about, let alone a movie, then should we not just abandon all pretense of civilization, grab our clubs and buffalo skins, and retreat to the caves of our prehistoric ancestors?"[47]

"The Truth Either Tortures Us or Sets Us Free"

The most common criticism of *Shattered Glass* was that it provides little insight into what drove Stephen Glass to lie. Glass's own explanation was that he tried to "deceive people in[to] thinking better of me." In response, Billy Ray said Glass's motivation "just doesn't interest me that much."[48] That lack of interest contributed to the movie's comparatively one-dimensional portrait of the young reporter as a sniveling weasel who received his just desserts. On the other hand, Chuck Lane's character is more fully rounded and softened through scenes with his wife and sick infant child, which the real-life Lane acknowledged were largely fictionalized.[49]

Thus, the film tells a straightforward tale of a sympathetic journalistic hero vanquishing an unsympathetic journalistic villain. That was consistent with the common press perception that Glass, like Jayson Blair and other fabricating reporters, was a "scoundrel" who had to be punished severely for his sins (as one journalist put it, "You cannot kill these creatures too many times").[50] It also was consistent with journalism ethics codes and the social responsibility model of the press: one news organization, through the initiative of its staff, had exposed the misdeeds of a competing news organization, and the editor at the competing organization had accepted responsibility by firing the wrongdoer and issuing a public apology.

However, just as *Shattered Glass* avoids an investigation of the psychological factors underlying Glass's deceptions, it also avoids significant examination of the social and cultural factors that may have contributed to the scandal. The movie alludes briefly to the financial pressures upon the *New Republic* ("Our losses are a joke," the publisher says). It notes that the median age of the staff was only twenty-six and that Glass was the youngest of all. It touches on the young staff's desire to make names for themselves and on the envy that some felt toward Glass's growing fame. It similarly shows the competitiveness among the online reporters at *Forbes* to get a piece of the story exposing Glass. And it subtly highlights the differences between Glass's splashy, personalized style of reporting and the drier, policy-oriented style favored by Lane.

Unexplored are questions regarding the magazine's cynical organizational culture and the editors' role in fostering it. For example, one critic charged that "junior staffers looking to [Michael] Kelly for editorial direction would see nasty and snide as the way to go,"[51] a far cry from the movie's depiction of him as a gentle, paternal figure. As for Lane, he not only had allowed some of Glass's fabricated articles to be published but also provided ironic titles, such as "Hack Heaven." "The editors were desperate for good stuff," an anonymous *New Republic* staffer said shortly after Glass's lies were uncovered. "A hungry dog doesn't sniff at his bowl before eating."[52] Samuel G. Freedman has written that alongside a deceitful reporter is often "an editor willing to suspend all the usual ethical norms, all the editorial due-diligence, if a writer can fulfill every preordained expectation."[53] *Shattered Glass* does not consider how such a climate could permit or even encourage deception. Instead, it shows Lane resisting Glass's attempts to envelop him in his web of lies and declaring with righteous indignation that the magazine will hold itself accountable for its performance.

One review of *Shattered Glass* ended by rhetorically asking, "What sort of culture elevates Glass for his entertainment value, punishes him for being too entertaining, rewards his notoriety, and then resurrects him again as a moral object lesson?"[54] The answer is a culture rife with the same contradictions that James Carey pointed toward in journalism, one that extols truth and professionalism while embracing "aggressiveness and star quality." When a Stephen Glass or Jayson Blair is caught taking the pursuit of stardom to a logical extreme, he is publicly pilloried. In following "the prescribed script of a ritual of atonement," Carey writes, the press resolves its "own internal contradictions symbolically, at least momentarily, by expulsion of the guilty."[55] Journalism is shown to be still worthy of its charter, able to deal with its own scoundrels just as it dealt with public scoundrels during Watergate. Truth is reasserted and order is restored; professional authority and autonomy are maintained. The deeper concerns that the scandals point toward are left largely unaddressed.

Of course, to expect a movie to come up with solutions to journalism's thorniest problems is unrealistic and unfair. There are those who have offered such solutions, some more radical than others. Media ethicists Clifford Christians, John Ferré, and Mark Fackler are proponents of communitarianism, which holds that "persons have certain inescapable claims on one another that cannot be renounced except at the cost of their humanity." Christians and his colleagues say the press and the citizenry should be "empowered for social transformation, not merely freed from external constraints," as libertarianism stipulated. Communitarian journalism advocates a reorientation away from individual autonomy and toward the common good, including "a fundamental restructuring of the organizational culture within which news is constituted" and "a decisive break with individualistic capitalism" geared only toward "fattening company coffers."[56] Consistent with the last point, media scholar and activist Robert McChesney has charged that the current media system "is not set up to create good journalism; it is set up to generate maximum profits for news media companies." He argues for "a strong policy bias toward encouraging more competitive markets," along with "strong policy measures and subsidies . . . to encourage a vibrant nonprofit and noncommercial media sector."[57]

As for journalistic deception, the *American Journalism Review* has suggested a host of possible remedies. They include clearer guidelines regarding how and when to attribute quotes or other information, a more team-oriented newsroom in which staffers are not made to feel as though they are competing for money or exposure, and more stringent editorial oversight for everyone, including established "stars" who might otherwise get a free pass. "Unfortunately, there's no simple set of instructions on how to build the perfect culture," the magazine concludes. "But merely handing out an ethics code isn't going to cut it."[58]

That is not to say that codes or movies such as *Shattered Glass* have no value in highlighting essential components of ethical journalism. Writer-director Billy Ray has said *Shattered Glass* is about the younger generation of journalists that "still has to prove itself." Not all are stars or star-wannabes, according to Ray; some are "grinders" who are "fighting the good fight." In turn, that highlights what for Ray is the central idea of the movie: "The truth either tortures us or sets us free. And it clearly did one thing to Stephen Glass and another thing to Chuck Lane."[59]

Shattered Glass is a reminder that whatever their shortcomings in presenting systematic critiques of the press, movies still can offer compelling studies of individual choices and show why they matter, even in an age of "truthiness." "The whole truth *is* out of reach," Sissela Bok has written. "But this fact has very little to do with our choices about whether to lie or to speak honestly, about what to say and what to hold back."[60] Those choices are especially important in journalism, in which individuals regularly make decisions reflecting either a commitment toward truth or toward "other principles—such as hunger for a good story or desire for career advancement."[61] *Shattered Glass* dramatically depicts what is at stake within news organizations and in the end shows the right choices being made.

More broadly, the movie speaks of ideals regarding truth and democracy that we cannot afford to abandon unless we are prepared to "retreat to the caves of our prehistoric ancestors."[62] The film may not address all that ails the press, but in making "ethical conviction tough and attractive,"[63] in suggesting that "grinders" are sometimes more valuable than stars, and in reminding us that truth telling remains the most important principle to defend in journalism, *Shattered Glass* takes the necessary first step.

NOTES

1. American Dialect Society, "*Truthiness* Voted 2005 Word of the Year by American Dialect Society," 6 January 2006, www.americandialect.org/Words_of_the_Year_2005.pdf (accessed 26 May 2006).

2. Frank Rich, "Truthiness 101: From Frey to Alito," *New York Times*, 22 January 2006, sec. 4, 16.

3. David Callahan, *The Cheating Culture* (Orlando, FL: Harcourt, 2004), 13.

4. Callahan, *The Cheating Culture*, 83–88; Lori Robertson, "Confronting the Culture," *American Journalism Review* 27, no. 4 (August–September 2005): 34–41; Seth Mnookin, *Hard Times: The Scandals at the New York Times and Their Meaning for American Media* (New York: Random House, 2004).

5. David Plotz, "Steve and Me," *Slate*, 30 September 2003, www.slate.com/id/2088948 (accessed 27 May 2006).

6. Bill Kovach and Tom Rosenstiel, *The Elements of Journalism* (New York: Crown, 2001), 37.

7. The following discussion is drawn from Matthew C. Ehrlich, "Hollywood and Journalistic Truthtelling," *Notre Dame Journal of Law, Ethics & Public Policy* 19, no. 2 (2005): 519–39, and Matthew C. Ehrlich, "*Shattered Glass*, Movies, and the Free Press Myth," *Journal of Communication Inquiry* 29, no. 2 (2005): 103–18.

8. Kovach and Rosenstiel, *Elements of Journalism*, 37, 71.

9. Jay Black, Bob Steele, and Ralph Barney, *Doing Ethics in Journalism*, 3rd ed. (Boston: Allyn and Bacon, 1999), 35–39.

10. Fred S. Siebert, "The Libertarian Theory," in *Four Theories of the Press: The Authoritarian, Libertarian, Social Responsibility, and Soviet Communist Concepts of What the Press Should Be and Do*, ed. Fred S. Siebert, Theodore Peterson, and Wilbur Schramm (Urbana: University of Illinois Press, 1963), 45.

11. Theodore Peterson, "The Social Responsibility Theory," in Siebert, Peterson, and Schramm, *Four Theories of the Press*, 93–94; John Nerone, ed., *Last Rights: Revisiting Four Theories of the Press* (Urbana: University of Illinois Press, 1995); Black, Steele, and Barney, *Doing Ethics in Journalism*.

12. Clifford G. Christians, "Social Dialogue and Media Ethics," *Ethical Perspectives* 7 (2000): 186; Clifford G. Christians, John P. Ferré, and P. Mark Fackler, *Good News: Social Ethics and the Press* (New York: Oxford University Press, 1993), 41.

13. Robertson, "Confronting the Culture," 37, 39.

14. Seow Ting Lee, "Lying to Tell the Truth: Journalists and the Social Context of Deception," *Mass Communication & Society* 7, no. 1 (2004): 111.

15. Clifford G. Christians, Kim B. Rotzoll, and Mark Fackler, *Media Ethics*, 2nd ed. (New York: Longman, 1987), 54.

16. See, for example, Jack Shafer, "The Fabulous Fabulists," *Slate*, 12 June 2003, www.slate.com/id/2084316 (accessed 29 May 2006).

17. *The Front Page* has been remade on screen three times, most notably as *His Girl Friday* (1940).

18. Joe Saltzman, *Frank Capra and the Image of the Journalist in American Film* (Los Angeles: University of Southern California, Norman Lear Center, Annenberg School for Communication, 2002), 146.

19. Buzz Bissinger, "Shattered Glass," *Vanity Fair*, September 1998, 176.

20. Stephen Glass, *The Fabulist* (New York: Simon and Schuster, 2003), 9.

21. Bissinger, "Shattered Glass," 189; Stephen Glass, "Spring Breakdown," *New Republic*, 31 March 1997, 18–20; Stephen Glass, "Monica Sells," *New Republic*, 13 April 1998, 10–11; Stephen Glass, "Hack Heaven," *New Republic*, 18 May 1998, 11–12.

22. Adam L. Penenberg, "Forbes Smokes Out Fake New Republic Story on Hackers," Forbes.com, 11 May 1998, www.forbes.com/1998/05/11/otw.html (accessed 29 May 2006).

23. Bissinger, "Shattered Glass," 180.

24. "To Our Readers," *New Republic*, 1 June 1998, 8–9.

25. Jonathan Chait, "Remembrance of Things Passed," *Washington Monthly*, July–August 2003, www.washingtonmonthly.com/features/2003/0307.chait.html (accessed 30 May 2006); Hanna Rosin, "Glass Houses," *Slate*, 21 May 2003, www.slate.com/id/2083348 (accessed 30 May 2006).

26. Nancy Day, "What Happened to the ABCs?" *Boston Globe*, 30 August 1998, E7; Ann Reilly Dowd, "The Great Pretender: How a Writer Fooled His Readers," *Columbia Journalism Review* (July–August 1998), http://backissues.cjrarchives.org/year/98/4/glass.asp (accessed 30 May 2006); Samuel G. Freedman, "Don't Reward Deceitful Writers," *USA Today*, 24 March 2004, 13A.

27. Tim Cavanaugh, "Is Brill's Content Going to Save the Press from Itself?" *Newsday*, 28 June 1998, B6; Reese Cleghorn, "Keeping Reporters Honest," *Baltimore Sun*, 23 July 1998, 17A.

28. Richard Blow, "Liberalism's Flagship Adrift at Sea," *Washington Monthly*, December 1997, www.findarticles.com/p/articles/mi_m1316/is_n12_v29/ai_20089206 (accessed 30 May 2006).

29. Eric Pooley, "Too Good to Be True," *Time*, 25 May 1998, 62.

30. David Shaw, "Is There Really No Defense against Lying Journalists?" *Los Angeles Times*, 18 May 2003, E14.

31. Ian Buruma, "Reality Cheque," *Financial Times Weekend Magazine*, 15 May 2004, 24.

32. James W. Carey, "Mirror of the Times," *Nation*, 16 June 2003, 5–6.

33. Chris Kaltenbach, "*Shattered Glass* Changed Paths," *Baltimore Sun*, 8 April 2004, 9T.

34. Billy Ray-Charles Lane commentary track, *Shattered Glass*, DVD, directed by Billy Ray (2003; Santa Monica, CA: Lions Gate Home Entertainment, 2004).

35. Jack Mathews, "Truth under Fire," *New York Daily News*, 1 September 2002, Showtime sec., 18; "Lions Gate Films Presents *Shattered Glass*" (unpublished publicity materials, Margaret Herrick Library, Academy of Motion Picture Arts and Sciences, Beverly Hills, CA, 2003), 9.

36. David Carr, "Authors of Their Own Demise," *New York Times*, 19 October 2003, sec. 2, 1; "Lions Gate Films," 5.

37. Billy Ray-Charles Lane commentary track, *Shattered Glass*, DVD; "Lions Gate Films," 5.

38. "Lions Gate Films," 8, 14.

39. Billy Ray-Charles Lane commentary track, *Shattered Glass*, DVD.

40. David Shaw, "Fabricators: Bewitched, Bothered and Bewildering," *Los Angeles Times*, 2 November 2003, E12.

41. Jim Lane, "House of Glass," *Sacramento News & Review*, 20 November 2003, www.newsreview.com/sacramento/Content?oid=oid%3A26181 (accessed 31 May 2006); David Edelstein, "Stephen's Bogus Journey," *Slate*, 30 October 2003, www.slate.com/id/2090544 (accessed 31 May 2006).

42. Wesley Morris, "Smart *Glass* Is Filled with Thrill," *Boston Globe*, 14 November 2003, C6; Glenn Kenny, "*Shattered Glass*," *Premiere*, 29 October 2003, www.premiere.com/article.asp?section_id=2&article_id=1291 (accessed 31 May 2006).

43. Ella Taylor, "Bullshit Detected," *Los Angeles Weekly*, 31 October–6 November 2003, Film sec., 38.

44. Frank Rich, "So Much for *The Front Page*," *New York Times*, 2 November 2003, sec. 2, 1.

45. Mark Bowden, "When the Front Page Meets the Big Screen," *Atlantic Monthly*, March 2004, 146, 150.

46. Anthony Lane, "Deceived," *New Yorker*, 3 November 2003, 104–105.

47. Peter Howell, "Big Game of Untruths and Consequences," *Toronto Star*, 28 November 2003, D3.

48. Douglas J. Rowe, "Picking Up the Pieces: Life Goes On for Disgraced Reporter," *Albany Times-Union*, 20 November 2003, P39.

49. Howard Kurtz, "Stephen Glass: The True Story," *Washington Post*, 7 October 2002, C1, C7.

50. William Powers, "Grinding Away," *National Journal* 35 (2003): 1712; Edelstein, "Stephen's Bogus Journey."

51. Blow, "Liberalism's Flagship Adrift at Sea," 27.

52. Pooley, "Too Good to Be True," 62.

53. Samuel G. Freedman, *Letters to a Young Journalist* (New York: Basic Books, 2006), 161–62.

54. J. Hoberman, "Bad Faith Is Back," *Village Voice*, 29 October–4 November 2003, C67.

55. Carey, "Mirror of the Times," 5–6.

56. Christians, Ferré, and Fackler, *Good News*, 14, 163.

57. Robert W. McChesney, *The Problem of the Media: U.S. Communication Politics in the Twenty-first Century* (New York: Monthly Review Press, 2004), 97, 195, 209.

58. Robertson, "Confronting the Culture, " 41.

59. Billy Ray-Charles Lane commentary track, *Shattered Glass*, DVD.

60. Sissela Bok, *Lying: Moral Choice in Public and Private Life* (New York: Vintage, 1999), 4.

61. Maggie Jones Patterson and Steve Urbanski, "What Jayson Blair and Janet Cooke Say about the Press and the Erosion of Public Trust" (paper presented at the annual meeting of the Association for Education in Journalism and Mass Communication, Toronto, Canada, August 2004), 7.

62. Howell, "Big Game of Untruth and Consequences," D3.

63. Morris, "Smart *Glass* Is Filled with Thrill," C6.

3

POLITICAL MANIPULATION OF THE MEDIA

Wag the Dog

Berrin A. Beasley

Barry Levinson's 1997 film *Wag the Dog* was designed to be a satire of politics and show business, but it has a clear message for journalists: you're being spun on a daily basis, and you either don't realize it, or you don't care. Whichever answer applies, and it may be a combination of both depending on the news outlet, journalism's code of ethics demands that journalists seek truth and provide a fair and comprehensive account of events and issues.[1] This is a journalist's fundamental responsibility, and *Wag the Dog* underscores the fact that many times journalists don't seek the whole truth; nor do they provide a comprehensive account of an event—otherwise, as depicted in the film, overwhelming public support for a manufactured war designed to boost a political candidate's ratings would never have happened. This chapter discusses the ways reporters are being fed spin and how different reporting techniques could have altered the scope of specific stories, all the while underscoring the relevant sections of the Society of Professional Journalists (SPJ) Code of Ethics regarding reporting responsibilities.

JOURNALISTS AS WATCHDOGS

For decades journalists have been known as the watchdogs of government,[2] meaning it's our responsibility to watch over elected and appointed officials to ensure they're acting both legally and ethically in the public's best interest.

Politicians are expected to enact the laws that govern us, spend our tax dollars in responsible ways, and sometimes even engage this country in war if the nation's safety is in jeopardy. Because the average American cannot be present physically while his or her state's legislature is in session or while Congress meets, Americans rely on the press to be there to report the daily decisions these politicians make and how those decisions influence our everyday lives. In theory, each American would watch over each elected and appointed representative, but in reality, that's just not possible, so reporters watch for us. That means journalists and their coverage of political figures are crucial to the health of our democracy because history has proven time and again that if you can control people's access to information, you can control people. *Wag the Dog* takes the concept of controlling people through information and tweaks it so that instead of controlling the public's access to information, the main characters of the film control the actual information people have access to, all for the purpose of misleading, and therefore distracting, the public from the potentially illegal and immoral activities of the film's president.

Now you can begin to understand the humor in the film's title. To "wag the dog" is to control the press[3] and therefore the information people have access to through the press. Ideally, the press controls the information, or to use the common comparison, the dog usually controls its tail, not the other way around. So, the film title provides viewers with a clue about the film's message: the watchdog can be misled, so that the tail ends up wagging the dog. And though the film is fiction, it provides some alarmingly plausible scenarios as to how easily the press can be misled.

CHANGE THE STORY, CHANGE THE LEAD

At the start of *Wag the Dog*, just fourteen days before the presidential election, a young girl accuses the president of sexually molesting her while she was touring the White House.[4] The president, whose reelection bid is on the line, asks Washington spin doctor Conrad Brean (Robert De Niro), aka "Mr. Fix It," to handle the situation. The film opens with Brean meeting with the president's staff. They explain the situation to him, and his first question is "Who has it?" meaning "which media outlets have the story?" White House staffer Winifred Ames (Anne Heche) asks Brean, "Don't you want to know if it's true?" Brean replies, "What difference does it make if it's true? It's a story and it breaks, and they're going to have to run with it."

This is Levinson's first indication to the audience that in politics, it doesn't matter if the story is true. What matters is how you handle the press, an important lesson indeed. Within the first ten minutes of the film, it's clear that Brean is a master manipulator and more than worthy of the title "Mr. Fix It." Brean quickly concocts a brilliantly simple strategy: distract the press by leading them on a wild goose chase after a story that doesn't exist, the B-3 bomber and its relationship to a potential crisis.

At this point in the story, the film's fictional president is in China for trade talks, but his plane is scheduled for immediate departure to the United States. Brean tells the White House press secretary to keep the president in China and away from the press and their questions about the girl's allegations by claiming the president is sick. "Get this out immediately before the story [about the girl] breaks so we're not responding to it," Brean orders. Then, Brean says the White House should claim the president is in China for trade relations and that his visit has nothing to do with the B-3 bomber. Staffers are confused about the B-3 bomber because there isn't one. When questioned about it, Brean replies, "Of course there's no B-3 bomber, and I don't know where these rumors get started," implying that staffers should continue denying the same story they're creating to distract the press. Then, he orders a staff member to leak information to the *Washington Post* about the B-3 bomber and the hope that the president won't decide to deploy it before it's fully tested because of the crisis. "What crisis?" Ames asks at this point, and Brean replies, "I'm working on that."

All in all, it's a masterful scene that fully articulates Noam Chomsky's claim that by relying on official government sources for information, the press can be manipulated by the same people they are charged with monitoring.[5] And in its most basic form, the distraction strategy will work because it plays on journalism's inherent weakness: the constant need for news, especially from the White House. The distraction strategy won't keep the girl's accusations from being reported, but journalism's basic definitions of what constitutes news[6] ensure that any story about the nation's potential involvement in a war, which is the crisis Brean creates, will trump a story about one person's claims of abuse. It's the "consequence" news value at work; stories that affect the greatest number of people get the most coverage, and because it's possible that U.S. citizens may be hurt or killed in a war, the importance of the story increases with the likelihood of direct physical danger.

Brean's strategy is interesting in that the press, while charged with providing the information the public needs to make informed decisions, is also a business, and profit is always its bottom line.[7] Spin doctors often use the drive for profits and the related competition to get news out first to attract the most readers, listeners, and viewers to manipulate the press. In this first scene, Brean plans to capitalize on the press's need to get the news first by leaking a story to a reporter at the *Washington Post* about the bogus B-3 bomber. Brean knows that journalists sometimes air or, in this case, publish leaks from confidential "White House" sources so they can break stories first. As long as there is a reliable source attached, the story may be aired with less corroboration than normal.

Traditionally, journalists are taught that they need to verify information via multiple sources before they go public with it.[8] But sometimes, when the information in question will capture the nation's attention and send readers or viewers to your news outlet versus the competition's, you run with it when you only have one or two sources, even if they're anonymous, as was the case with outed CIA operative Valerie Plame.[9] Investigations have since revealed that Richard L. Armitage, a former deputy secretary of state under the Bush administration, was the primary source who told columnist Robert Novak about Plame's employment with the CIA, thus blowing her cover and perhaps endangering her and everyone who worked with her. This is a prime example of how the White House uses journalists to disclose information and how journalists use government sources, even anonymous sources, to gather information they share with the public.

Another example of the use of anonymous sources to keep a story in the press appears in the scene where Brean and Ames are en route from Hollywood producer Stanley Motss's (Dustin Hoffman) home in California to Nashville. While traveling in the car, they're watching a small TV on which a television reporter is standing live in front of the White House, telling viewers that, according to his source, the president is looking for a "swift, painless and victorious conclusion to the war." And while the reporter's source refuses to go on the record, which means reveal his or her name, the reporter assures his viewers that his source is "from the highest level." This is yet another instance of sloppy reporting that facilitates Brean's propaganda campaign designed to distract Americans from the real issue, the "Firefly girl" who has accused the president of sexually molesting her.[10]

Journalists attribute information so that news consumers will know where the information originated and can decide on the veracity and usefulness of that information based on its source. When information is relayed to readers, listeners, and viewers via anonymous sources, consumers have no way of judging its legitimacy. Viewers then must rely on the skills and ethics of the reporter to verify the information, but reporters can be misled by skillful public relations (PR) practitioners and spin doctors. As a result, the public may also be misled, which is why the SPJ Code of Ethics states,

"Journalists should identify sources whenever feasible. The public is entitled to as much information as possible on sources' reliability."

Brean's tactic of leaking information to the press is nothing new; what's new, or at least unethical, about it is that some of the information leaked is untrue. So what? Journalists are trained to corroborate every piece of information or fact acquired. They're expected to question everyone and everything. But in *Wag the Dog*, the journalists fail in their ethical responsibility as watchdogs early on by not adequately investigating the president's alleged illness, the B-3 bomber, and the war in Albania. Big stories like these are often published with minimal sourcing and verification in the name of the public's right and need to know, especially when the competition has got the story, too. In subsequent days, reporters should have been investigating every piece of information thoroughly, as well as questioning the sources' motives and identifying sources whenever possible. They didn't, and because of their failure, Brean was able to pull off a highly polished propaganda campaign that directed journalists and voters away from the president's potentially illegal and immoral behavior and toward the manufactured war with Albania.

"SEEK TRUTH AND REPORT IT"

As a rule, journalists should always question the ethics of politicians and public relations practitioners because these two groups consistently have their own best interests at heart.[11] In recognizing that, it's the responsibility of the journalist to act ethically. According to the SPJ Code of Ethics, "Members of the Society of Professional Journalists believe that public enlightenment is the forerunner of justice and the foundation of democracy. The duty of the journalist is to further those ends by seeking truth and providing a fair and comprehensive account of events and issues." Two ways to do that, as the code explains, are to "test the accuracy of information from all sources" and "identify sources whenever feasible." Bearing these directives in mind, it's feasible that if the film's journalists had been doing their jobs properly by investigating the claims made by White House staffers regarding the B-3 bomber and the impending crisis with Albania, rather than bowing down to the pressures of competition and ratings, Mr. Fix It wouldn't have been able to. Instead, he is frighteningly effective. For a crisis, he concocts a war against Albania because, to paraphrase Brean from the film, who has ever heard of them and what have they ever done for us?

Shortly after meeting with the president's staff at the White House, Brean and Ames fly to California to meet with Motss, the Hollywood producer who can manufacture the war. Brean tells Motss he wants a pageant "like the Oscars," which indicates that Brean is willing to spare no expense to make the war with Albania look and feel real.

At Motss's Hollywood mansion, Motss and Brean develop the backstory to the war, the details necessary to make it seem real. They decide that Albania wants to destroy the American way of life, and the B-3 bomber deployment is possible because it has just been discovered that Albania has a suitcase bomb.[12] To add drama to their story, Brean and Motss decide the bomb will have been found in Canada as part of an attempt by Albania to smuggle the bomb into the United States.

The presence of weapons of mass destruction to justify war is, ironically, what some claim to be the basis of the Valerie Plame scandal. They contend Plame's cover was blown by the Bush White House in retaliation for her husband's opinion column in the *New York Times* suggesting that "the Bush administration misrepresented intelligence findings in order to bolster a pre-established agenda to invade Iraq."[13] The United States invaded Iraq on March 19, 2003, just days after the United Nations asked for more time to verify reports of chemical and biological weapons in Iraq. Plame's husband, retired U.S. ambassador Joseph C. Wilson, had investigated at the request of the CIA whether Saddam Hussein had attempted to buy ingredients necessary to create nuclear weapons. He concluded Hussein had not. Plame's cover was blown eight days after Wilson's column appeared, although other journalists have said that Plame's name and occupation were revealed to them by White House officials one month prior to the column's publication, the same time that Wilson began anonymously revealing to the press that one of Bush's most compelling reasons for invading Iraq, weapons of mass destruction, was unsubstantiated. Sometimes life imitates art, which makes the study of *Wag the Dog*'s manipulation of the press a worthy educational endeavor.

Brean knows that "seeing is believing," and who better to provide the audio and video of a fake war than a Hollywood professional with access to all the necessary sources and experience? This is another neat example of how to manipulate the press because, in this digital age, seeing is not believing. Any kind of digital image can be altered, and modifications can be as simple as cropping an image to make it better fit the available space or as complex as adding someone to the image who was never there or removing the image of someone who was there.[14]

While much of the general public may still be ignorant of the power of digital editing, journalists have no such excuse. They use these editing tools daily and should realize that images must be verified as thoroughly as any fact. To do otherwise is in direct violation of the SPJ Code of Ethics, which reads, "Never distort the content of news photos or video. Image enhancement for technical clarity is always permissible." The code also states, "Avoid misleading re-enactments or staged news events. If re-enactment is necessary to tell a story, label it."

Levinson masterfully demonstrates the power of digital editing to create a real-looking fictional news event. He shows Motss producing video of a screaming Albanian girl fleeing from her burning village, sirens wailing in the background, which will be released to news outlets as a concrete image of the war. The girl is dressed in costume and told to run toward the camera. Motss directs the crew to shoot the footage with a hand-held camera so that it appears grainy, like real news footage. When the video is finished, the girl will be holding a kitten, which will be added digitally later, but during the shooting, she's holding a bag of tortilla chips. There's also nothing behind her to run from except a blue screen; the village, complete with a bridge, running water, and burning buildings, will also be added later from the digital archive.[15] Ames asks when the video will be finished, and she's told in a few hours. Levinson is driving home the point that it doesn't take long to create pseudonews for those with the tools and the know-how to do so.

The film's very next scene shows a television news anchor airing the faux footage as a legitimate news story. The anchor has been duped into believing the footage is real, which has been Brean's goal all along. Good journalists would have followed their ethical responsibilities and done something the film's fictional news anchor does not: include the source of the video either in the voice-over or by the use of a super.[16] In *Wag the Dog*, the journalist fails to question the origin of the video footage, thus enabling the charade to continue and even lending it credibility. Many television news broadcasts do include video news releases (VNRs), which are press releases for television, but ethical journalists cite the source of the footage so that viewers don't perceive the VNRs as original work by the news station and therefore free from bias. In reality, TV news broadcasters often air VNRs without identifying them as such, thus compromising their integrity and making the manipulation of the press by spin doctors that much easier.

Another tactic Brean and Ames use to keep the press off the "Firefly girl" story and on "Albania" is to stage an emotional photo op[17] for the president's return to the United States. Now that the nation's press, and therefore its people, are focused on the war with Albania, it's safe to bring the president back from China, so they decide to have a young Albanian girl and her grandmother greet the president as he steps off the plane. The girl will offer the president the first cut of wheat, a traditional Albanian harvest gift. Brean even wants it to be raining for dramatic effect when the little girl makes the presentation, so Ames has the president's plane redirected from Andrews Air Force Base to Boca Raton, Florida, where it's forecast to rain. By creating this emotion-laden photo opportunity, Brean and Ames are manipulating the kinds of images and information that journalists will be reporting during the potentially controversial return of the president. This is spin in action, and journalists must deal with it every day. In this case, journalists are expected to chronicle the president's return to the United States. Brean and Ames know this, and they use it to their advantage by planning, down to the smallest detail, images that will make the president seem a kind, sympathetic character rather than the kind of man who might have molested a young girl.

In the process of planning the details of the president's return, however, Brean and Ames's car is stopped by the CIA, who lay out the evidence indicating that there is no war. Brean's reply is, "Of course there is war. I'm watching it on TV." The line is priceless. It reminds us of the danger of relying on old maxims like "seeing is believing." Finally, Brean convinces the CIA agents to let them go, and he and Ames arrive in Nashville just in time to see, via airport TV sets, the president accepting a sheaf of wheat from a young Albanian girl in the rain. The TV reporter says, "It's quite an emotional moment here," which is exactly what Brean and Ames had planned.

Shortly after Brean arrives in Nashville—he's there for the recording of a song about the right to defend America's borders—he learns, again via TV news, that the war in Albania is over. This is a shock to him because neither Brean nor Motss had planned for the war to end before the president's re-election. The announcement is made by Sen. John Neal, who is running for president and says the CIA has confirmed that the situation in Albania has been resolved. That's when Brean realizes that the CIA has beaten him at his own game by using the media to end the war. Ideally, journalists would never have lent credibility to the war in the first place by covering it without question, but since they did, it would have been nice for those same journalists to uncover the setup through serious investigative reporting. Instead, Levinson again depicts the press as being played, this time by the CIA.

But Motss isn't willing to accept someone else's putting an end to "his picture." Instead, he conceives of the CIA's move as the end of his film's first act. For act two, Motss, Brean, and others create the idea of a hero, a solider left behind enemy lines and held hostage by the same Albanian terrorists who started the war. Together, they create a marketing campaign around the "old shoe" concept. A special programs soldier named William

Schumann (Get it? Shoe? Schumann?) is selected to be the soldier left behind. A song is written and recorded about an old shoe, and the recording is placed in the Library of Congress as a 1930 folk song. Its presence is leaked to a CBS news employee, who finds and broadcasts it, just as Brean has planned. A picture of Schumann being held hostage is released to the press, and in the picture, Schumann's sweater is strategically torn using Morse code to convey the phrase "courage Mom." Brean and Motss hang sets of shoes from trees as symbols of Sergeant Schumann. With only eight days to go until the election, it's a brilliant strategy to keep the nation's press and people focused on the war via the president's effort to bring home Willie Schumann.

The strategy works. Days pass in which the nation, via its press, remains focused on showing its support for the missing soldier. Then, with two days to go before the election, Brean and Motss decide it's time to bring the lost soldier home. Their plan is to have Schumann brought to Brean's private plane and taken to a hospital for evaluation until after the election. Motss explains the need to keep Schumann out of sight until then: "It's the contract. With the election—whether they know it or not—is, 'Vote for me Tuesday. Wednesday, I will produce Schumann.'" Here again, Levinson is reminding the audience that this entire charade has been planned by a media spin doctor and a Hollywood producer to mislead the American public substantially until after the election. All it took to do so was knowledge of how the press operates and the ability to tell good stories.

In reality, the ability to tell good stories should always be trumped by reporters' adherence to the ethics of journalism—by testing the accuracy of information from all sources, by identifying sources whenever feasible, by always questioning sources' motives before promising anonymity, by not using faked or stage audio or video. If at any point in the "war" reporters had seriously executed their ethical responsibilities, they would easily have exposed Brean's charade.

As Election Day creeps closer, new problems arise that challenge the success of the Albanian distraction campaign. Sergeant William Schumann, when finally delivered to Brean's private plane, is revealed to be a mentally ill soldier imprisoned for the rape of a nun—so much for the vaunted image of a war hero. True to character, Motss realizes that Schumann's illness could be an advantage. A soldier who has been imprisoned and tortured will exhibit mental and emotional distress, he argues. Just as Ames and Brean start to buy Motss's argument, their plane crashes in a terrible lightning storm. On the ground, Brean, Motss, Ames, and Schumann are rescued by a farmer, who takes them to a nearby country store. There, Brean phones in a make-believe explanation of what happened to the flight. Within moments, the owner of the general store is watching a White House press conference where Brean's words are repeated verbatim to the American public. The press secretary explains that there was a plane crash. The Federal Aviation Administration is investigating possible pilot error. Sergeant Schumann was injured and will need to be hospitalized.

Suddenly, the owner hears his daughter scream, and everyone realizes that Schumann, who had been left unattended, is now missing. The father races toward his daughter, gun in hand, and kills Schumann for the attempted rape. Ever the creative team, Brean, Ames, and Motss use this unexpected turn of events to their advantage by bringing Schumann home as a dead war hero. The press plays up pictures of the flag-draped coffin and military burial, and the president is reelected to office. End of film.

REAL TRICKS OF THE PR TRADE

But not the end of the lesson. Although the film's storyline is outlandish at times and the characters two-dimensional, the concept behind the film is not only plausible but entirely possible. Public relations practitioners are persuaders by profession.[18] They are not bound by the same expectation of objectivity that most journalists are, and they're certainly not expected to adhere to the same set of ethical guidelines.[19] In fact, public relations practitioners get paid to manipulate the media, and that's clearly the role Conrad Brean fills for the president.

In real life, PR practitioners coach their clients on how to "handle" the press. These aggressive tactics work because of what reporter and editor Alicia Mundy cites as the "three general weaknesses on the media's part: mistakes in reporting or a perception of the reporter as disorganized; intermedia competitive jealousy, which is pathetically easy to manipulate; and the increasing tendency by many editors (particularly for magazines), TV executives (particularly local news general managers), and internal attorneys to 'cave' in the face of even vague suggestions of legal threats."[20] Mundy is writing about tactics she learned from PR practitioners at an Investigative Reporters and Editors[21] conference, where panelists revealed how they had deliberately attempted to control where and when clients' bad news would appear in the press. One way to do that from the White House? By releasing hundreds of official documents to reporters late on Friday afternoons with any potentially embarrassing information buried inside. Reporters get overwhelmed by the amount of information provided in the documents and, having only a short while before a story is due, are unable to review the material adequately.

Panelists also said they pitted one news outlet against another by playing on the competition factor. For example, by releasing a story to a smaller paper in a market, the larger, or leading, paper looks scooped and has to play catch up by either finding a new angle on a story that is now old or ignoring the story altogether. That's a tough place to be in an industry that maintains readers or viewers by claiming to get the story first.

PR practitioners also manipulate the press in other ways. A lucrative side industry to public relations is media training,[22] where practitioners charge between $4,000 and $10,000 a day to train clients to deal with the press. Clients are taught how to wrest control of an interview from a reporter, how to dodge questions by giving responses that fit with the message they plan to deliver, how to eat up time in an interview by telling a story that supports one's planned message, and how to avoid tough follow-up questions by staying on message. Today's reporter faces pressure to avoid being too tough an interviewer because then the "must get guests" will go over to the "easier" competitor.

GOOD REPORTING REQUIRES GOOD ETHICS

Given all these ways in which the press can be manipulated, Levinson's film is no real stretch for the imagination. Indeed, it capitalizes on the myriad ways in which journalists can be used to advance specific political or business agendas at the expense of the public's right to know. The only surefire method for preventing such manipulation is the execution of solid, ethical reporting. By "testing the accuracy of information from all sources," by "identifying sources whenever possible," by "questioning sources' motives before promising anonymity," by "avoiding misleading re-enactments or staged news events," reporters are better able to ensure that public enlightenment continues to be the "forerunner of justice and the foundation of democracy."

Good reporters aren't drawn off serious charges levied against the president by sudden leaks about new bombers and a potential foreign crisis. Good reporters aren't fooled by fabricated footage of a young girl fleeing from terrorists or anonymous sources who claim to know the president's intentions. Good reporters ask hard questions: Did the president sexually molest the Firefly girl? Where did this video of the terrorist attack come from? If Albania has nuclear capabilities, why hasn't the president said something about it before now? Good journalists follow their instincts—and their ethics—when covering a story, especially a story about a manufactured war designed to boost a political candidate's ratings before an election.

NOTES

1. The generally accepted code of ethics for journalists, both print and electronic, was developed by the Society of Professional Journalists and may be found at www.spg.org.

2. For a detailed discussion of the watchdog function of the press, see the book by David L. Protess, Fay Lomax Cook, Jack. C. Doppelt, James S. Etterna, Margaret T. Gordon, Donna R. Leff, and Peter Miller, *The Journalism of Outrage: Investigative Reporting and Agenda Building in America* (New York: Guilford Press, 1991).

3. For a brief history of the origin of the phrase, see www.wordorigins.org.

4. This film was released approximately one month before the Clinton-Lewinsky White House sex scandal broke, which means the film was not based on Monicagate.

5. For more information on Chomsky's perspective, see his *Necessary Illusions* (Boston: Southend Press, 1989).

6. Many basic reporting texts discuss what constitutes news. One good text is Melvin Mencher's *News Reporting and Writing,* 10th ed. (Boston: McGraw-Hill, 2006).

7. For more information regarding the corporate influence on the media, including its effects on the practice of journalism, read Ben Bagdikian's *The Media Monopoly*, 6th ed. (Boston: Beacon Press, 2004).

8. Bill Kovach and Tom Rosenstiel, *The Elements of Journalism* (New York: Crown Publishers, 2001), 73. In their book, Kovach and Rosenstiel discuss the "discipline of verification" as "seeking multiple witnesses to an event, disclosing as much as possible about sources, and asking many sides for comment," among other practices. For another practical application of the discipline of verification, see Michele McLellan's *The Newspaper Credibility Handbook: Practical Ways to Build Reader Trust* (Reston, VA: American Society of Newspaper Editors' Journalism Credibility Project, 2001).

9. Neil A. Lewis, "First Source of C.I.A. Leak Admits Role, Lawyer Says," *New York Times*, 30 August 2006, A12.

10. For more on the widespread use of anonymous sources, including by leading news organizations, see Al Neuharth, "Evil of Journalism: Anonymous Sources," *USA Today*, www.usatoday.com/news/opinion/columnist/neuharth/2004-01-16-neuharth_x.htm (accessed 6 June 2006).

11. Alicia Mundy, "Games P.R. People Play: Corporate Damage Control Turns Tough," *Columbia Journalism Review* (September–October 2003): 10–11.

12. A suitcase bomb is a compact, portable bomb, either conventional or nuclear, that can be small enough to fit inside a suitcase.

13. Joseph C. Wilson VI, "What I Didn't Find in Africa," *New York Times*, 6 July 2003, sec. 4, 9.

14. For more information on digitally editing still photos, see Michelle Perkins, *Digital Camera Tricks and Special Effects 101: Creative Techniques for Shooting and Image Editing* (New York: Amherst Media, 2006). For more information on

digitally editing video, see Robert M. Goodman and Patrick McGrath's *Editing Digital Video: The Complete Creative and Technical Guide* (New York: McGraw-Hill, 2003).

15. A digital archive is a collection or library of digital images, either still or moving, that can be accessed on demand by users. Production companies often build and keep their own digital archives for business purposes.

16. A *voice-over* in broadcasting occurs when either an anchor or reporter reads copy during a video segment. A *super* in broadcasting refers to the superimposition of lettering over video; usually it includes the names and titles of the people in the video but can also identify the source for the video being aired. For more information on broadcast terms, see Robert A. Papper's *Broadcast News Writing Stylebook*, 6th ed. (Needham Heights, MA: Allyn & Bacon, 2006).

17. A *photo op* is a photo opportunity created by public relations practitioners for news outlets to garner news coverage for their clients. For more information about photo ops, other pseudo–news events, and the ways in which the press may be manipulated, read Richard Jackson Harris's *A Cognitive Psychology of Mass Communication*, 4th ed. (Mahwah, NJ: Lawrence Erlbaum Associates, 2004), 187–222.

18. The Public Relations Society of America's Statement of Professional Values, which, according to the statement, forms "the foundation for the Member Code of Ethics" and sets the "industry standard for the professional practice of public relations," begins with the concept of *advocacy*. Advocacy for PR practitioners is defined in the statement as serving "the public interest by acting as responsible advocates for those we represent" and as providing "a voice in the marketplace of ideas, facts, and viewpoints to aid informed public debate." Public Relations Society of America, "PRSA Member Code of Ethics 2000," http://prsa.org/_About/ethics/preamble.asp?ident=eth3 (accessed 17 October 2006).

19. To read the Public Relations Society of America's Code of Ethics, visit http://prsa.org/_About/ethics/preamble.asp?ident=eth3.

20. Mundy, "Games P.R. People Play," 10–11.

21. For more information on the Investigative Reporters and Editors (IRE) organization, visit www.ire.org. Mundy is referencing the 2003 IRE Annual Conference in Washington, D.C., June 5–8.

22. Trudy Lieberman, "Answer the &%$#° Question!" *Columbia Journalism Review* (January–February 2004): 40–44.

4

WHAT IS GOOD WORK?

Absence of Malice

S. Holly Stocking

It is said good journalists must be a little disobedient now and then. They must break the unspoken rules of being nice and deferential, especially as sources are always going to keep secrets, and some of those secrets the public needs to know.

This perspective was especially popular back in the early 1970s, when the enrollments of journalism schools swelled with students who sought to emulate the derring-do of government watchdogs Bob Woodward and Carl Bernstein, and journalism professors assigned as must-reading investigative reporter Robert Scheer's electrifying call for reporters to lie, cheat, and steal if it means getting the goods on the bad guys.[1] And this perspective must have lingered in the mind of former newspaper editor Kurt Luedtke when he wrote the script for the 1981 film *Absence of Malice*.

Malice casts Sally Field as a female rule breaker who fancies herself a journalistic watchdog of the government agencies she covers. Field's character, Meg Carter, is a reporter for a major Miami newspaper, someone who delights in breaking docile female stereotypes and, from the get-go, hungers for stories that officials don't want her to have.

Carter has a well-developed "nose for news." From a casual conversation with a secretary, she sniffs out that a special strike force may be investigating a local liquor wholesaler, Mike Gallagher (Paul Newman), in the disappearance and presumed murder of a union leader. She is relentless in her pursuit of information about the government investigation. At a bar with a member of the strike force, she slyly injects questions about Gallagher into a meeting the man had thought was purely social. Later, in a calculated bluff to test her hunch that Gallagher may be suspected of murdering the longshoreman, she confronts the head of the task force. "Michael Gallagher," she says, and then, seeking confirmation of her suspicions, *"the guy who hit Diaz"* (italics added). When the strike force leader fails to bite and leaves her alone in his office, the reporter does not hesitate to do what her source obviously intended for her to do: She snoops through a file on the investigation that he has deliberately left on his desk.

On the surface, Carter appears to have the qualities of a hard-hitting journalistic watchdog. She is inquisitive, feisty, and resourceful and refuses, presumably for the sake the public's right to know, to play the role of Oh-So-Polite-Nice-Girl-Who-Never-Breaks-the-Rules-Ever.

The problem is, despite three years on the job, Carter hasn't a clue about the rules of good journalism or about the kind of rule breaking more thoughtful journalists can—and do—justify on occasion.[2] She is a journalist who spouts the public's right to know without thinking about the public's right to good work by those who have been given privileges under the First Amendment to keep our government's nose clean. She lusts after the big story, heedless of the power journalists wield to do harm and clearly ignorant of standards, both technical and ethical, spoken and unspoken, that many working journalists aspire to live up to. And her compatriots at the newspaper, her feckless editor Mac (Josef Sommer) and a cynical corporate attorney, Davidek (John Harkins), do scandalously little to help her become mindful of the larger ramifications of her actions.

Thankfully, by the end of the movie, Carter appears to realize her missteps, but not before she has victimized two innocent people and she and her paper have been besmirched. Would that she had learned her lessons earlier. But then, we wouldn't have had the movie, which is rich in lessons about how to do, or rather how not to do, good work.

GOOD WORK DEFINED

Good work, in the view of psychologists Howard Gardner, Mihaly Csikszentmihalyi, and William Damon, consists of labor that earns high marks both technically and morally. Put another way, it is work that is both excellent in quality and socially responsible, work that is "good" in two senses of the word.[3]

As Gardner and his coauthors point out, it is possible to do work that is technically excellent but morally dubious, as when a lawyer wins most of her cases but, in the process, cuts one ethical corner after another and takes only clients who can line her pockets. Conversely, it is possible to do work that is morally excellent but technically flawed, as when a lawyer takes on all clients regardless of income and hews to high ethical standards but has trouble making a persuasive legal argument. Particularly in times of change and uncertainty, these authors say, achieving excellence in both realms can be difficult.[4]

But it can also be difficult for individuals who simply don't know—or don't care—what is expected of them. In *Absence of Malice*, Meg Carter, out of ignorance and hubris and working in a shop that fosters both, does journalistic work that is highly dubious in both the technical and moral arenas. In matters of reporting, where touching all the important informational bases and getting the facts right are foundational rules of information gathering, Carter's work fails miserably.

To be fair, she is not indifferent to some kinds of accuracy. Early in the movie, she carefully chooses the words she will use to describe Gallagher, the crimes he may be suspected of, and the unnamed sources for her information on the inquiry. In every other way, however, she violates the most basic journalistic rules of evidence. In a conversation with her editor, she only briefly questions the government official's motives for leaving out for her prying eyes the file on his unit's investigation of Gallagher. It doesn't occur to her that her source may have launched the investigation for his own questionable purposes (as it turns out, to smoke out the real criminals responsible for the disappearance of the union leader). As a result, she wrongly assumes that the government has an evidentiary basis for conducting the investigation. Worse, she doesn't make even the most basic efforts to solicit a comment from Gallagher until a corporate lawyer, in a scene that gives the movie its title, suggests she might want to check her story with him. "If he talks, we'll include his denials," the lawyer counsels. "If he declines to speak, we can hardly be responsible for errors. If we fail to reach him, we've tried." As a matter of law, he argues, "the truth is irrelevant"; what matters is creating the appearance of fairness to demonstrate absence of malice. Or to put it more crassly, the rules of law (forget the rules of good reporting or ethics) will cover the corporate fanny. "We can say what we like about him; he can't do us harm. Democracy is served." Astonishingly (we're talking Journalism 101 here), it is only then that Carter agrees to make this crucial phone call. Just as incredibly, when Gallagher is not immediately available, a one-sided, one-source story is rushed into print.

If the journalist's technical lapses in reporting loom large in this film, so do her moral ones. She doesn't think twice about wearing a hidden microphone when interviewing a source. She blithely snoops through the deliberately leaked file, then uses the information contained there without disclosing or justifying her actions to readers. She cultivates close personal relationships with news sources, replete with wining and dining and sexual seduction. All of this is questionable under professional codes of ethics that urge journalists to tell the truth and to refrain from conflicts of interest that could compromise their independence and undermine their credibility. Megan Carter clearly didn't go to journalism school. (Or if she did, she slept through class.) Even in the less ethically vigilant 1980s when the film was released, such actions were often discussed and debated in journalism classes because of their potential to contaminate the trust necessary between journalists and their sources and journalists and their publics.

Perhaps nowhere are Carter's technical and moral shortcomings more apparent than in the meeting with Gallagher's vulnerable friend from childhood, Teresa Perrone (Melinda Dillon). Perrone has read Carter's stories about the investigation and knows the stories have wreaked havoc on Gallagher's business. She also knows Gallagher is innocent because he was with her in Atlanta on the day the man disappeared, helping her to get an abortion. In a city park where she and Carter have arranged to meet, Perrone approaches the reporter, hoping she will use the information to write a story that exonerates her friend.

Naively, Perrone expects that because Carter wrote her earlier story based on anonymous sources, she will do the same with her. But reflecting real-life journalists' tendency to privilege "official" over unofficial sources, Carter balks.

> Carter: I can't write a story that says someone claims Michael Gallagher is innocent and won't say how or why or even give a name.
> Perrone: But you printed that other story!
> Carter: That was different. I knew where it came from.
> Perrone: You don't believe me?

Explaining that she's never met Perrone before, Carter says in no uncertain terms that she doesn't. "You want me to write he's innocent, but I can't use your name. You say you were with him and won't tell me where. Now what would *you* do?"

Stymied, Perrone wonders if she were to tell Carter, just her, would it have to be in the paper? The information, she stresses, doesn't have a thing to do with the missing union leader. It's private. To her credit, Carter won't make promises she can't keep, but says she'll speak to her editors about it.

Perrone: I don't understand. Couldn't you say you spoke to someone who was with him the whole time?

Carter: I'm a reporter! You're talking to a newspaper right now, do you understand? Look, if you have some information about where Michael Gallagher was that night and want to help him . . .

Perrone (softly): You don't understand. There was this guy . . .

In quiet desperation, she reveals that Gallagher was with her for three days in Atlanta when she had the abortion. Suddenly interested, Carter reaches into her handbag for her reporter's notebook. "That is not such a terrible thing," she says. "It's 1981. People will understand."

"Are you crazy?" Perrone snaps, incredulous because she comes from a traditional Catholic family and holds a responsible position in a Catholic school. "Not my people. Not my father. I don't even understand it."

Dismissing a final plea to not write the story, Carter asks for ticket stubs or receipts or anything to prove the story, but before she can even finish her sentence, a distraught Perrone gets up and wanders away.

At this point, some teachers of journalism ethics might stop the film and ask (as I have done), "If you were the reporter, would you run with the story Teresa Perrone just gave you? The source has a strong alibi for Michael Gallagher. If you present her story, the business and reputation of an innocent man may be salvaged. On the other hand, if you write the story, you divulge the secret of a woman who clearly believes the truth could devastate her loved ones."

On the surface, this is a classic dilemma for the ethics textbooks, a case in which the value of truth telling undermines the value of minimizing harm and one that requires the kind of systematic moral reasoning encouraged by journalism schools everywhere. But the fictional reporter never engages in such reasoning. Pressured by her editor, who insists that the only reason he believes the story is because of the abortion, Carter swiftly ends the discussion, silencing both conscience and moral imagination. The story goes to press, and Perrone, who was more vulnerable than anyone knew, slits her wrists and dies.

THE RULES OF GOOD WORK

If good work requires attention to both the technical aspects of one's job and to the moral implications of one's work, bad work clearly requires indifference to one or both of these. Given Meg Carter's obvious lack of proficiency in reporting and her lack of moral awareness, we can only conclude that far from doing "good" work, this fictional journalist has done the kind of work that reinforces public perceptions of journalists as arrogant, uncaring, and incapable of getting it right.

As more than one real-world journalist pointed out after the film was released in 1981, this view of journalists is a gross distortion of the much more complex reality. To be sure, there are individual journalists as devoid of humility, empathy, and reporting acumen as the reporter in this film. It may even be the case, as some critics have contended, that there are more journalists in today's competitive 24/7 news cycle who fit this story-at-any-costs stereotype than there were in 1981.[5] But ours is also an era of widely publicized media scandals with resulting concerns about media credibility. Given such concerns, there remain legions of journalists who are loath to cut corners and who aspire instead to do good work. Put another way, the field continues to be populated by journalists who aspire to practice according to technical and ethical ideals outlined in their profession's codes of ethics.[6] Although codes of ethics are mere window dressing in some shops,[7] in others, especially newsrooms with traditions of ethical excellence, journalists can and do take the ideals they express seriously.[8] In many cases, such standards are ones they initially learned about in journalism school.[9]

In my own media-ethics classes, I usually follow a showing of the first half of the film (through the Teresa Perrone case) with an examination of the most ubiquitous code of journalism ethics, that of the Society of Professional Journalists (SPJ). I also show the students organizational codes of ethics, which, unlike the professional-level codes, typically carry sanctions for employees who violate them. While codes of ethics can be difficult to interpret and are obviously limited in the guidance they can offer,[10] it quickly becomes clear that had Meg Carter or her superiors had a clue about the guidelines in the vast majority of these codes, she might have done things very differently.

The SPJ code includes, for example, the following provisions that would have offered Carter clear direction in some of the circumstances in which she found herself:

- Diligently seek out subjects of news stories to give them the opportunity to respond to allegations of wrongdoing.
- Avoid undercover or other surreptitious methods of gathering information, except when traditional methods will not yield information vital to the public.
- Remain free of associations and activities that may compromise integrity or damage credibility.[11]

The guidance offered by other provisions of the code is less clear. Take the Perrone case. On the one hand, the code counsels journalists to seek truth and report it, but on the other hand, it counsels reporters to minimize harm by respecting the privacy of people who are not public figures. As in many real-world ethical dilemmas, it can thus appear impossible in this case both to print the truth and to minimize harm to Perrone and her family. Indeed, Carter's editor expresses this very view, but as a glib truism.

In situations like this one, when codes offer contradictory advice, one hopes that journalists will take the time to think long and hard about the options available to them. Whether or not they are formally schooled in classical ethical theory (as most students who study journalism are these days), one hopes that they will thoughtfully consider, as a utilitarian might, the consequences of their actions for everyone involved. Additionally, one hopes they will ask themselves, as a rule- or duty-based philosopher would, if the actions they are considering are ones that respect the dignity of others and that they would want all journalists to follow. At the very least, one hopes that they will exercise a little moral imagination, asking as an Aristotelian philosopher would, for example, if there is an imaginative middle way between extremes (in this particular situation, an option that might allow a journalist both to tell the truth and to minimize harm).[12] As it happens, my students come to several middle courses in the Perrone case, including the fairly obvious one of tapping Gallagher for hotel receipts that would prove his innocence. Meg Carter and her editor, however, seem clueless not only about journalistic rules of thumb but also about ways to think through ethical dilemmas, ways that, in this case, might have prevented a needless death.

When I teach this film, I don't show the aftermath of the Teresa Perrone tragedy until the last day of class. By this time, the students have been exposed not only to ethical codes across media but also to numerous cases in which codes are too ambiguous to offer guidance and so require both systematic moral reasoning (which students learn) and moral imagination (which they practice). Each student has studied a media professional to explore the extent to which the professional did or did not do good work as judged by peers and evaluated against stated professional standards of the time. Each has explored the conditions, including family values, the presence or absence of mentors, and economic factors, that helped or hindered the professional to do good work. Each also has examined his or her own personal ideals and has thought about the conditions, including pressures from superiors, that can undermine these.

In addition, the students have mulled over cases in which some kinds of rule breaking have been morally justified to a public that may not always understand the checks and balances journalists are expected to provide under the First Amendment. These sometimes include well-known instances like the Pentagon Papers case, but more commonly include more pedestrian cases in which ethically questionable techniques, such as undercover reporting or hidden microphones and cameras, might be justified. The students have learned, in other words, to distinguish between technical and moral guidelines that professionals are expected to follow in most instances and guidelines that may on occasion need to be jettisoned for the public good. They have grappled with the relationship of personal values to professional values. And they have learned the kind of conditions they need to find or create for themselves to do good work. The last half of the film, seen through such learning, drives these lessons home.

Toward the end of *Absence of Malice*, Meg Carter meets for the first time a professional ethical dilemma that she both recognizes and takes seriously. And for the first time, she briefly searches for something outside her own limited view and that of her ethically impaired superiors to guide her. "I keep thinking there must be some rules to tell me what I'm supposed to do now," she says, "but maybe not." Still clueless concerning widely accepted professional ideals and systematic moral reasoning, Carter chooses to minimize harm to an anonymous source whose motives she has come to trust over revealing the source's identity to a government official. It's a hard-won decision from the gut, one that finally lives up to professional ideals, even as it comes too late to save her from losing her job.

In the closing scene, a chastened Carter tells Gallagher, her former lover, source, and subject, "I know you think what I do for a living is nothing. But it really isn't nothing. I just did it badly."

If there is any redeeming value in this film, it comes with this line. Out of ignorance and hubris, and, significantly, in a work environment that fostered both,[13] this fictional journalist did do her work badly. Legally, she may have acted without malice, but technically and morally, she did not do good work. One can only hope these are lessons students will remember as they leave this overly simplified "reel" world to find work in the far more challenging "real" one.

NOTES

1. Ken Auletta, "Bribe, Seduce, Lie, Steal: Anything to Get the Story?" *More* (March 1977): 14–20.

2. In a series of surveys, American journalists have expressed willingness occasionally to adopt a range of ethically questionable reporting practices to gain an important story. But this does not imply that the journalists approve of the routine use of such practices. The journalists were asked which practices they might "on occasion" justify for an important story and which they might reject under any circumstances. David H. Weaver, Randal A. Beam, Bonnie J. Brownlee, Paul S. Voakes, and G. Cleveland Wilhoit, *The American Journalist in the 21st Century: U.S. News People at the Dawn of a New Mellennium* (Mahwah, NJ: Lawrence Erlbaum Associates, 2007), 157–73.

3. Howard Gardner, Mihaly Csikszentmihalyi, and William Damon, *Good Work: When Excellence and Ethics Meet* (New York: Basic Books, 2001), xi.

4. Howard Gardner, "Good Work Well Done: A Psychological Study," *The Chronicle of Higher Education,* 22 February 2002, B7.

5. For a discussion of critics' contentions, see Howard Good, *Girl Reporter: Gender, Journalism, and the Movies* (Lanham, MD: Scarecrow Press, 1999), 118–20.

6. Building on the notions of "good work" of Gardner, Csikszentmihalyi, and Damon (2001), Lee Wilkins and Bonnie Brennen have called codes of ethics in journalism "a professional statement of what constitutes good work." See Lee Wilkins and Bonnie Brennen, "Conflicted Interests, Contested Terrain: Journalism Ethics Then and Now," *Journalism Studies* 5, no. 3 (2004): 297.

7. David Pritchard and Madelyn Peroni Morgan, "Impact of Ethics Codes on Judgments by Journalists: A Natural Experiment," *Journalism Quarterly* 66 (1989): 941.

8. David E. Boeyink, "Codes and Culture at the *Courier-Journal*: Complexity in Ethical Decision Making," *Journal of Mass Media Ethics* 13, no. 3 (1994): 165–82.

9. Weaver et al., *The American Journalist in the 21st Century*, 159–62.

10. Jay Black and Ralph D. Barney, "The Case Against Mass Media Codes of Ethics," *Journal of Mass Media Ethics* 1, no. 1 (1985–1986): 27–36.

11. Society of Professional Journalists, "Society of Professional Journalists Code of Ethics," www.spj.org/ethicscode.asp (accessed 15 December 2006).

12. For a textbook account of classical ethical theories applied to journalistic decision-making, see Clifford G. Christians, Kim B. Rotzoll, Mark Fackler, Kathy Brittain McKee, and Robert H. Woods Jr., *Media Ethics: Cases and Moral Reasoning,* 7th ed. (Boston: Pearson Education, 2005). See also Louis Alvin Day, *Ethics in Media Communications: Cases and Controversies,* 5th ed. (Belmont, CA: Thomson, 2006), and Philip Patterson and Lee Wilkins, *Media Ethics: Issues and Cases,* 5th ed. (Boston: McGraw-Hill, 2005).

13. Social influences have been found to play a much greater role in the ethical decision-making of journalists than factors idiosyncratic to the individual. See Paul S. Voakes, "Social Influences on Journalists' Decision Making in Ethical Situations," *Journal of Mass Media Ethics* 12, no. 1 (1997): 18–35.

5

DECEPTION AND UNDERCOVER JOURNALISM

Mr. Deeds Goes to Town and *Mr. Deeds*

Joe Saltzman

Most journalists become uncomfortable when discussing undercover journalism. They don't like it because, like adultery, you can't really do it without deception. And deceptive behavior is in direct conflict with the journalist's obligation to be accurate and fair, to try to tell the truth as the facts dictate. So, most journalists take the safe road, saying undercover journalism should be avoided except in extreme cases, that it should be done only when there is no other way to get the story or not at all.

Ethicists point out that deception in undercover journalism takes three specific forms:

Active deception. Reporters purposefully stage events to reveal wrongdoing, such as getting prostitutes to bring men to their rooms and then exposing the customers. This is rarely done.

Passive deception. Reporters fail to identify themselves and act as if they are officials or just plain citizens. The reporter gets information from people without disclosing who he or she is. People assume the reporter is a police officer at a crime scene, a doctor at a hospital, or a grieving parent at an accident site. The reporter never deliberately tells a lie and, when asked, usually admits to being a reporter.

Masquerading. Reporters pose as someone else. This is the most typical form of undercover reporting, especially in movies and on television.

The reporter pretends to be a patient in a hospital or insane asylum, a worker in a sweatshop, or a participant in an illegal operation.[1]

UNDERCOVER JOURNALISM IN HISTORY

Some of the best investigative reporters in the history of journalism went undercover for the best of reasons—to inform the public about wrongdoing by business or government. Journalists who used deception to get the goods on the bad guys often were treated like heroes, winning accolades and the top journalistic prizes.[2] In the 1890s, Nellie Bly (her name was not even real; she was actually Elizabeth Cochrane) posed as an insane woman so she could expose conditions in New York City's notorious Blackwell's Island Insane Asylum.[3] Annie Laurie (whose real name was Winifred Black) disguised herself as an indigent patient to expose improper conduct by the staff of San Francisco's city hospital. These women exposed so many corrupt practices that the technique was given its own name: stunt journalism.[4]

In the 1930s, the *Chicago Times* repeated Bly's undercover report on a mental institution, an exposé destined to recur throughout much of the twentieth century.[5] Stunt journalism became commonplace. Undercover reports continually resulted in "best of the year" journalism stories. In 1971, William Jones of the *Chicago Tribune* won the coveted Pulitzer Prize after he took a job as an ambulance driver to show how police and ambulance companies were in collusion. During the 1970s, the *Tribune* won additional Pulitzers for stories exposing voter fraud (in which reporters posed as election judges) and patient abuse in hospitals (in which reporters worked as hospital employees). Legendary CBS anchorman Walter Cronkite voted under false names twice in the same election to expose election fraud. *Miami Herald* reporters went undercover to expose housing discrimination.

Reporters from the *Wilmington* (North Carolina) *Morning Star* in 1983 decided to stage a terrorist assault on a nearby military base. They left notes pointing out that if they had been terrorists, they could have planted bombs inside one of the buildings. The *Chicago Sun-Times* sent female journalists into clinics in downtown Chicago that performed costly abortions on women who were not pregnant. In 1995, a *Wall Street Journal* reporter won a Pulitzer Prize for a series that included his undercover work in a chicken plant. In 1997, a *New York Times* reporter got a job in a garment factory and catalogued the brutal fifteen-hour workdays. In 2005, the *Spokane Spokesman-Review* used undercover methods to entrap the mayor by having a computer expert pretend to be a minor and organize a sexual liaison online with the mayor.

Even when effective, however, undercover reporting did not always win ethical approval. In 1978, the *Chicago Sun-Times* set up a bar called the Mirage, staffed it with undercover journalists, and watched as various city officials demanded bribes for their services. The story caused a national sensation, but the Pulitzer advisory board refused to give the *Sun-Times* a Pulitzer Prize because it believed that by honoring this kind of undercover reporting, it would be endorsing it. One board member, Eugene C. Patterson, called undercover reporting "a fashionable trend I don't like to see encouraged. . . . The press as a whole pays a price in credibility when a newspaper that editorially calls for government in the sunshine and candor in business shows itself disposed to shade the truth or mask its motives."[6]

In the 1990s, ABC News' *Prime Time Live* used undercover reporters and hidden cameras to document charges that some Food Lion stores sold tainted meat and spoiled fish. This controversial case resulted in a major lawsuit. The supermarket chain did not claim that the story was false or malicious. It sued ABC for fraud because the researcher lied on her application. The jury agreed, awarding Food Lion $5.5 million in punitive damages in 1997. Two years later, a divided federal appeals court threw out all but $2 of the damages.

By the 1990s, there was a good deal of hand-wringing and soul-searching over undercover reporting. David Halberstam, who won a Pulitzer Prize for his reporting from Vietnam for the *New York Times*, writes, "We didn't want anyone to speak to us with any misimpression of who we were."[7] Valerie Hyman, a former TV journalist and ethics teacher at the Poynter Institute, adds, "If truth-telling is one of the values we hold dear as journalists, then we have to think awfully hard before we decide to be deceptive in our pursuit of telling the truth."[8] As Professor Ron F. Smith puts it in *Groping for Ethics in Journalism*, "People are not allowed to sneak onto restricted military bases, lie to school officials or apply for passports under phony names. Yet journalists have done these things without being arrested or punished."[9] More and more journalists became reluctant to reward or even sanction such practices. Former *Washington Post* executive editor Benjamin Bradlee sums it up: "In a day in which we are spending thousands of man hours uncovering deception, we simply cannot deceive. How can newspapers fight for honesty and integrity when they themselves are less than honest in getting a story? When cops pose as newspapermen, we get goddamn sore. Quite properly so. So how can we pose as something we're not?"[10]

There is no denying, however, that from the beginning undercover reporting produced exciting and newsworthy stories. The movies were quick to realize that undercover journalism made for sensational dramas. In *For*

the Sunday Edition (1910), a reporter disguises himself as a convict and infiltrates a gang.[11] In quick order, a reporter for the *Daily Star* infiltrates a
suicide club and is almost killed before his colleagues rescue him in *The
Queen of Spades* (1912).[12] In *A Newspaper Nemesis* (1915), a female reporter enters the underworld and is almost captured by a killer before being rescued by a policeman she later marries.[13] In *The Lost House* (1915),
a male reporter fakes insanity so he can be committed to an asylum to rescue a woman and get the story.[14]

In the 1930s, a cub reporter goes undercover to investigate the psychic
rackets (*Sucker Money*, 1933). In a role reversal, a spoiled society boy pretends to be a "hotshot reporter" in *Badge of Honor* (1934), getting away
with all sorts of outrages by explaining, "Well, a newspaperman can do a little bit of everything." In *Blackwell's Island* (1939), a determined reporter
has himself framed to go to prison to expose a gangster's prison rackets.

In *Gentleman's Agreement* (1947), a magazine writer played by Gregory
Peck pretends he is Jewish in order to write about the effects of bigotry.
That same year, in *Violence*, a female magazine reporter joins a public service organization to prove it's a front for racketeers. In perhaps the most realistic film based on a true story, *Call Northside 777* (1948), P. J. McNeal
(James Stewart) uses passive deception to get information from the police
by simply picking up a phone in the police department and asking to see a
file denied to him as a reporter. He gets the information before being exposed. It was common practice for reporters to make calls from the pressroom in police headquarters and introduce themselves by saying they were
calling from police headquarters. The ruse often worked—people assumed
they were talking as police officials.[15]

In *Chain Gang* (1950), a reporter exposes political corruption by posing
as a convict and joining a prison chain gang. In *Shock Corridor* (1963), an
ambitious journalist is determined to win a Pulitzer Prize by solving a murder committed in a lunatic asylum. He gets himself declared insane and
ends up with the Pulitzer Prize, but in the process he loses his sanity and is
committed to the asylum for life. In 1964's *Black Like Me*, a film based on
a true story, magazine writer John Horton (James Whitmore) takes treat-
ments to darken his skin and poses as an African American in the deep
South to show how African Americans are abused.

In 1970s movies, reporters went undercover to expose conspiracies no one
believed were possible. A freelance journalist joins a powerful organization of
former Nazis to expose their future plans in *The Odessa File* (1974). A determined reporter played by Warren Beatty discovers a conspiracy to take over
the country but is killed before he can expose it in *The Parallax View* (1974).

Perhaps the most blatant example of undercover reporting, active and passive deception, and masquerading can be found in two films based on a series of books written by Gregory MacDonald. In the first, *Fletch* (1985), Irwin "Fletch" Fletcher (Chevy Chase) is a smart-alecky investigative reporter for a Los Angeles newspaper who continually changes his identity and poses as someone else to get the story. And with each new identity comes a new, albeit hilarious, name: Mr. Babar, Dr. Rosenpenis, Igor Stravinsky, Don Corleone, and Harry S. Truman. Fletch violates almost every rule of journalism, from deceiving everyone he interviews to breaking and entering so he can shoot pictures of some important stolen documents. But he always gets the story.

Undercover journalists also are featured in movies based on true exploits. In *A Bunny's Tale* (1985), Gloria Steinem (Kirstie Alley) becomes a Playboy bunny to give readers an inside look into what female employees of the Playboy clubs go through to please the boss as well as the customers. In *Her Life as a Man* (1984), Carol Lynn Mithers (Robyn Douglas) poses as a man to get a job on a sports magazine and publishes the results in a *Village Voice* article.

But no reporter speaks more to the issues of undercover reporting and deception than Babe Bennett (Jean Arthur) in *Mr. Deeds Goes to Town* (1936) and its crass remake, *Mr. Deeds* (2002). In both films, she is involved in every aspect of undercover reporting: active deception (she takes an active role in arranging events to get her story), passive deception (she fails to tell the millionaire she is following that she is a newspaper reporter), and masquerading (she pretends to be someone she isn't). In *Mr. Deeds Goes to Town*, she masquerades as an out-of-work stenographer named Mary Dawson, and in *Mr. Deeds*, as a school nurse named Pam Dawson.

In *Mr. Deeds Goes to Town*,[16] *Daily Mail* city editor MacWade (George Bancroft) urges Bennett to get front-page stories on a man who just inherited millions. The Pulitzer Prize–winning reporter tells her two photographers to follow her and "grab whatever you can get." As millionaire Longfellow Deeds (Gary Cooper) comes out of his house, Bennett staggers toward him and falls to the ground. She tells him her sad story, and they go off together, the photographers close behind. What happens next is splattered across the front page of the morning paper. Bennett explains how she got the exclusive:

> Bennett: It took some high-powered acting, believe me. I was the world's sweetest ingénue.
> Editor MacWade: Is he really that big a sap?
> Bennett: He's the original. There are no carbon copies of that one.

The editor doesn't care about her deceit. He is ecstatic. His newspaper is scooping the town: "Cinderella Man! Babe, you stuck a tag on that hick that'll stick to him the rest of his life." They both laugh, and Bennett says, "If we could sell tickets, we'd make a fortune." The ethical ramifications of a reporter's pretending to be someone else to get a story don't concern either of them and didn't seem to matter much to 1930s audiences. The editor is deliriously happy with his ace reporter, but cautions her not to show her face in the office again: "I'll tell everybody you're on your vacation. They'll never know where the stories are coming from. Stick close to him, Babe. You can get an exclusive story out of him every day for a month. We'll have the other papers crazy."

More often than not, competition among newspapers resulted in the kind of unethical journalism depicted in *Mr. Deeds Goes to Town* rather than in journalistic excellence. Undercover reporting may have provided an important public service by exposing corruption and dishonesty, but the primary purpose of stunt journalism was to scoop the competition by printing an exclusive story that no one else in town knew anything about.

Babe's stories continue to make front-page headlines. Deeds doesn't suspect a thing. He thinks the stories are being written by a nasty male reporter. "I'd like to go down to that newspaper and punch the fellow in the nose that's writing that stuff," he tells Babe. Later she says, "You're worried about those articles they're writing about you, aren't you?" He tries to reassure her: "Oh, I'm not worrying anymore. I suppose they'll go on writing 'em till they get tired. You don't believe all that stuff, do you?" A guilty Bennett answers, "Oh, they just do it to sell the newspapers, you know." He thinks about what she has said. "What puzzles me is why people seem to get so much pleasure out of hurting each other. Why don't they try liking each other once in a while?" Bennett has no answer.

Back at her friend's apartment, Bennett has a moral crisis: she's can't seem to write a story that ordinarily would write itself. She's falling in love with either the "dumbest, stupidest, most imbecilic idiot in the world—or else he's the grandest thing alive. I can't make him out." Her friend says, "You started out to be a successful newspaperwoman, didn't you?" Bennett acts as if she's looking for a fight: "Yeah, then what?" "Search me," says her friend. Bennett then shows that the hard-hearted reporter is really a softie: "He's got goodness. . . . Do you know what that is? No, of course you don't. We've forgotten. We're too busy being smart-alecks. Too busy in a crazy competition for nothing."

In this scene, Babe hits upon one of the key ethical dilemmas involved in undercover reporting, how deception is a premeditated assault on a person's privacy and dignity and violates basic trust between human beings. No amount of rationalization about the merits of undercover reporting can disguise the fact that the reporter is lying to someone who trusts and believes her, and this violation irreparably damages the reporter's credibility and image as someone who pledges to the public that stories will be written with accuracy and fairness.

After Babe's epiphany, director Frank Capra goes to a montage of Bennett typing her story and its going to press, followed by more photographs and headlines ("Cinderella Man Fire-Eating Demon—Punches Photographer"). Readers are laughing. Bennett decides to stop writing stories about the man she loves. City editor MacWade doesn't understand any of this. When he finds out Deeds has proposed to her, he shouts, "Why, Babe— that's terrific. 'Cinderella Man Woos Mystery Girl! Who Is the Mysterious Girl That . . .'" Bennett yells back, "Print one line of that and I'll blow your place up." MacWade responds, "Sorry, Babe. Sorry. I just got carried away. That's too bad. It would have made a swell story. So he proposed to you, huh? What a twist! You set out to nail him—and he . . ." Bennett bitterly agrees, "Yeah. Funny twist, isn't it?" MacWade asks, "Hey, you haven't gone and fallen for that mug, have you?" Bennett's silence says it all.

When Bennett adds, "I'm gonna tell him the truth," the city editor can't believe what he's hearing. "Tell him you're Babe Bennett? Tell him you've been making a stooge out of him? . . . You're crazy! You can't do that." Bennett says, "He'll probably kick me right down the stairs. I only hope he does." MacWade answers, "I'll put you on another job. You need never see him again, huh?" But Bennett has it bad. "Well, it was fun while it lasted, Mac. I'll clean out my desk."

Public relations (PR) man Lionel Cobb (Lionel Stander) finds out that Mary Dawson is really Babe Bennett and confronts the naive Deeds: "I don't mind you making a sap out of yourself, but you made one out of me, too. . . . Mary Dawson, my eye. That dame took you for a sleigh ride that New York will laugh about for years. She's the slickest, two-timing, double-crossing . . ." Deeds grabs him, but the furious Cobb says, "All right, go ahead, sock away and then try to laugh this off." He shows him a newspaper clipping with Bennett's photograph and caption: "Louise (Babe) Bennett, wins Pulitzer Prize for reportorial job on Macklyn love triangle." Cobb tells him the truth: "She's the star reporter on the *Mail*. Every time you opened your kisser, you gave her another story. She's the dame who slapped that moniker on you—Cinderella Man. You've been making love to a double dose of cyanide." When Bennett admits she's a reporter, Deeds is stunned. The dejected millionaire decides to give his fortune away to the poor and unemployed. Deeds goes into a deep depression, and Bennett wants to help him, but PR man Cobb tells her, "As swell a guy as ever hit this town and you crucified him for a couple of stinking headlines. You've done your bit—now stay out of his way!"

The moneymen who manage Deeds's fortune go to court to have Deeds declared insane and new heirs named. The repentant reporter wants to help Deeds, but he refuses to see her. At the trial, the lawyer trying to put Deeds away uses Bennett's series of articles as a prime exhibit "written by a newspaperwoman who was an eyewitness to his conduct ever since he came to New York." He quotes from her articles and shows the court the incriminating photographs. Bennett tries to testify on Deeds's behalf because he refuses to testify for himself. On the stand, she is manipulated when she tries to explain that she believes in Deeds, that she resigned from the *Morning Mail* and is quitting journalism because of what she did. But the lawyer forces her to admit that the stories she wrote did indeed take place.

As the trial comes to a close, Bennett refuses to remain silent. She insists on speaking, and the judge finally lets her. She makes an emotional appeal, explaining that the reason Deeds won't speak up on his behalf is that he is so hurt. "He's been hurt by everybody he's met since he came here, principally by me. He's been the victim of every conniving crook in town. The newspapers pounced on him—made him a target for their feeble humor. I was smarter than the rest of them. I got closer to him, so I could laugh louder. Why shouldn't he keep quiet? Every time he said anything, it was twisted around to sound imbecilic. He can thank me for it. I handed the gang a grand laugh. It's a fitting climax to my sense of humor." Bennett's heartfelt testimony persuades Deeds to testify in his own defense, and his testimony convinces everyone that, regardless of the headlines, he is not insane. All is forgiven, and the reporter and the millionaire fight the courtroom crowd to declare their love for each other.

There is a sweetness about the characters in *Mr. Deeds Goes to Town* that covers a multitude of sins. The female reporter lies shamelessly to an innocent, making a fool of him in one sensational story after another. Midway through the movie, she realizes that she has violated not only professional ethics but, perhaps even more importantly, personal ethics. She has become someone she doesn't like very much—a lying, deceitful person. If she had behaved this way to get a story that might have saved lives or exposed corruption, she might have felt better about herself. The story not only isn't significant, but also does terrible harm to a decent person she has grown to love. At the end of the film, she repents, leaving in doubt that she will stay in a profession that has so perverted her values.

In the remake, *Mr. Deeds,* nothing much has changed except the technology and the viciousness of the new medium, television. Babe Bennett (Winona Ryder) is now a tabloid TV journalist who deceives the millionaire (Adam Sandler) to get exclusive stories for the TV program *Inside Access.* Tabloid TV host Mac McGrath (Jared Harris) replaces the newspaper editor, and he'll do anything to get an audience-pleasing, sensational story. He assigns the Longfellow Deeds story to "his most vivacious reporter," who tells her cameraman, Marty (Allen Covert), "I need this story. I'm flat broke, and Mac is going to fire me." She pretends to be mugged—by her cameraman disguised as the mugger. Deeds saves her, surprising both reporter and cameraman by beating up the mugger. Bennett tells Deeds she is a virginal school nurse, and when they chat about their past lives, she makes up everything, awkwardly telling him she's from a small town in Iowa called Winchestertonfieldville.

On their first date, Bennett tapes a video camera between her breasts to get exclusive pictures. McGrath takes the video footage and spices it up to make Deeds look like an idiot. Bennett continuously makes up one outrageous lie after another. During one phone call, she tells Deeds she was "brought up never to drink alcohol, not even rum raisin ice cream" as she takes a drink from a bottle of beer. When they go bike riding in the park, she makes up a story about growing up in a big Victorian house right off Main Street with blue shutters and a red door with a tire swing in the front yard. She tells him about the time she fell out of an apple tree and broke her arm and how her father scooped her up and took her to Dr. Pepper. The one time she is honest with Deeds is when she explains a childhood ambition: "When I was a kid, I wanted to be a news reporter. . . . I used to go around interviewing everyone and writing notes in my little Holly Hobbie notebook. People didn't like that. I got beat up a lot. . . . But my Grandma said to me, 'One day, honey, you're going to grow up and work for *60 Minutes* and make a difference in the world.'" Deeds tells her she does make a difference every day as a school nurse: "Don't give up hope. You'll be a reporter some day if you really want to."

When Deeds goes to a fire and saves a batch of cats and their owner, the TV tabloid show host McGrath recuts the video to make him look like a fool, ending the program by calling him "our jackass of the week." Bennett is furious when she sees what McGrath has done. "That's not what I shot," she screams. McGrath tells her, "Your first cut was great, but I needed to spice it up a bit." Bennett responds, "The truth was a great story. He saved that woman and her seven cats. He was heroic." McGrath retorts, "Heroic is nice. Depraved and insane is better." She gets angry because none of what is happening is fair: "He is such a sweet guy. . . . He doesn't deserve this." She throws the hidden camera on the floor, and the bemused cameraman Marty picks it up.

In an absurd plot twist, Deeds finds Bennett's mythical hometown of Winchestertonfieldville. The townspeople think they remember her. Then, Deeds finds the exact house she described. She pretends it is her old house: "So many memories. Where to begin?" When they return to the city, she tries to tell Deeds that she's a reporter. "I don't want to hurt you anymore," she says. Deeds gives her a greeting card saying how much he loves her. She reads it and cries. Cameraman Marty records the scene without the reporter's knowledge. Marty says to himself, "Sucker."

Bennett goes to see McGrath in the control room: "I'm in love with him. And I'm going to see him tonight and I'm telling him everything." McGrath brags about his Mercedes, his Fifth Avenue apartment, and his sexy girlfriend: "And that bullshit you're talking about paid for all of it." Bennett responds, "Good for you, Mac. But I'm still telling him." McGrath answers, "Babe Bennett falls in love. I'm happy for you. I am. Going to miss you Babe. Something fierce." McGrath then exposes Babe on national television.

Deeds, preparing an engagement party at Madison Square Garden, sees the broadcast on the big screen. McGrath tells the audience, "What happens when a reporter becomes part of what she's reporting? What happens when a journalist falls in love with an idiot? That's Longfellow Deeds with Pam Dawson . . . but, wait, doesn't Pam Dawson bear a striking resemblance to Babe Bennett? A producer here at *Inside Access*. In fact, the two are one and the same." A dejected Deeds gives all his money away and leaves town. Bennett follows him, gets beaten up by his female friend, and falls into a frozen lake. Deeds saves her but doesn't want to see her anymore. At the climactic stockholders' meeting, Bennett shows up, exposing the villain. Deeds and Bennett reconcile, and they go back to his hometown to live. Again love triumphs over all, even deception, lies, and the worst aspects of undercover reporting. This is not a story involving national security, unsafe conditions in a hospital or insane asylum, corrupt business practices, or any other problem affecting the public welfare. It is undercover reporting that serves no public interest, just gossip and entertainment.

UNDERCOVER JOURNALISM TODAY

More and more journalists now believe that undercover journalism has undermined a journalist's primary mission: to be honest and truthful with the audience. Some journalists, however, believe that undercover journalism still has its place. Don Hewitt, creator of the pioneering TV newsmagazine *60 Minutes*, believes that when it comes to stories involving the public interest, the ends often justify the means. "It's the small crime versus the greater good," he explains. "If you catch someone violating 'thou shall not steal' by your 'thou shall not lie,' that's a pretty good trade-off."[17] But even by this more flexible standard, *Mr. Deeds Goes to Town* and *Mr. Deeds* fail miserably.

This is a real dilemma for most journalists. On the one hand, undercover reporting amounts to unethical behavior—deceiving people who think they can talk freely to you because you are not a reporter who will tattle on them. On the other, there are stories important to the public welfare that cannot be reported in any other way. The question is whether the ends justify the means. Absolutists believe that the ends never justify unsavory means. Others make a decision on a case-by-case basis. Too often, the decision is made based on nonjournalistic motives—getting a bigger audience and making more money. Undercover reporting usually results in high-profile stories the public loves. *A Current Affair*, *Hard Copy*, *Inside Edition*, and other entertainment news shows ferociously lampooned in *Mr. Deeds* have seen their ratings soar whenever they have used hidden cameras.

In its handbook *Doing Ethics in Journalism*, the Society of Professional Journalists (SPJ) has come up with guidelines for deciding when deception by a journalist is justified:

When the information obtained is of profound importance. It must be of vital public interest, such as revealing great "system failure" at the top levels, or it must prevent profound harm to individuals

When the journalists involved are willing to disclose the nature of the deception and the reason for it

When the individuals involved and their news organizations apply excellence, through outstanding craftsmanship as well as commitment of the time and funding needed to pursue the story fully

When the harm prevented by the information revealed through deception outweighs any harm caused by the act of deception

When the journalists involved have conducted a meaningful, collaborative, and deliberate discussion in which they weigh the consequences (short- and long-term) of the deception on those being deceived; the impact on journalistic credibility; the motivations for their actions; the deceptive act in relation to their editorial mission; the legal implications of the action; and the consistency of their reasoning and their action

The SPJ handbook also suggests some criteria that cannot be used to justify deception:

Winning a prize
Getting the story with less expense of time and resources
Doing it because "others already did it"
Believing the subjects of the story are themselves unethical[18]

Ethicists believe that the "fundamental question is whether deception is the best way to get the story."[19] Many journalists maintain that undercover reporting should be the last resort, only used when all other means are exhausted, and most seem to agree that the story has to be of major significance and in the public interest for undercover reporting and deception to even be considered. If Babe Bennett and her editor in *Mr. Deeds Goes to Town* or Pam Dawson and the TV host-producer in *Mr. Deeds* had sat down and considered these questions and guidelines, they would have been poor journalists to do what they ended up doing. If the story had had great significance to the public, rather than being about a man who had inherited millions, some of their methods might have been justified. Most journalists agree, however, that there is no room in journalism, be it for print, broadcasting, or new media, for deception when the story is trivial and insignificant to the daily lives of most Americans.

There should be, however, a place for undercover journalism in situations where the story is of importance to the public welfare. Journalists who do more than just regurgitate a company or government news release know how hard it is to get accurate stories, especially if that company or government agency is involved in wrongdoing. It has become popular for less-than-courageous people who work in the news media to point to the erosion of constitutional protections for such reporting. It is too easy for a cowardly or financially strapped editor or publisher simply to say no to undercover investigative reporting and to move on to the next story. If this happens, the loser will be the public.

The trivialization of undercover reporting as illustrated by both *Deeds* films, in countless TV programs and movies, and in real-life examples may have affected its credibility with the public, which has become more and more suspicious of and concerned about journalists who violate a person's privacy and trust, who lie to get a story. Because of this kind of deception, the public tends to forget that undercover reporting has resulted in stories that reveal massive corruption and malfeasance in government and business. And often undercover journalism is the only way to discover and report on these stories.

For the last century, courageous journalists have risked their lives to uncover corruption and wrongdoing. They were once considered honorable and given a hero's welcome when the job was done. Even then, too few journalists were willing to take the risks necessary to do such exposés. The future of this kind of investigative reporting, the last resort of the crusading journalist and the last hope for the public's right to know, could fade if undercover journalism is rejected completely.

NOTES

1. Ron F. Smith, *Groping for Ethics in Journalism*, 4th ed. (Ames: Iowa State University Press, 1999), 215–18.

2. Joe Saltzman, "A Chill Settles over Investigative Journalism," *Magazine of the Society for the Advancement of Education* 126 (July 1997): 29.

3. Her three articles for the old *New York World* were headlined "Ten Days in a Mad-House."

4. Howard Good, *Girl Reporter: Gender, Journalism, and the Movies* (Lanham, MD: Scarecrow Press, 1998), 50–51. Good points out that the term *stunt journalism* was probably more of a gender issue than a deceptive practice. It embodied the prejudice of the day that it was unladylike to be a reporter. When male reporters did similar reporting, it was labeled "investigative journalism."

5. Silas Bent, *Newspaper Crusaders: A Neglected Story* (New York: Whittlesey House, 1939), 198. Bent's story was headlined "Seven Days in a Madhouse." Bent acknowledged that his undercover report caused the *Times*'s circulation to go up considerably, "but that was of minor importance in comparison with the drastic cleanup of the institution."

6. Quoted in Smith, *Groping for Ethics in Journalism*, 220.

7. David Halberstam, "Dangerous Liaisons," *Columbia Journalism Review* (July–August 1989): 31.

8. Kenneth Clark, "Hidden Meanings: Increasing Use of Secret Cameras and Microphones Raises Ethical Questions about TV Journalists," *Chicago Tribune*, 30 June 1992, C1.

9. Smith, *Groping for Ethics in Journalism*, 223.

10. David Shaw, "Deception—Honest Tool of Reporting?" *Los Angeles Times*, 20 September 1979, 1A.

11. Richard Ness, *From Headline Hunter to Superman: A Journalism Filmography* (Lanham, MD: Scarecrow Press, 1997), 8.

12. Ness, *From Headline Hunter to Superman*, 9.

13. Ness, *From Headline Hunter to Superman*, 13, 52–53, 61.

14. Ness, *From Headline Hunter to Superman*, 18.

15. Smith, *Groping for Ethics in Journalism*, 217.

16. Joe Saltzman, *Frank Capra and the Image of the Journalist in American Film* (Los Angeles: Norman Lear Center, 2002), 68–73, 89–91. See this book for a more complete analysis of the film.

17. Colman McCarthy, "Getting the Truth Untruthfully," *Washington Post*, 22 December 1992, D21.

18. Jay Black, Bob Steele, and Ralph Barney, *Doing Ethics in Journalism* (Greencastle, IN: Sigma Delta Chi Foundation, 1993), 112–13.

19. Smith, *Groping for Ethics in Journalism,*, 225.

6

COVERING SPORTS

The Pride of the Yankees

John Carvalho

Every journalist craves access. The Beltway reporter wants a prominent seat at White House press briefings. The entertainment reporter wants to be on the red carpet, not shouting names from behind a velvet rope. And the sports reporter wants to hang out in the clubhouse with sports heroes while the public cheers from a distance.

But access can come with a price. Judith Miller of the *New York Times* got a phone call from Lewis "Scooter" Libby, a top aide to Vice President Dick Cheney. He allegedly confirmed to her that the wife of a Bush administration critic was an undercover CIA agent. As a result, she ended up with an inside scoop—and spent time in jail for refusing to reveal the name of her anonymous source to the investigating prosecutor. When she finally did reveal Libby's name with his permission, she was criticized by fellow journalists, who saw manipulation on every side of the transaction, including hers.

The same thing happens in other forms of journalism. Agents and studio publicists play entertainment journalists off each other, with flattery and promises of access, to help their celebrity clients. For sports journalists, criticism of their work has intensified as more is learned about the baseball steroids scandal. In 1998, when Mark McGwire and Sammy Sosa were dueling for the all-time season home run record, the sports media ignored rumors of steroid use by McGwire, Sosa, and other baseball players. A decade later, these same sports journalists are reexamining their actions, wondering if they ended up failing in their obligation to readers.[1] "In hindsight, I screwed up," writes sportswriter Ken Rosenthal, formerly of the *Baltimore Sun*. "That is our greatest sin, extolling these guys as something more than they were. Some of us had a feeling that something was amiss. We are more guilty of making McGwire and Sosa into heroes when they weren't."[2] Granted, sportswriters got carried away in this case. Different forms of peer pressure can force a journalist into an uncomfortable position. Sometimes it's friendship; in other cases, it's pressure from fellow media members to "play ball" and overlook stories. Every journalist must decide which is worth pursuing, friendship or a story. Access is valuable to a reporter; friendships are valuable to every human being.

Ethical codes encourage journalists to maintain a professional distance from their sources. The Society of Professional Journalists Code of Ethics urges journalists to "act independently." It stresses, "Journalists should be free of obligation to any interest other than the public's right to know." It also cautions, "Remain free of associations and activities that may compromise integrity or damage credibility." One of the trickiest causes of conflicts of interests is friendship. It's not that there is anything wrong with journalists' having friends, but when your sources become your friends, or vice versa, matters can get complicated.

This situation arises in one of the most popular sports biopics of all time, *The Pride of the Yankees*. Released in 1942, soon after the death of its main character, Lou Gehrig (Gary Cooper), the film tells a classic tale about a humble, all-American athlete whose life was cut short by the tragic disease that now bears his name. But *The Pride of the Yankees* also provides a look at what happens when a journalist gets close to a source. One of the major characters is Sam Blake (Walter Brennan), a journalist for an unnamed newspaper. At every important moment in Gehrig's life, Sam is there. To one film historian, Blake serves as "the historical muse who witnesses and records. Sam Blake represents one of the functions of the friend, that of the chronicler of the great deeds of the hero."[3]

The first time we see Blake, he is in the office of Columbia University's head baseball coach. The coach is begging Blake not to write about Gehrig, worried that the publicity will result in a pro contract that will lure Gehrig away. Blake not only ignores the coach's wishes, but he also informs Gehrig that the Yankees are interested in signing him and is there when Gehrig signs the contract. As Gehrig's career continues, Blake becomes a close friend and confidant. The two share a sleeping room on the team's train during road trips. Blake also introduces Gehrig to his future wife, Eleanor Twitchell (Teresa Wright), and encourages the courtship. He even serves as best man at their wedding.

Now, Sam Blake is not a real person; he is one of those convenient, do-everything characters that keep films from having casts that are too large and hard for audiences to keep track of. Even more, Blake is not based on any such person in Gehrig's life. If Gehrig had any mentors (and he probably didn't), none were journalists.

From a professional perspective, that is a relief. While Sam Blake might be a positive character to the audience, he is an ethical nightmare as a sports journalist. Any of his professional peers, recognizing the close friendship he was developing with Gehrig, would warn Blake that he was getting too close to his source and that eventually the friendship would put him in an ethically compromising position.

Gehrig's teammate, Babe Ruth, benefited from such a close relationship with sportswriters. In 1925, Ruth was hospitalized with what doctors ultimately diagnosed as an intestinal abscess. The diagnosis was probably accurate, but the buildup generated rumors. Ruth first fell ill on the Yankees' return train trip from spring training. Until his surgery, rumors spread that Ruth was suffering from a sexually transmitted disease. Even a Yankees team official told reporters, off the record, that Babe was suffering from syphilis. Ruth was notorious for his sexual behavior. That same year, his wife was hospitalized with a "nervous condition," and the two ultimately separated. But none of this was reported by sportswriters. They and Ruth worked together to create an image of Ruth as a Jazz Age sports hero and role model.[4]

Of course, some sports reporters go in the other direction. Instead of worshipping sports figures, they approach sports with a cynicism that refuses to acknowledge its positive aspects. For an example of an ubercynical sportswriter, check out Robert Duvall's character, Max Mercy, in the 1984 film *The Natural*. Max has lost faith in baseball to the point where he is cooperating with gamblers and tries to convince slugger Roy Hobbs (Robert Redford) to join them. In the 1920s, if Grantland Rice represented the romantic "gee whiz" school of sports writing, then W. O. McGeehan led the skeptical "aw nuts" school, refusing to grant immortality to every sports hero who could swing a bat or run with a football.[5] In *The Pride of the Yankees*, Hank Hanneman (Dan Duryea) represents the "aw nuts" school. At every point in Gehrig's career, Hanneman serves as a cynical foil to Sam Blake. Hanneman openly mocks Gehrig, preferring Ruth's hard living to Gehrig's clean image.

The *New York Herald-Tribune* often ran Rice's and McGeehan's columns on the same page, letting readers identify their own ground between the two approaches.[6] That's a good model for professional ethics. I'm not suggesting that sports journalists adopt a cynical "aw nuts" approach any more than I would advocate a praise-happy "gee whiz" approach that would ignore steroid use or careless behavior by athletes. The middle of the road is not such a bad place to be in this case as it gives you the ethical flexibility to evaluate a story's value.

The young sportswriter is more likely to start with the "gee whiz" approach. Speaking from experience, I can attest that the first few years in sportswriting can be tough. The transition from bleachers to press box can be heady. You enter a professional relationship with the athletes you used to cheer for. A young journalist can consider a young pro athlete more of a peer. The situation can quickly veer toward conflicts of interest. Allow yourself to become too buddy-buddy with the athletes you write about, and you can end up in difficult situations.

In *The Pride of the Yankees*, Sam Blake finds himself there. When Gehrig learns he has a fatal disease, Blake is with him. (Ironically, Gehrig's wife is not; does that seem odd to anyone else?) Blake agrees to help Gehrig mislead the other sportswriters about the nature and severity of his disease. "I'll cook something up," Blake promises. The audience, already close to tears in the emotion of what is a truly powerful scene, might consider Gehrig lucky to have such a loyal friend, but any journalists in the audience might feel a moral twinge. They would see a sports journalist promising to deceive his peers and his audience. Concerned readers would turn to Blake for information on Gehrig, and Blake would lie to them. It is one thing for team public relations personnel or family members to protect an athlete's privacy, but a journalist's loyalties are supposed to lie elsewhere. Typically, if a sportswriter begins to develop such a close friendship with a source, his or her supervisor (and probably coworkers) will issue a stern warning: do not get too close. Sam Blake ends up too close and apparently does not even realize the situation's ethical implications.

For a better example of professional ethics in sports, check out the 1988 film *Eight Men Out*, directed by John Sayles. It depicts the "Black Sox" scandal, in which members of the Chicago White Sox accepted money from gamblers in exchange for throwing the 1919 World Series. The two prominent sports journalists in *Eight Men Out*, Ring Lardner (played by Sayles himself) and Hugh Fullerton (played by author Studs Terkel), maintain an objective independence that allows them to ask tough questions. Their relationship with the players is professional but not cold. Lardner's disappointment is apparent when he realizes one of the players he knows best, Eddie Cicotte (David Strathairn), is involved in throwing games, but that doesn't stop him from questioning Cicotte directly about rumors of a fix.

> Lardner: You really took a shelling out there today.
> Cicotte: Ah, they got their raps in.
> Lardner: That one Ruther caught hold of looked like you tossed it in underhand.
> Cicotte: It didn't break.
> Lardner: You didn't put anything on it. Why should it break?
> Cicotte (embarrassed): Did you bring me up here to tell me I had a lousy day?
> Lardner (pausing, looking at a baseball): I want to know if the series is on the level, Eddie.
> Cicotte: What if I told you we're doing our best?
> Lardner: I'll believe you.
> Cicotte: We played like a bunch of bushers today, but nobody is in the bag.
> Lardner: Don't be sore at me for asking, okay?
> Cicotte: Aw, we're just dumb ballplayers. We need a mug like you to keep us honest.

That interview shows Lardner's professional ethic in practice—a mutual respect that allows him to ask tough questions without appearing hostile or cynical.

Whenever we discuss conflicts of interest involving friendships, my students throw up the same red flag: "Can I be friends with *anyone*? Isn't every friendship a potential conflict of interest?" From their perspective, a career in journalism would turn them into social outcasts, friendless hermits.

First, some reassurance (and then some lifestyle advice): you don't have to give up your friends to be an ethical journalist. That would be too much of a sacrifice. One of the reasons friendships can get complicated is that young journalists, running hard on passionate enthusiasm, tend to put in long hours. As a result, their friendships are often with coworkers and sources. Now, the lifestyle advice: develop a network of friends outside of the office, friends who have no connection to your work. That can provide balance to your life, while avoiding the ethical implications of being too friendly with sources.

At times, however, you will have to be vigilant, lest you or your friend compromise either your friendship or your careers. Obviously, if you follow the advice above, most of your friends will live their lives quite happily far below the media radar. But in those cases where a friend ends up the focus of media attention, and you are the media, tread carefully. Think seriously about all of the loyalties involved: to your friend, to your newspaper, to your audience, to your profession, to yourself. Different situations cause different loyalties to emerge as the most important to consider.

Blake finds himself in the midst of other ethically compromising situations in the film, with the same negative results. At one point, he confronts Hanneman about a column, supposedly written by Babe Ruth, that dismisses a home run Gehrig hit as "accidental." The exchange that takes place between the two is worthy of an elementary school playground:

> Blake: Look at that: "Gehrig's accidental home run yesterday."
> Hanneman: I'm only putting down what Babe Ruth says.
> Blake: Well, you don't need paper for that. You can write all the Babe ever thought on a piece of confetti.
> Hanneman: That was pretty brainy, I suppose—you having Gehrig call Ruth the "Ex-King of Swat."
> Blake: That's fact; Gehrig's writing fact.
> Hanneman: Okay, Ruth will show you some facts in his column tomorrow.
> Blake: Well, any facts Ruth dreams up will be topped by Lou Gehrig without borrowing your opium pipe.

It almost sounds like a 1930s version of those ESPN shout fests, doesn't it? But Blake and Hanneman are talking about ghostwriting, a form of fakery that had been around since the early twentieth century. Ghostwriting itself is not the problem; when the ghostwriter is not identified, however, that deceives the readers into thinking that the athlete wrote the article, which is often not the case. That is exactly how newspapers played it up in the 1920s and 1930s: "Buy our newspaper! Read what Babe Ruth wrote today!"

The assumption, based on the conversation between Hanneman and Blake, would be that they indeed wrote columns for Ruth and Gehrig, respectively. None of Gehrig's biographies indicate that he had a column published under his name, ghostwritten or not. Ruth was a popular newspaper columnist and frequently employed unidentified ghostwriters.[7] In fact, one of his ghostwriters was probably Ford Frick, a columnist for the *New York Evening Journal*. That is the same Ford Frick who, as commissioner of baseball, directed that Roger Maris's 162-game season home run record not replace Ruth's 154-game record. Instead, Frick directed that "some distinctive mark" accompany Maris's record.[8] Coincidence? That's another ethical question.

The ghostwriting situation is not that far from the conflict of interest we have been discussing. If you develop a friendship with a professional athlete, he or she might come to you for help with some writing or other promotional project. The addition of a ghostwriter's byline could seem clumsy. Would you feel pressured to allow such a deception for the sake of a friend?

In Gehrig's time, athletes wrote columns in newspapers. Today, many athletes maintain their own blogs. It's a convenient way to sidestep the mainstream media and write directly to fans. Barry Bonds does not have to answer tough questions about steroid use on his blog[9] (and don't get me started on the "reality" show, *Bonds on Bonds*, that ESPN broadcast early in the 2006 season). Even Mark Cuban, the controversial owner of the Dallas Mavericks (and high-tech pioneer) maintains a blog[10] that is as quirky as Cuban; when I checked it out, he was discussing the physics of the new National Basketball Association game ball. The National Football League Players Association[11] and Major League Baseball[12] maintain player blogs as well.

Even these efforts to free players from dependence on traditional media can present ethical challenges. What if a player asked you to look at a rough draft of his blog entry to make sure it didn't read too dumb? Would you provide your professional services free of charge to a highly paid pro athlete?

Some might ask, what is the fuss all about? Today's sports culture—professional in particular, but college is close behind—is founded on a close working relationship between media and athlete. And we are talking about a form of entertainment here, not world peace or rampant disease. Can't we lighten up?

The most purist of sports fans would argue that sports fans need a watchdog media as much as voters do. Fans assume that they are watching pure competition. When anything corrupts sports, who is more qualified to uncover it than sports journalists? And let's not forget the tremendous amount of money that goes into sports every year. According to Forbes.com, the Washington Redskins are the highest valued professional football team, with a current value of $1.26 billion,[13] while the New York Yankees led Major League Baseball with a value of $1.026 billion.[14] NBC will pay $2 billion to broadcast the 2010 Winter Olympics and 2012 Summer Olympics.[15] With so much money being spent, sports needs a watchdog as much as government and business do. Sadly, then, when it comes to journalism ethics, Sam Blake strayed far outside the lines. He let his friendship with Lou Gehrig compromise his responsibilities as a journalist. The audience might applaud the actions of a loyal friend; most journalists would cringe.

Unless you're an unrepentant grinch, part of you will reach out to any individual who treats you with respect, on and off the job. But reach carefully. Otherwise you might end up with your hand bitten—by the athletes you help.

NOTES

1. Allan Wolper, "Reporters Lament the Steroid Secret," *Editor & Publisher* 138 (August 2005): 8, 22.

2. Joe Strupp, "Caught Not Looking," *Editor & Publisher* (October 2006): 42–47.

3. George F. Custen, *Bio/Pics* (New Brunswick, NJ: Rutgers University Press, 1992), 163.

4. Paul Aron, *Did Babe Ruth Call His Shot? And Other Unsolved Mysteries of Baseball* (Hoboken, NJ: John Wiley & Sons, 2005), 51–55.

5. Mark Inabinett, *Grantland Rice and His Heroes: The Sportswriter as Mythmaker in the 1920s* (Knoxville: University of Tennessee Press, 1994), 21–22.

6. Inabinett, *Grantland Rice and His Heroes*, 110.

7. Jonathan Eig, *Luckiest Man: The Life and Death of Lou Gehrig* (New York: Simon and Schuster, 2005), 119.

8. "Ruth's Record Can Be Broken Only in 154 Games, Frick Rules," *New York Times*, 18 July 1961, 20.

9. Barry Bonds, "Barry's Journal," October 4, 2006, BarryBonds.com, http://barrybonds.mlb.com/players/bonds_barry/journal/latest.html (accessed 28 October 2006).

10. "Blog Maverick: The Mark Cuban Weblog," www.blogmaverick.com (accessed 28 October 2006).

11. "Players," NFLPlayers.com, www.nflplayers.com/players/journals.aspx (accessed 28 October 2006).

12. "The Player Blog," http://players.mlblogs.com (accessed 28 October 2006). Unfortunately, this blog is no longer active.

13. "NFL Team Valuations," Forbes.com, www.forbes.com/lists/2005/30/Rank_1.html (accessed 29 August 2006).

14. "Baseball Team Valuations," Forbes.com, www.forbes.com/lists/2006/33/Rank_1.html (accessed 29 August 2006).

15. Vicki Michaelis, "U.S. Games Boost Bottom Line," *USA Today*, 30 June 2005, C9.

WHEN JOURNALISTS ARE FIRST RESPONDERS

Die Hard and Die Hard 2

Bill Reader

It's sometimes said that news reporters are the sort of people who run toward whatever everybody else is running away from. Within the ranks of journalism, that's a statement of pride, signifying that the best reporters often put their responsibility to inform the public above their own safety and comfort. What journalists see as selfless bravery, however, others often see as foolhardy meddling based on questionable ethics. That perception certainly is held by the other people who run toward things that everybody else flees—police, firefighters, medics, and other "first responders" to emergency situations.

Although journalists and emergency workers are often first on the scene, whether journalists belong there is a matter of debate. The tension between police and the press has been well documented, and the research reveals that while journalists rely on police for providing information and police rely on journalists to make their work known to the public,[1] there exists between them considerable distrust and resentment.[2] Police officers complain that journalists engage in sensationalism, are often inaccurate, sometimes compromise criminal investigations, are insensitive toward victims, and have little or no concern about how negative reports of police behavior can undermine public trust in law enforcement.[3] Journalists often complain that police are obstructionist to the public's right to know. That mutual resentment has been found even among college students in the respective fields of journalism and criminal justice,[4] suggesting that the suspicion

police have for journalists, and vice versa, may be endemic to both professions.

The distrust often spikes during *critical incidents*, defined as rare situations of extraordinary levels of mayhem, such as "natural disasters, hostage
situations, suicides, high-profile homicides, hazardous materials spills and
terrorist attacks."[5] During such dangerous and newsworthy situations, the
conflicting goals of journalists seeking information and police trying to es-
tablish control have "historically resulted in hostility, suspicion, and occasional violence."[6] For example, the April 1995 bombing of the Murrah Federal Building in Oklahoma City presented examples of such hostilities, as a
team of criminal justice scholars have recounted: "As quickly as police and
rescue personnel worked to secure the site, hordes of local and national
journalists flocked excitedly to the scene, replete with bright lights, cameras, and an insatiable need for immediate coverage and information from
authorities."[7]

Although written by an ostensibly objective team of researchers, that description presents an all-too-common negative framing of the media's role
in such situations. While the authorities were trying to "do their jobs" of
"protecting evidence, aiding victims, and interviewing witnesses," their
work was frustrated by "hordes" of journalists "flocking excitedly" out of
some "insatiable need."[8] Such rhetoric all but calls journalists vultures (the
researchers actually referred to such reporting as a "piranha-like assault").[9]
Like so many studies of first-responder journalism, that one ignores or dis-
counts any notion that journalists might have moral motives for covering
such critical incidents.

The caricature of journalists as uncaring scavengers figures prominently
in the blockbuster action films *Die Hard* and *Die Hard 2: Die Harder*, in
which the heroic efforts led by off-duty cop John McClane (Bruce Willis's
breakout role as an action hero) are complicated by journalists, particularly
an arrogant, aggressive TV reporter named Richard "Dick" Thornburg
(William Atherton). Although a second-tier character used to facilitate minor plot twists and add some cathartic comic relief (by being ridiculed, ver-
bally abused, and punched in the face by "good guys" in the films), Thornburg anchors a story arc across both films in which journalists are portrayed
as meddlesome, rude, pushy, exploitative, uninformed, and potentially dangerous. The journalists in these films seem willing to do anything to get the
story, from crossing police lines and breaking into secure areas to intimi-
dating innocent housekeepers and ignoring flight attendants on commercial
jets. And their resulting news reports to the public give the violent villains
(who, of course, are tuned in) a competitive edge over the good guys.

Whereas the goal of the police in the films is to seize control of crisis situations, protect the innocent, stop the bad guys, and restore order, the journalists seem more interested in fostering chaos, inciting panic, and exploiting situations for their own personal glory. The subtext is obvious: in times of crisis, journalists only make matters worse for first responders.

Less obvious in the films is the notion that journalists also are first responders and, like firefighters, medics, and police officers, have distinct jobs in critical incidents that, when approached ethically, can be of profound service to the public. First-responder journalists are in a position to warn the public of danger, to verify and (if necessary) correct statements from authorities and other media, to put a human face on the stoic, abstract reports from officials, and to document traumatic situations in ways that facilitate collective understanding and eventual healing. Those benefits are easy to overlook in the heat of the moment, when sirens are blaring, lights are flashing, and people are screaming.

Few people realize that first-responder journalists face many of the same physical and emotional risks as emergency workers, yet still feel obligated to be on the scene to "do the job." A reporter and a news photographer covering the 9/11 attacks on the World Trade Center told a researcher that they felt obligated to be on the scene along with the police and fire crews they had covered for years.[10] The two journalists did not just take pictures and gather eyewitness accounts of the death and destruction; they also "pulled people from the rubble, made calls for help, tried to save people high up in the Towers, dug for remains, and handed out water."[11] In previous years, both journalists had developed close professional and even personal relationships with police officers and firefighters (including some who died on 9/11), such that the photographer characterized his work that day as a "sacred obligation"[12] to the first-response teams, and the reporter said, "It was great to have the image of [the] reality of these brave men" to make the public aware that "if you are in trouble there are people who will come and give their lives for you."[13]

The personal toll of responding to such incidents also is similar among journalists and emergency workers. Like firefighters, medics, and police, first-responder journalists often find themselves facing incidents involving injury, destruction, and grisly death.[14] A survey of journalists found 86 percent had experienced traumatic incidents while on the job, and some exhibited self-reported symptoms of post-traumatic stress disorder.[15] While covering critical incidents, journalists may deal with the horrors in much the same way as police and firefighters: they may draw on their professional training and experience to engage the situation, exhibit signs of "psychological numbness" to avoid being hampered or paralyzed by emotions at the scene, and tap into their sense of camaraderie to "get the job done."[16] Research on real-world journalists reveals that most of those who "swarm" to the scenes of critical incidents are far from the uncaring scavengers depicted in such films as *Die Hard* and *Die Hard 2*. Rather, they are human beings willing to risk physical and emotional injury to serve the public good.

RETHINKING NEWS COVERAGE IN *DIE HARD*

Unfortunately, the negative portrayal of first-responder journalists in *Die Hard* has become more than a simple mischaracterization. Since its wildly successful release in 1988, *Die Hard* has inspired other big-budget action films. (Australian film critic Terry Oberg noted that many films have adopted the *Die Hard* formula, lamenting that "*Passenger 57* was *Die Hard*-on-a-plane, *Under Siege* was *Die Hard*-on-a-boat, and *Speed* was *Die Hard*-on-a-bus").[17] Based on the 1979 novel *Nothing Lasts Forever* by Roderick Thorp and set in late-1980s Los Angeles in an ultramodern corporate high rise called the Nakatomi Plaza, *Die Hard* pits off-duty New York cop John McClane against a dozen highly trained, well-equipped terrorists, who capture the building and take its occupants hostage. In one daring action sequence after another, McClane foils the terrorists' plans to steal millions of dollars and then blow up the building and the hostages to mask their escape. McClane's task is complicated by a number of factors: his estranged wife, Holly, is one of the hostages; the terrorists have locked up the building's elevators, security gates, and communications networks, making it impossible for McClane to escape or call for help; and he is severely outnumbered and outgunned as the terrorists/thieves are armed with assault rifles, plastic explosives, and rocket launchers. The primary antagonists are the slick European terrorists/thieves led by Hans Gruber (Alan Rickman), but a number of lesser antagonists unwittingly compromise McClane's heroic efforts. Those tangential "villains" include an incompetent deputy police chief, Dwayne T. Robinson (Paul Gleason), whose by-the-book bravado endangers his own men as well as McClane; two overconfident FBI agents who further "help" the terrorists with their extreme measures; and the aggressive TV news reporter Richard "Dick" Thornburg.

Of all the characters in the film, Thornburg is the only one given no redeeming qualities. Gruber is almost an antihero: refined, cunning, and charismatic. His fellow terrorists/thieves impress with their flawless martial arts, smile-inducing witticisms, and high-tech know-how. The bungling deputy chief clearly has good intentions to resolve the situation by the book, even if "the book" is well known to the terrorists. The swaggering FBI agents (Grand L. Bush and Robert Davi) deliver some deadpan one-liners that elicit laughs and some respect, even as they callously discuss "acceptable" losses of hostages.

But Thornburg is afforded no sympathetic attributes. His interest in pursuing the story appears to be motivated only by his desire to beat the competing news stations and win personal accolades. At no point does he seem concerned about the dangers of the situation, sympathetic toward the hostages and their families, or concerned for the safety of the police officers trying to resolve the crisis. Public service seems wholly absent from his motives. Moreover, Thornburg is rude and demanding of everybody he encounters, and his dialogue is neither clever nor memorable. Most poignantly, his broadcasts unwittingly tip off the terrorists to McClane's and his wife's identities, putting both in even more danger.

Thornburg is more than just a character you love to hate. He is the prototype for another stock bad guy in popular culture, the media vulture (akin to strict principals in high-school comedies or gossipy housewives in suburban dramas). Now common in so many movies and television shows, the press-as-piranha role encourages people to take a negative attitude toward journalism in the real world. When critical incidents do occur, and we stop what we are doing to tune in the special reports on TV, we have a need and desire for the journalists' work. But we also feel resentment toward those journalists. We can't help but see the despicable Dick Thornburg reporting the news, and we don't like what we see.

Thornburg first appears about halfway through *Die Hard*, sitting on a desk in the newsroom of his TV station, KFLW. He is on the phone trying to firm up plans for a dinner date, bragging, "Monica, I can get us a table. Wolfgang and I are very close friends. I interviewed him, for God's sake." Over a nearby CB scanner, he hears a frantic policeman reporting gunfire at the Nakatomi Plaza building. Thornburg drops the phone without saying anything to his potential date and runs off as if to pursue the story.

After cutting to the main action between McClane and the terrorists for several minutes, the film returns to Thornburg, who is chasing his dismissive news director through the chaotic newsroom just before the evening newscast is to go on air. Thornburg aggressively tries to get permission to use a news van and crew to pursue the story at the Nakatomi Plaza, saying, "I can get the jump on everybody if I get a remote," a van equipped with editing and broadcasting technology. The news director seems unwilling to accommodate him until Thornburg says, "Alright, look, Sam, I'll tell you what. If you don't want to give me a truck, I'll go and I'll steal a truck." The journalists next appear in a scene at the police line outside the Nakatomi Plaza. Their presence is announced by one of the officers, who says, "TV's here," to which the deputy chief responds, "Oh, shit." The scene then cuts to an image of a TV van swerving to get around police officers waving their arms to stop it.

The next journalism scene starts on a small television in the office used as the terrorists' command center. The screen shows Thornburg in front of his camera outside the building, starting his report with "This is Richard Thornburg live from Century City. Tonight, Los Angeles has joined the sad and worldwide fraternity of cities whose only membership requirement is to suffer the anguish of international terrorism." As Thornburg talks, the movie camera pans back to view his report through another TV being watched by a chauffeur waiting in a limousine in the building's parking garage, suggesting that the broadcast is being watched not just by the terrorists or the hostages, but also by people who may be in danger.

As the action continues, an overconfident SWAT commander orders his team to go in, only to see them gunned down by the terrorists. The SWAT commander then calls in an urban assault vehicle, which the terrorists destroy with a rocket launcher. Thornburg's crew films the fiery destruction of the SWAT vehicle and the massive explosion that follows. Thornburg's response is a curt "Please tell me you got that!" to his camera operator, who says he did, leading Thornburg to gloat, "Eat your heart out, Channel Five."

Like the police around him, Thornburg has learned that one of the hostages in the building is fighting the terrorists. Upon learning about Mc-Clane by listening in on his communications with the police on site, Thornburg turns to a female assistant and says, "Get on the phone to Harry in New York. C'mon baby, move! Move!" The assistant soon returns, smiling with self-satisfaction, and presents all manner of biographical details about McClane from his personnel file at the New York Police Department, including his estranged wife's home address in Los Angeles.

We next see Thornburg and his crew wedged in the door of the McClane home, trying to convince the housekeeper to let them in to interview the McClanes' young children. When denied entry, Thornburg threatens the Hispanic-sounding woman: "You let us in right now, or I call the INS. *Comprende*?" Seeing her nervous reaction, Thornburg appears to soften and, assuming a compassionate tone, says, "Look, this is the last time these kids will have to speak to their parents. Alright?" The housekeeper reluctantly lets Thornburg and crew enter.

The report from the house shows Thornburg interviewing the McClanes' daughter: "You know, your mom and dad are very important people.

They're very brave people. So is there something you would like to say to them?" The little girl says plaintively, "Come home." Unbeknownst to Thornburg, the report reveals to the terrorists that the hostage "Holly" is McClane's wife, and the terrorists attempt to use her as a human shield against McClane's efforts to stop them.

Thornburg doesn't appear again until the very end of the film when, as the McClanes stagger triumphantly from the damaged building, he runs up to them yelling, "Mr. McClane! Mr. McClane! After this incredible ordeal, what are your feelings?" Through the TV news camera, Thornburg is seen extending and holding his microphone in front of McClane's face. Holly responds with a quick punch to Thornburg's nose. In the background, police officers start laughing, and Thornburg looks into the camera and says sarcastically, "Did you get that?"

A JERK, BUT NO COWARD

Die Hard star Bruce Willis is no fan of the news media, being quoted in May 2006 as saying, "We go for the sensational now in the news. If it's not sensational or tantalizing or making fun of someone, it seldom gets into the news. I don't watch the news anyway. I have it turned off, and I feel so much better for it."[18] Similar sentiments have been expressed by the film's director, John McTiernan, who, in the commentary on the 2001 DVD of *Die Hard*, says, "It's become a cliché now that, y'know, reporters are not necessarily nice people. But it was astonishing then. Some reviewers were just excoriated because we were making fun of the press." Yet the same criticisms can be made of the police in the film, especially the deputy chief and the two FBI agents, who also come across as "not nice." The fact is that all professions, including professions staffed by "heroes," such as cops and firefighters, have members who "are not necessarily nice people." That doesn't mean that their work is of no value.

In *Die Hard*, if we look beyond Thornburg's thoroughly unpleasant personality, we can see how his actions could be seen as selfless, morally defensible, and of profound social benefit. From the very start, he is portrayed as a journalist willing to put his personal life on hold when duty calls (he hangs up on his date to pursue the news of terrorists firing machine guns). Thornburg also risks his professional security by arguing zealously with his news director and coworkers, all of whom seem uninterested and even hostile toward Thornburg's call to action. His behavior brings to mind Warren Breed's landmark study, "Social Control in the Newsroom," in which Breed suggested that journalists might not challenge the questionable actions of coworkers and superiors for a number of reasons: loyalty to their bosses, fear of punishment, desire for promotion, unwillingness to disrupt an otherwise pleasant working environment, and a lack of colleagues willing to stand with the objector.[19] Thornburg could easily be characterized as a jerk, but he's no coward.

Once on the scene, the nature of Thornburg's public service becomes apparent. By getting to the critical incident almost immediately after the police, he and his camera crew position themselves so that police must both protect and be responsible to the public. On the face of it, that might seem only to make the police's job more difficult, but keep in mind that such a critical incident would pose a serious public risk as well:

- In the film, terrorists are firing high-powered machine guns and rockets into the air and at police in the streets. The effective range of such weapons is measured in miles. If the situation had been real, anybody within a miles-wide radius of the office tower could have been at risk of getting hit by stray bullets.
- The Nakatomi Plaza ostensibly contains the offices of other businesses, whose personnel, equipment, and documents would also be in danger. News of such risk could allow employees of those businesses to initiate any emergency plans they may have for high-risk scenarios, such as freezing assets or securing remote databases.
- Of course, in crisis situations, friends and family of people who live or work in the affected buildings want to ascertain whether their loved ones are safe. In such cases, family and friends commonly look in the background of TV images to catch glimpses of their loved ones or to seek more detailed information from news reports.

Because other first responders often are more focused on the emergency, they may not consider or appreciate the importance of alerting the general public. And even if they do, they will rely on the first-responder journalists who are on hand to get that information out quickly and with authority.

Beyond alerting the public, Thornburg also plays a "watchdog" role by recording the many failures of the police. Had the *Die Hard* scenario been real, there would have been considerable public concern about how both local and federal law enforcement responded to the situation, from the deputy chief who ignored warnings from McClane about the terrorists' weapons to the FBI agents whose attempted helicopter assault on the terrorists resulted in a massive explosion and the deaths of at least the agents and their flight crew. Though unflattering to police, such reporting can also spark public demands for internal investigations of police procedures and can lead to reforms that will in the end protect first-response officers and boost public confidence in police leaders. If journalists just report from their newsrooms by relying solely on press releases, there is no guarantee that information about commanders' incompetence will be accurate or even made public.

AMBULANCE CHASERS, HEROES, OR "JUST DOING THEIR JOB"?

It would be a stretch to lionize first-responder journalists in the same way our culture celebrates the heroism of those who fight fires, render medical assistance, and stop bad guys. Suggesting that we should likely would generate outright hostility, as these comments from one reader of the *Seattle Times* show: "To elevate the ambulance chasers of the press as first responders when they simply sit on the sidelines and file stories of the tragedy without lifting a finger to provide real help to the suffering aside from shoving a microphone in their faces is to make a cruel joke of the term."[20]

Yet there are examples of first-responder journalists preventing injuries, destruction, and even deaths. Consider the role of journalists in New Orleans in early September 2005, after Hurricane Katrina raged along the Louisiana and Mississippi coasts. Immediately after the storm cleared, national media reported that New Orleans had "dodged a bullet," based on reports from journalists who were staying in hotels in the largely untouched French Quarter and downtown areas. But first-responder journalists who rushed to evacuation sites, such as New Orleans's convention center and Superdome arena, quickly corrected that initial error—New Orleans had been devastated, with tens of thousands of people trapped in the flooded city. While government officials were making claims that aid was being provided and the situation was under control, on-the-scene reporters presented evidence to the contrary.[21] They were in a position to provide real-time reports about the tragedy, from such basic information as which evacuation routes were open to gripping testimony from victims who were suffering with no relief in sight.[22] Although much of New Orleans was under water, journalists managed to get into, out of, and around the city, refuting with firsthand evidence government claims that help was delayed because rescue trucks couldn't get into the city. In fact, some journalists even told government officials which roads were passable.[23]

Journalists also rendered actual aid to victims. Syndicated columnist Leonard Pitts Jr. of the *Miami Herald*, dispatched to the Gulf Coast to cover the hurricane's aftermath, recalled purchasing water, food, and other supplies to take with him not just for himself but also for any victims he encountered.[24] According to Mizell Stewart III, editor-at-large for Knight Ridder newspapers at the time, reporters for the Biloxi (Mississippi) *Sun Herald* not only passed out emergency supplies as they moved around their storm-ravaged communities but also gave away copies of their newspaper, which was the only source of information many victims had about where to seek shelter, medical assistance, or other relief.[25]

Journalists also were able to perform a watchdog role by revealing public officials and police officers who were exploiting the chaos. Recalls one journalist from the *Times-Picayune* newspaper, "When our own reporting team crossed the river on that Tuesday morning to head back downtown, scarcely an hour after we had evacuated our building, they came upon police and citizens at a downtown Wal-Mart. Mistaking it for a command post and relief center, [the reporters] charged breezily into a massive and systematic looting spree. The police were not there to stop it. They were there to participate. When somebody shouted out, 'The *Times-Picayune*'s taking pictures. Let's go out back and take care of business,' [the reporters] *knew*, first, that it was time to go, and second, that the city was now completely out of control."[26]

Perhaps the most important role of journalists, however, is to humanize such tragedies. The business editor of the *Sun Herald* said her experiences covering Hurricane Katrina taught her that first-responder journalists are there to "listen to as many people as you can—standing in line with them, in every day situations . . . to learn what they're talking about—their problems, their needs."[27] Another journalist at the *Sun Herald* recalls, "There are two lessons I learned that cannot be segregated in my mind because they overlap. . . . The first is journalism's absolute necessity in this information-laden world. It fills the void where people in sympathy, empathy and who are living the disaster need to see, feel and hear what is happening. The second is to sometimes kick-start the conversation. There are so many things happening all at once, journalism serves as a tool to focus the communal conscience. People need to be told what is important, what to concentrate on and how to address it."[28]

Although journalists can, and sometimes do, cause problems at disaster scenes, they also can serve several valuable functions:

- *Warning the public:* Journalists on the scene of critical incidents often are in positions to provide real-time reports of dangerous situations, such as flash floods, spreading conflagrations, violent mobs, clogged evacuation routes, the locations of stranded victims, and the like. As trained, professional observers, journalists at minimum can provide additional eyes and ears to help emergency workers locate victims or witnesses and to identify previously unreported hazardous situations. Sometimes journalists even witness crimes in progress and may agree to provide police with photographs or video of the incidents, even though they are under no legal obligation to do so. Besides possibly assisting authorities directly, journalists also can equip citizens with information that can help them make immediate decisions to protect themselves, their friends and families, and their property.

- *Monitoring and verifying official claims:* As in the case of the New Orleans journalists who said their presence at the scene of post-Katrina looting revealed police officers were participating in the crime, the eyes (and especially cameras) of journalists can sometimes deter reckless or unprofessional behaviors by other first responders. Those journalists also are in positions to verify, document, and, if necessary, refute the claims of authorities, eyewitnesses, and also other journalists.
- *Relaying timely information from authorities to the public:* As authorities on the scene engage and investigate situations, they will invariably have information that they need to make public as quickly as possible. In those situations, first-responder journalists form a bridge between the police and public, which is perhaps "the true audience of concern for law enforcement administrators."[29] Such quick publication of information may spur emergency evacuations, resolve public confusion about the scope of incidents, and rally the public to assist by looking out for signs of additional risk. Moreover, timely releases of information to the public via news media can help police officers enhance public trust that police are "on the job" and "in control."[30]
- *Documenting history in the making:* Critical incidents are not just emergencies to be dealt with quickly; they also are moments of profound historical significance. Although the raw emotions generated during and immediately after such incidents can be painful, as time goes on the images and eyewitness accounts gathered by journalists become the texts through which people contemplate and understand those events. Photojournalists in downtown Manhattan on 9/11 captured horrifying images of people jumping from the towering infernos of the World Trade Center, of mobs running from mushrooming clouds of dust and debris as the towers collapsed, and of artifacts in the rubble that dramatically attested to the scope of the human toll. In the

days and weeks after the attacks, the publication of such images was controversial and heart wrenching. Years later, those images are important reminders of what happened that day and provide a shared discourse through which the world can reflect upon the horror.

FROM *DIE HARD* TO THE REAL WORLD

Of course, the *Die Hard* character Thornburg does make some unethical choices that would have done real harm had the situation not been a fiction. His remark after the first large explosion ("Eat your heart out, Channel Five") is crass and, if made public, could have undermined the benefits of the coverage and further eroded public trust in the news media. His behavior at the McClane household violates several tenets of the ethics codes of both the Radio Television News Directors Association (RTNDA)[31] and the Society of Professional Journalists (SPJ)[32] regarding reporting on critical incidents, interviewing children, and endangering victims. And his final act of sticking a microphone in the face of a victim and asking, "How do you feel?" is insensitive, inappropriate, and inane.

Thornburg's character is never fully developed; he is only constructed in brief moments scattered throughout the first film, and he is largely the object of ridicule in the second. But given the enduring popularity of the *Die Hard* films and their influence on the films that have followed, it would be folly to dismiss him as "just a minor character." It would be interesting to ask random people if they think the Thornburg character is a realistic portrayal of what TV reporters are really like. The responses would likely be sobering.

Missing from both the *Die Hard* movies and many real-world discussions of journalistic behavior is not how journalists should behave at critical incidents, but rather why they should cover such incidents. Professional advice from such notable journalism ethicists as the Poynter Institute's Bob Steele and Joe Hight, managing editor of the *Oklahoman* and president of the executive committee of the Dart Center for Journalism and Trauma, often is framed as "don't get in the way" and "listen to the police."[33] Professional codes of ethics, including those of the RTNDA and SPJ, also seem to focus entirely on how first-responder journalists should behave on the scene, with no suggestion as to why they should be there in the first place.

Although the advice of Steele, Hight, and others is thoughtful and useful, it doesn't help journalists understand the ethical arguments in support of their presence on the scene or their obligations to society at those critical incidents. In fact, nonjournalists could misread advice like "ask if the value of a live, on-the-scene report is really justifiable compared to the harm that could occur"[34] as meaning that the press should defer to the authorities, regardless of whether the authorities may be overlooking public interests. What if a SWAT team's action inadvertently endangers the public? What if more harm could be done by not going live on the scene? What if a few bad-apple officers exploit a situation to cover up their own wrongdoing? Those are the kinds of serious questions rarely asked by emergency workers or the people tuning in to watch such incidents unfold on the news.

In *Die Hard*, the negative portrayal of the press is based on an assumption that journalists have no useful role to play in emergency situations. When a critical incident occurs, nobody questions why police cordon off the area, why firefighters smash windows or break down doors, or why ambulances are allowed to exceed speed limits and run traffic lights. But it seems people always question why journalists rush to the incidents. And beyond throwing out generic arguments based on First Amendment rights and the public's right to know, most journalists themselves may not understand why they should be there either.

If journalists are to feel proud that they so often run toward what everybody else is running away from, they need to be fully aware of their mission. The best time to think of that mission isn't live on the scene, when emotions are high and the dangers real, or after an incident, when the newsroom is barraged with angry phone calls and e-mails from the audience, but perhaps on the sofa in front of the television, watching a silly old action movie and thinking seriously about why journalists must be among the first to respond.

NOTES

1. Steven Chermak and Alexander Weiss, "Maintaining Legitimacy Using External Communication Strategies: An Analysis of Police-Media Relations," *Journal of Criminal Justice* 33, no. 5 (September–October 2005): 501–12.

2. Gerald W. Garner, *The Police Meet the Press* (Springfield, IL: C. C. Thomas, 1984).

3. J. E. Guffey, "The Police and the Media: Proposal for Managing Conflict Productively," *American Journal of Police* 11, no. 1 (1992): 33–51.

4. William L. Selke and G. Marshall Bartoszek, "Police and Media Relations: The Seeds of Conflict," *Criminal Justice Review* 9, no. 2 (1984): 25–30.

5. Tory Caeti, John Liederbach, and Steven S. Bellew, "Police-Media Relations at Critical Incidents: Interviews from Oklahoma City," *International Journal of Police Science & Management* 7, no. 2 (2005): 86–97.

6. Caeti, Liederbach, and Bellew, "Police-Media Relations at Critical Incidents," 87.

7. Caeti, Liederbach, and Bellew, "Police-Media Relations at Critical Incidents," 87.

8. Caeti, Liederbach, and Bellew, "Police-Media Relations at Critical Incidents," 87.

9. Caeti, Liederbach, and Bellew, "Police-Media Relations at Critical Incidents," 86.

10. Tovia G. Freedman, "Voices of 9/11 First Responders: Patterns of Collective Resilience," *Clinical Social Work Journal* 32, no. 4 (Winter 2004): 377–93.

11. Freedman, "Voices of 9/11 First Responders," 383.

12. Freedman, "Voices of 9/11 First Responders," 383.

13. Freedman, "Voices of 9/11 First Responders," 389.

14. Chermak and Weiss, "Maintaining Legitimacy Using External Communication Strategies"; Jim Ruiz and D. F. Treadwell, "The Perp Walk: Due Process v. Freedom of the Press," *Criminal Justice Ethics* 21, no. 2 (Summer/Fall 2002): 44–56.

15. Richard A. Simpson and James G. Boggs, "An Exploratory Study of Traumatic Stress among Newspaper Journalists," *Journalism & Mass Communication Monographs* 1, no. 1 (Spring 1999): 1–26.

16. Freedman, "Voices of 9/11 First Responders."

17. Terry Oberg, "Where Have All the He-Men Gone?" *Courier Mail* (Queensland, Australia), 14 April 2001, M9.

18. "Willis' News Strike," Internet Movie Database, 9 May 2006, www.imdb .com/news/wenn/2006-05-09#celeb4 (accessed 30 September 2006).

19. Warren Breed, "Social Control in the Newsroom," *Social Forces* 33, no. 4 (1955): 326–35.

20. Michael R. Fancher, "The Role of Journalism in the Midst of Disasters," *Seattle Times*, 25 September 2005, A2A.

21. Steven Carter, "New Orleans Newspaper Blasts FEMA," *Oregonian*, 5 September 2005, A12.

22. Alessandra Stanley, "Reporters Turn from Deference to Outrage," *New York Times*, 5 September 2005, A14.

23. Carter, "New Orleans Newspaper Blasts FEMA."

24. Leonard Pitts Jr., personal communication, October 2005.

25. Mizell Stewart III, personal communication, October 2005.

26. James O'Byrne, "Katrina: The Power of the Press against the Wrath of Nature," Poynteronline, www.poynter.org/content/content_view.asp?id=106352 (accessed 30 September 2006).

27. Candace Clark, "Lessons from Katrina," Poynteronline, www.poynter.org/ column.asp?id=68&aid=93926 (accessed 30 September 2006).

28. Clark, "Lessons from Katrina."

29. Caeti, Liederbach, and Bellew, "Police-Media Relations at Critical Incidents," 96.

30. L. Gaines, M. Southerland, and J. Angel, *Police Administration* (New York: McGraw-Hill, 2003).

31. Radio Television News Directors Association, "Code of Ethics," www.rtnda .org/ethics/coe.shtml (accessed 30 September 2006).

32. Society of Professional Journalists, "Code of Ethics," www.spj.org/ethicscode .asp (accessed 30 September 2006).

33. Bob Steele, "Guidelines for Covering Hostage-Taking Crises, Prison Uprisings, Terrorist Actions," Poynteronline, www.poynter.org/content/content_view .asp?id=4640 (accessed 30 September 2006).

34. Joe Hight, "First Responders," Dart Center for Journalism and Trauma, www.dartcenter (accessed 30 September 2006).

8

STYLE OVER SUBSTANCE

Broadcast News

Lee Anne Peck

Forty years ago, Fred Friendly, a former CBS News president, published his book *Due to Circumstances Beyond Our Control*, in which he shared his disheartening thoughts about networks needing to "get the ratings and make as much money as [they] can." Those were the words of Friendly's onetime boss, James Aubrey, president of the CBS Television Network.[1] When Aubrey decided on February 10, 1966, to run an "ancient rerun" of the sitcom *I Love Lucy* instead of the Senate Foreign Relations Committee hearings on Vietnam, Friendly quit.[2]

James L. Brooks, writer and director of the 1987 film *Broadcast News*, worked briefly as a writer for CBS News in New York before moving to Los Angeles in 1966 to become a screenwriter. Almost twenty years after his 1960s CBS stint, he returned to the news business—not as a writer but as an observer.[3] What evolved from his experiences was the screenplay for *Broadcast News*, a movie presenting worst-case scenarios for network news of the 1980s and foreshadowing broadcast news of the future.

Broadcast News tackles the battle between journalistic and business values and injects a workplace romance into the conflict. Other network-news dilemmas the movie confronts include news versus entertainment, good-looking anchors with questionable news backgrounds (flash over substance), the dumbing down of society via television, and the faking of the news. Throughout the movie, ethical dilemmas reign, and viewers will learn why falsifying a seemingly trivial personal reaction is verboten.[4]

Broadcast News is foremost a comedy—and an enjoyable one at that. As one reviewer said, "This picture should delight a sizable audience looking for a thoughtful night out as well as a good laugh."[5] Brooks, who has been the executive producer of *The Simpsons*, has always written and/or produced comedies, whether they be half-hour TV sitcoms, such as *The Mary Tyler Moore Show* and *Taxi*, or movies, such as *Big*, *The War of the Roses*, *Jerry Maguire*, and *As Good As It Gets*. No matter what subject Brooks tackles, however, his efforts always seem to ring true. With *Broadcast News*, the interactions of the characters seem "priceless and achingly authentic."[6]

A TRIP TO PLATO'S CAVE

Broadcast News has three main characters: Jane Craig (Holly Hunter), a producer at a network's Washington, D.C., news bureau; Aaron Altman (Albert Brooks—no relation to James L. Brooks), a reporter working at the D.C. office who allegedly lacks the looks needed to be an anchor; and Tom Grunick (William Hurt), an anchor and reporter at the D.C. bureau who doesn't understand what he reads on the air but has the good looks people at home want to see. Jack Nicholson plays the network's national anchor, Bill Rorich, based in New York City. The movie examines how these "professionals" operate on and off the job and how the TV industry works.[7]

Toward the beginning of the movie, Jane speaks before her peers at a broadcasting conference. After trying to engage her restless and inattentive audience with a discussion of what's troubling about TV news, she puts aside her note cards and describes a situation somewhat similar to Friendly's in the 1960s:

> I was going to talk about other trends . . . the magazine shows, news as profit, the historic influence of *Entertainment Tonight*, the hope, the dream, the question. . . . Oh, I was going to show you a tape—a story that was carried by all networks on the same night—the same night not one network noted a major policy change in Salt II nuclear disarmament talks. . . . Here's what they ran instead.[8]

Video monitors show a spectacular Japanese domino championship, and the audience claps and squeals with delight. Poor Jane—her peers just don't get it. She notes that, yes, the domino championship makes for good film, but "it's just not news."

The scene reminds one of Plato's "Allegory of the Cave" from Book VII of *The Republic,* a tome that describes Plato's ideas of a just society.[9] To recap the story: In a deep cave, men have been chained by their legs and necks to a wall; they cannot move and can only look straight ahead. A fire burns behind these prisoners, and the light from the fire reflects above them on the wall. Between the fire and the prisoners is a walkway bordered by a screen. Behind this screen, puppeteers walk, carrying high above them artificial objects. These items project above the screen on the prisoners' wall. For the prisoners, these shadows are their reality—or their beliefs.

For the purposes of this chapter, the cave is a community. The prisoners are members of the public, and the puppeteers are journalists doing what they're told. The daylight outside the cave is true knowledge. The shadows the public sees on the wall are what the journalists provide them.

Both Friendly of CBS and Jane of *Broadcast News* believe a journalist's or news organization's job is to provide "prisoners" with the information they need to function in society. In other words, they would say journalists need to go beyond merely providing entertainment for the public. The networks showing the domino competition instead of covering nuclear disarmament talks illustrates this problem.

In Plato's allegory, a prisoner escapes from the cave and sees the real world outside. He becomes enlightened, so to speak; the shadows are no longer his reality. When he returns to the cave to explain what he saw to the other prisoners, they are incredulous. Plato would say ethical journalists need to be like the prisoner who escapes, coming back to the cave and sharing the truth—whether it's entertaining or not. They should know "the important role that they play in what is essentially a civilizing process."[10]

After Jane's speech, the good-looking Tom introduces himself to her. She asks him to dinner with motives other than talking shop. Tom believes he has a decent on-air presence and "talks well enough."[11] However, he confides that he often doesn't understand the news he reads. Jane finally sees beyond Tom's good looks and realizes he's unqualified and a fraud. "So you're not well educated and you have almost no experience and you can't write. . . . It is hard for me to advise you since you personify something that I truly think is dangerous. . . . Just what do you want from me? Permission to be a fake?" she asks.[12] Tom leaves but calls later to tell her what he'd been trying to share all evening: he's been hired by her network and will work at the Washington bureau.

Later, Jane and Aaron rant about Tom's hiring and lament the dumbing down of their bureau—and the news in general. Jane and Aaron both have the highest news standards, and for Aaron, Tom represents "the devil."[13]

However, Jane continues to have romantic feelings for Tom, no matter how hard she tries to ignore them, while Aaron has romantic feelings for Jane. But why is Tom a network devil? Aaron explains it well:

> What do you think the devil will look like if he's around? . . . He will be attractive. He'll be nice and helpful. He'll get a job where he influences a God-fearing nation. . . . He'll just bit by bit lower our standards where they're important. Just coax along flash over substance. Just a tiny little bit. And he'll talk about all of us really being salesmen.[14]

Tom is not the prisoner who escapes the cave. He is a puppeteer told what to say and do by invisible producers.[15] When the unqualified Tom is not told what to do and tackles an assignment on his own, the consequences are, at best, mixed.

THE TEARS

As the storyline progresses, viewers see the clueless Tom reporting and anchoring. He decides to do a report without guidance, a piece on date rape for the evening news. When it airs, Tom is shown interviewing a victim with tears in his eyes. Aaron blatantly announces, "Can I turn on the news for a second? Oh, wait a minute. Sex, tears—this must be the news."[16]

Jump ahead almost twenty years to today. CNN's "star" newsperson Anderson Cooper gazes out from the June 2006 cover of *Vanity Fair*. Who is this guy—a journalist or a celebrity? "The main knock against [Cooper] is that he seems created out of whole cloth by a P. R. machine the way the old Hollywood studios once created stars through media campaigns," writes Neal Gabler of Salon.com.[17] *People* magazine named him one of the sexiest men of the year, and he has done a photo shoot for *Details* magazine and appeared on many TV talk shows.

Gabler believes that CNN is not just boosting an anchor "but changing the very paradigm of television news."[18] Cooper is a celebrity and he "emotes," Gabler writes. He points out that when news anchor Walter Cronkite teared up announcing President John F. Kennedy's death, it was a signature moment in American culture. Today, emoting anchors show up regularly on network, local, and cable news.

Dan Neil writes in the *Los Angeles Times* that when he looks at the blurry-eyed Cooper on the cover of *Vanity Fair*, he "can't help thinking of James L. Brooks' movie *Broadcast News*, in which William Hurt's character sheds an empathetic tear and becomes a star." He also points out that Cooper—"propelled to the info-pop empery with his trembling, awed and ireful coverage of the Katrina disaster in New Orleans—is mining the same vein of trumped-up pathos."[19] Neil calls him "the newscaster as professional mourner" and admonishes, "I don't need you to show me that you care. I need you to tell me what you know." In other words, give the public some insight, please.

Katie Couric, who was hired away from NBC's *Today* morning program to anchor the *CBS Evening News* in September 2006, has also been "sold as a star."[20] Her dating life is reported just as aggressively as any celebrity's. Plus, she's an emoter, too, Gabler says. She's the highest-paid news anchor on television, earning $15 million a year.[21] *New York Times* television writer Jacques Steinberg notes that "Ms. Couric—despite arriving on a wave of marketing hype that would have cost CBS more than $10 million had it not owned the network on which her endless promotional spots were broad-cast—lolled in third place [in the November sweeps], as Mr. Rather had for more than a decade, with 7.8 million viewers."[22] Her previous perky de-meanor on the *Today* program perhaps deflates her credibility as an evening news anchor. Is she a prisoner who escapes the darkness of the cave or merely a puppeteer?

THE SWEAT

Speaking of overpaid anchors: when Aaron is taken aside by his boss Ernie and told firings at the D.C. bureau are imminent—"They're not going by seniority. There's a recklessness in the air"[23]—he asks for the chance to an-chor. If he can prove himself both an excellent reporter and anchorperson, he might be more valuable to the network and keep his job.

Again, twenty years later, mass layoffs in newsrooms have become a reg-ular topic in various publications and broadcasts—and in the newsrooms themselves. Most recently, NBC Universal announced that it would lay off about four hundred people in its news division.[24] Layoffs began in late 2006 as part of a wider plan, NBCU 2.0, which hopes to save $750 million by cut-ting seven hundred jobs (5 percent of the total workforce) throughout the company by 2008 while creating less expensive prime-time programs.[25] Lo-cal D.C. station WRC, part of NBC Universal, began eliminating staffers in fall 2006; most of those asked to leave were older employees. "The station can pare its payroll substantially by replacing older, higher-salaried veterans with younger, less-expensive on-air personalities who theoretically will help

WRC attract younger viewers that the advertisers seek," reports the *Washington Post*.[26] But will cutting experienced news people at the station turn viewers off? Will credibility be lost? WRC anchor Wendy Rieger laments, "People forget that's what journalism is all about. It's not about pretty faces and the hot stand-up. It's about the story and the integrity of the craft and that's what's leaving the building. Who's left to set an example for the people coming up behind us?"[27] Someone like *Broadcast News*'s Aaron Altman? Although his journalistic motives and values are the highest, his future in network news turns out to be bleak.

Because everyone at the bureau wants to attend the Correspondents' Dinner, Ernie says Aaron can anchor the weekend news. Ironically, Tom coaches Aaron for his on-air performance, and the coaching turns into "a locker-room pep talk."[28] "And remember—you're not just reading the news or narrating. Everybody has to sell a little. You're selling them this idea of you," Tom says. "You know, what you're sort of saying is, 'Trust me. I'm, uh, credible.' So whenever you catch yourself just reading . . . stop and start selling a little."[29] As uncomfortable as this training from Tom makes Aaron, he accepts it to show the network what he can do.

Unfortunately, during his live broadcast on the weekend news, Aaron begins to sweat—profusely. He oozes "a Niagara of flop-sweat."[30] The sweating is so bad that people call the station to make sure Aaron is not having a heart attack. He tells Jane later that his "central nervous system was telling him something." "Sweat pouring down my face, makeup falling into my eyes, people turning on this fusillade of blow dryers on my head," he says. "All so I could read introductions to other people's stories."[31] The experience helps Aaron realize he still wants to report stories, to be the ethical journalist who leaves the cave and shares the truth. The slick anchor persona does not suit him.

NO PLACE FOR LOVE?

All this sweating on air, however, is happening while Tom and Jane attend the Correspondents' Dinner. They are two corners of a love triangle that includes Aaron. *Variety* describes the triangle in its 1987 review of *Broadcast News*: "Jane loves Tom but hates his work. Aaron loves his work and loves Jane and hates Tom. Tom loves himself and loves Jane. In short, it's a case of scrambled emotions among people who heretofore have substituted work for pleasure."[32] As Howard Good points out in his book *The Drunken Journalist*, these characters are "frantic overachievers, careerists with an aching void at the center of their lives."[33]

Jane leaves Tom at the dinner to go to Aaron's house to ask how the anchoring went. She promises to meet Tom later at his apartment. After learning that Aaron's stint went poorly, Jane reveals to Aaron she has to meet Tom with whom she thinks she may be in love. All hell breaks loose. "If things had gone well for me tonight, then I probably wouldn't be saying any of this," Aaron says. "I grant you everything. But give me this. . . . He personifies everything that you've been fighting against. And I'm in love with you. How do you like that? I buried the lead."[34]

The next week, the official firings happen. Bill Rorich, the network's multimillion-dollar anchor, comes from New York to soften the blows and keep up morale. Bill tells the station manager, Paul Moore (Peter Hackes), the layoffs are brutal and adds, "All because they couldn't program Wednesday nights." Paul replies, "You can make it a little less brutal by knocking a million dollars or so off your salary." Seeing the shocked look on Bill's face after this comment, Paul apologizes: "Just a bad joke. I'm sorry."[35] But he knows the reality of the situation.

As some staffers are given their notices, others are given promotions, namely Jane and Tom. Tom is being sent to the network's London bureau to continue his grooming, and Jane is given Ernie's job as bureau chief. Aaron, still maintaining his journalistic standards, quits before he can be fired. "They told me they'd keep me because they could plug me into any story and my salary was in line," he tells Tom, who seems oblivious to the fact that a move to London is actually a promotion. Tom has seen similar firings at every station he's worked for. Aaron, incredulous at Tom's nonchalance, asks Tom, "Can I ask you something? You only had one crew on the date-rape piece, right?"[36] "Yes," Tom says and immediately moves on to discussing the farewell party. However, Aaron knows that some unethical behavior has taken place on Tom's part during the rape piece. With only one crew, the camera only can record one person at a time. How did the camera get Tom's tears?

Nonetheless, Aaron has a good job lead with the number-two station in Portland, Oregon. He explains later to Jane, "The general manager says he wants to be every bit as good as the networks. Personally, I think he should aim higher."[37] Aaron also shares with Jane, who plans to take a weeklong vacation with Tom before starting her new job, the information he has about Tom's date-rape piece. He tries to help her remember her journalistic values one more time—to go beyond her star-crossed lover behavior. "Jane, do you know how Tom had tears in his eyes in that interview he did with that girl?" he asks. "Ask yourself how we were able to see that when he only had one camera, and it was pointed at the girl during the whole interview. I'm fairly sure I was right to tell you."[38]

IT *IS* VERBOTEN

With heartstrings tugging, Jane returns to the bureau's videotape library to see if what Aaron has said is true. She discovers Tom did fake his tears. Jane meets him at the airport the next day for their weeklong island trip. As Tom rises from a bench to greet her, she fights to remain calm. The conversation that ensues is the most powerful by far in clarifying the danger a person such as Tom presents to the television news industry.

> Jane: I'm not going.
> Tom: Why?
> Jane: I saw the taped outtakes of the interview with the girl. I know you "acted" your reaction after the interview.
> Tom: I felt funny about it afterward. It's verboten, huh? I thought since I did it for real the first time—but I get you. That's not the reason you're not coming?
> Jane: Of course it's the reason. It's terrible what you did.
> Tom: We disagree on how god-awful it was. Why don't you come with me, and we can disagree and get a tan at the same time?
> Jane: Jesus, if you're glib about this, I'm going to lose it. I was up all night and—
> Tom: Jane, Jane, Jane, Jane, Jane, Jane . . .
> Jane: It made me ill what you did. You could get fired for things like that.
> Tom: I got promoted for things like that.
> Jane: Working up tears for a news piece cutaway. . . . You totally crossed the line between—
> Tom: It's hard not to cross it. They keep moving the little sucker, don't they?
> Jane: It's amazing. You commit this incredible breach of ethics, and you act as if I'm nitpicking. Try and get this. When you edited that—
> Tom: I'm leaving now. Gate 43.[39]

AUTHENTIC OR NOT?

After *Broadcast News*'s release, the reviews were mostly positive. The main question asked was whether this storyline was true to life. The answers varied. In a 1988 interview with *People Weekly*, Tom Brokaw of NBC admitted some parts of *Broadcast News* were real but questioned airhead anchor Tom's character. Things really can't be that bad, he said. The two other major network anchors in 1988, Dan Rather and Peter Jennings, declined to comment for the *People* article.[40]

Mike Wallace of *60 Minutes* told *People* he found Tom unrealistic but the film "very realistic—the ambience, the egos, the pressures."[41] The article also stressed that those in the TV news business do blame "any flash-over-substance emphasis . . . with the new, bottom-line-minded network owners, who have no special feeling for TV journalism."[42] Brokaw admitted that he was not comfortable with the show-business aspects of anchoring but said "they come with the territory. . . . Hell, even Walter Cronkite did the 'Mary Tyler Moore' show."[43]

Bonnie Anderson, *News Flash* author and former CNN manager and correspondent, discusses how TV news today fakes "the small stuff."[44] The boundary between news and entertainment is blurry; Anderson calls this area the "Bad" because it's in the middle between the Good and the Ugly. Over time, she says, the Bad has become acceptable to broadcast news people.[45] "A cardinal rule of ethical television journalism has always been the video should be honest, nothing faked," Anderson explains.[46]

But Anderson gives many examples of fake footage the public (prisoners) see every day on their TVs (the shadows on the wall), such as shots set up in advance, video of events that did not happen naturally, interviews taped with one camera crew (as was Tom's date-rape interview). Her point is this: although these are seemingly small abuses that save money, they deceive viewers.[47] "Just how big a role should profit play for parent companies?" Anderson asks. "If news divisions or networks don't have the budget to cover the news events they're responsible for bringing to the public, then the profit-pushers have crossed the line. 'Selling' news to viewers is not the same as selling widgets. . . . The integrity of the news organization must be maintained for much more important and honorable reasons—for the good of democracy."[48]

What can one take from the movie *Broadcast News*? One won't watch the nightly network newscasts in the same way again, movie reviewer Peter Travers wrote.[49] "*Broadcast News* is sounding an alarm to a nation that wants it news delivered sitcom style," he explained. "Believe, if you want, the disclaimer that this movie is a fiction with no relation to real events."[50] Even CNN's emoter, Anderson Cooper, has said *Broadcast News* "is in the know."[51]

Just as the movie foreshadows, broadcast news in America today—be it done by networks, local stations, or cable—is in a precarious state.[52] Rebecca MacKinnon, who quit her job as a CNN bureau chief because she questioned CNN's motto of "the most trusted name in news," says, "The business model for democratized news of the future is completely unclear."[53] Many

people, from politicians to corporate heads, want to profit "from the puppeteer's show."[54]

"Citizens of a democracy need to know what their government is up to
and the implications of its actions," MacKinnon says. "Informing the public
courageously and responsibly is our patriotic duty as journalists."[55] TV journalists need to remember their role as those who escape from the cave. Responsible journalism means quality, truthful journalism, not "shadows."
Consider the following from Plato's allegory:

> And suppose someone tells [the escaped prisoner] that what he's been seeing
> all this time has no substance, and that he's now closer to reality and is see-
> ing more accurately, because of the greater reality of the things in front of his
> eyes—what do you think his reaction would be? . . . Once he'd distinguished
> between the two conditions and modes of existence, he'd congratulate any-
> one he found in the second state and feel sorry for anyone in the first state.[56]

The twenty-year-old *Broadcast News* shows viewers many of the conflicts
and ethical dilemmas with which network news people struggle. Because of
technology, how the news is transmitted and received keeps changing.
However, the basic principles and values of the profession of journalism will
remain the same, and this film gives viewers a good reminder of them.

NOTES

1. Fred W. Friendly, *Due to Circumstances Beyond Our Control* (New York:
Random House, 1967), xii.

2. Friendly, *Due to Circumstances*, xxv.

3. Rachel Abramowitz, "The Filmmaker Series: James L. Brooks," *Premiere*,
January 1998, 48–49.

4. James L. Brooks, *Broadcast News: The Screenplay* (New York: Vintage
Books, 1988), 165.

5. Jagr, "*Broadcast News*: Well-Acted Look at TV Journalism Lacks a Satisfying
Windup," *Variety*, 9 December 1987, 13.

6. Jagr, "*Broadcast News*," 13.

7. Don Kaye, "*Broadcast News*: Synopsis," MSN Movies, http://tv.msn.com/
movies (accessed 11 August 2006).

8. Brooks, *Broadcast News*, 20.

9. Plato, *The Republic* (Oxford: Oxford University Press, 1993), 240.

10. Jay Newman, *The Journalist in Plato's Cave* (Cranbury, NJ: Associated University Presses, 1989), 17.

11. Brooks, *Broadcast News*, 24.

12. Brooks, *Broadcast News*, 25.

13. Brooks, *Broadcast News*, 139.

14. Brooks, *Broadcast News*, 139.

15. Jane Hall and Brad Darrach, "The News about *Broadcast*," *People Weekly*, 1 February 1988, 62.

16. Brooks, *Broadcast News*, 113.

17. Neal Gabler, "Method Anchor," Salon.com, August 23, 2006, www.salon.com (accessed 11 November 2006).

18. Gabler, "Method Anchor."

19. Dan Neil, "'I' on America," *Los Angeles Times*, 2 June 2006, http://www.latimes.com (accessed 21 December 2006).

20. Gabler, "Method Anchor."

21. Jacques Steinberg, "In November Sweeps, NBC's Williams Is First among Anchors," 9 December 2006, *New York Times*, http://www.nytimes.com (accessed 30 December 2006).

22. Jacques Steinberg, "Dizzying Adventures on the Anchor Carousel," *New York Times*, 24 December 2006, http://www.nytimes.com (accessed 30 December 2006).

23. Brooks, *Broadcast News*, 117.

24. Matea Gold, "Staffers at NBC News Are Bracing for Layoffs," *Los Angeles Times*, 14 November 2006, http//:www.latimes.com (accessed 22 December 2006).

25. Gold, "Staffers at NBC News."

26. Paul Farhi, "WRC Cuts Change Face of Local News," *Washington Post*, 29 November 2006, C1.

27. Farhi, "WRC Cuts," C1.

28. Brooks, *Broadcast News*, 121.

29. Brooks, *Broadcast News*, 121.

30. Hall and Darrach, "The News about *Broadcast*," 62.

31. Brooks, *Broadcast News*, 137.

32. Jagr, "*Broadcast News*," 13.

33. Howard Good, *The Drunken Journalist* (Lanham, MD: Scarecrow Press, 2000), 136.

34. Brooks, *Broadcast News*, 140.

35. Brooks, *Broadcast News*, 150.

36. Brooks, *Broadcast News*, 154.

37. Brooks, *Broadcast News*, 160.

38. Brooks, *Broadcast News*, 162.

39. Brooks, *Broadcast News*, 164–66.

40. Hall and Darrach, "The News about *Broadcast*," 62.

41. Hall and Darrach, "The News about *Broadcast*," 62.

42. Hall and Darrach, "The News about *Broadcast*," 62.

43. Hall and Darrach, "The News about *Broadcast*," 62.

44. Bonnie M. Anderson, *News Flash: Journalism, Infotainment, and the Bottom-Line Business of Broadcast News* (San Francisco: Jossey-Bass, 2004), 98.

45. Anderson, *News Flash*, 99.

46. Anderson, *News Flash*, 99.

47. Anderson, *News Flash*, 100.

48. Anderson, *News Flash*, 233.

49. Peter Travers, "*Broadcast News*," *People Weekly*, 21 December 1987, 10.

50. Travers, "*Broadcast News*," 10.

51. Cristy Lytal, "What Is the Perfect Journalism Movie?" *Premiere*, June 2005, 30.

52. Rebecca MacKinnon, "The Precarious State of Television News," *Nieman Reports* 59, no. 1 (Spring 2005): 88.

53. MacKinnon, "The Precarious State," 90.

54. Newman, *The Journalist in Plato's Cave*, 90.

55. MacKinnon, "The Precarious State," 90.

56. Plato, *The Republic*, 241.

9

ETHICS IN BLACK AND WHITE

Good Night, and Good Luck

Michael Dillon

In *Good Night, and Good Luck*, the patron saint of broadcast journalism
Edward R. Murrow, ringed in halos of cigarette smoke, slays the dragon of
McCarthyism, infusing the infant medium of television with instant gravi-
tas and shifting the locus of politics from print to video. (It's been downhill
ever since.) In real life, though, Murrow was more picador than dragon
slayer, delivering the political deathblow to anti-Communist demagogue
Sen. Joseph McCarthy after the politician had already been staggered by
others.

The film's climax, a televised duel between Murrow and McCarthy,
makes it appear that the senator's Communist witch hunt ended in a
clash of individuals, mano a mano, on Main Street at high noon. Those
riveting scenes, in which Murrow debunks the "junior senator from Wisconsin" (Murrow was a master of subtly disparaging rhetoric) and a chill-
ingly paranoid McCarthy seals his own doom by accepting Murrow's in-
vitation to address the American public directly over the airwaves, are
dramatic and accurate—as far as cinematic compression allows.[1] In reality, the anticommunism movement and American journalism's response
to it were, for the most part, morally ambiguous. Had it been otherwise,
McCarthy's reign of terror would likely not have lasted for more than
four years.

In fact, before the media, in the person of Murrow, could destroy Mc-
Carthy, it first had to create him.

ROOTS OF THE CONFLICT

Good Night, and Good Luck, as did the Edward R. Murrow it portrays, de-mands a great deal from its audience. Without an understanding of the backstory—the circumstances and details that led to the clash depicted in the film—it is at best confusing and at worst misleading. So, before plung-ing into the plot, we'll spend a bit of time exploring the context in which the dramatic collision of journalist and demagogue unfolded.

Republican Sen. Joseph McCarthy may well have believed the anti-Com-munist ravings that brought him to prominence in 1950. In the early days of the atomic age, when the threat of annihilation hung over the political landscape, there was good reason to fear the Communists. McCarthy ex-ploited that fear to the advantage of himself and his political party, which had been out of power since Franklin D. Roosevelt had assumed the pres-idency in 1933, seventeen years earlier.

In brief, several political and historical forces led to the rise of rabid an-ticommunism after World War II:

- Fear of communism had deep roots. In 1919, exploiting wartime hys-teria and the Bolshevik Revolution in Russia, U.S. Attorney General A. Mitchell Palmer ordered the arrest and deportation, without trial, of people he suspected had Communist sympathies. There was much talk of communism as the "Red Menace."
- After World War I, many thoughtful intellectuals in Europe and the United States, seeking relief from the excesses of Darwinian capital-ism, turned to communism and socialism. They also feared fascism more than communism and supported the Communists in their strug-gles with the Fascist axis of Germany, Italy, and Spain. In the Spanish Civil War of the 1930s, idealistic Americans formed the Abraham Lin-coln Brigade to aid the Communist side against the Fascist govern-ment. It was an altruistic act that would, in the 1940s and 1950s, haunt those who survived it.[2]
- Communism appeared ascendant. The Soviet Union's sphere of influ-ence in Eastern Europe was growing. In 1948, the United States had to organize an airlift to supply its sector of Berlin, which was ringed by Soviet forces, a manifestation of the "Iron Curtain" dividing commu-nism from democracy. China, our ally in the Pacific during World War II, had also fallen to communism, as had North Korea. Julius and Ethel Rosenberg, American Communists convicted of giving atomic secrets to the Soviets, were executed after a highly publicized trial.[3]

- In the view of rabid anti-Communist Republicans like McCarthy, there could be only one reason for the rise of communism: the Democrats. Hadn't they been in power for almost two decades? Hadn't all these developments happened on their watch? Hadn't some of those idealistic Lincoln Brigade types from the 1930s ascended to power in government, in Hollywood, in the media? It was time for payback.

Fearmongering cannot occur without a vulnerable public whose fears can be exploited. During the 1950s, Americans were seemingly dancing on the edge of an abyss. True, thanks to the jolt World War II had provided to the economy, they were enjoying an unprecedented affluence. But, at the same time, headlines warning of impending nuclear conflict compelled schools to run bomb drills in which students dove under their desks and waited for a white flash that never came. Signs pointing to public fallout shelters appeared everywhere, and a significant number of Americans built their own shelters, raising fears of an every-man-for-himself scenario when Armageddon arrived. Popular culture also stoked fear. Science fiction movies depicted hideous mutations caused by atomic fallout or stealthy infiltration by alien beings who were obvious stand-ins for Communists.

Into this maelstrom stepped McCarthy, who owed much of his success to a lazy, and even willfully manipulative, news media. McCarthy first announced to the world that he possessed a list of 205 Communists in the U.S. State Department at a political rally in West Virginia. It was late in the evening, and a sole reporter from the Associated Press (AP) was covering the event. Without time to corroborate McCarthy's claim, he wrote a story about it, and the AP sent it over the wires. The dynamite had been there all along. Now, McCarthy, with the media's help, had lit the fuse.

As a member of the House Un-American Activities Committee (HUAC), McCarthy launched investigations of the State Department, Hollywood, and the army. Employees who had merely dabbled in socialism in the 1930s were fired. Others under the threat of being blacklisted were forced to sign loyalty oaths and pressured to "name names," that is, implicate friends who might have Communist connections in their past. According to Harvard Law School dean Erwin Griswold, "Senator McCarthy was judge, jury, prosecutor, castigator, and press agent all in one."[4]

The media was not exempt from this inquisition. Sponsors fearful of government and consumer backlash pressured media companies, including CBS, to ferret out Communists and demand loyalty oaths. A secret document dubbed "Red Channels" served as a blacklist in the media industry. CBS forced Murrow to sign a loyalty oath, and he, in turn, was forced to require the men and women who worked for him to sign. Meanwhile, Mc-Carthy leveled widespread accusations against government officials and popular entertainers. The number of Communists he claimed for the State Department was ever shifting.

FILLING A VACUUM

The Edward R. Murrow of *Good Night, and Good Luck* (portrayed with eerie precision by David Strathairn) is a contained, taciturn figure whose worries and woes can be read in the creases of his face. Those lines were etched in part by countless difficult compromises as he navigated the rapids of McCarthyism.

Ethics is often regarded as a quest to find *the* right way to resolve a conflict or navigate a dilemma. Some ethical models, such as Kant's categorical imperative, which directs us to make no decisions we would not have become universal laws, appear quite rigid. But other models are predicated on compromise.

Philosopher Jeremy Bentham exhorted people to choose that action which brings the greatest happiness to the greatest number. Similarly, John Stuart Mill set as the goal of his utilitarian ethics the maximization of good and the minimization of harm. In both conceptions, it is assumed that a minority of people will end up unhappy and harmed. If ethics demanded that all decisions benefit all people equally, it would be a quixotic and futile pursuit indeed.

Eighteenth-century philosopher Edmund Burke declared, "All that is necessary for the triumph of evil is that good men do nothing." In fact, sometimes some evil triumphs, and some people get hurt, even when good men do something. *Good Night, and Good Luck* is a case study in calculating who must be harmed so that a majority might be spared.

The Edward R. Murrow of legend, the one invoked by critics of today's shrieking and shallow local TV news, is an omnipotent and omniscient dispenser of journalistic justice, almost a Christ figure. The real man was, of course, far more complex and flawed. He also had less personal power than the mythmakers acknowledge. Murrow was a public figure of towering stature, but he did not own the pedestal upon which he stood—William S. Paley, president of the Columbia Broadcasting System, held title to that.

Instead, Murrow worked within a web of corporate hierarchy, government regulation, bitter partisan politics, journalistic norms, the vagaries of mass taste, and the all-important ratings that defined success in television.

Murrow felt this web closing in not only on him, and not only on the media, but also on democracy itself. In the scene in which he receives an award from television executives, Murrow appeals to the conscience of his audience, even though he knows it will likely do no good.

> It is my desire, if not my duty, to try to talk to you journeymen with some candor about what is happening to radio and television. Our history will be what we make of it. And if there are any historians about fifty or a hundred years from now and there should be preserved the kinescopes of one week of all three networks, they will there find recorded in black and white, and in color, evidence of decadence, escapism and insulation from the realities of the world in which we live. We are currently wealthy, fat, comfortable, and complacent. We have a built-in allergy to unpleasant or disturbing information. Our mass media reflect this.

Despite the low fare that dominated television in its infancy (and continues to reign today), Murrow was among a minority who believed that television could serve as an instrument of public education and illumination. Steeped in the Enlightenment sensibility that shaped the Declaration of Independence and the Constitution, Murrow believed public communicators had an obligation to do more than just amuse and enthrall the public.

In that same speech to indifferent executives, Murrow expressed his vision of the medium's potential: "This instrument can teach. It can illuminate and it can even inspire. But it can do so only to the extent that humans are determined to use it towards those ends. Otherwise, it is merely wires and lights in a box." Those who aspire to use the public platform of television and other powerful media should consider whether they have what it takes to think and act "outside the box."

A WEB OF OBLIGATIONS

Whether revered or anonymous, media workers operate in a complex web of economic, social, political, and cultural realities. They have obligations to their employers, their audience, their profession's standards, the conventions of the medium they work in, and the public at large. Let's look at the multiple forces that confronted Murrow in his conflict with McCarthy and discuss how each shaped the ethical minefield through which he navigated in the mid-1950s as depicted in *Good Night, and Good Luck.*

The Fallacy of "Public" Ownership

In Murrow's time, CBS was owned by William Paley, the network's founder. Murrow's controversial documentaries about politics, racial prejudice, and, increasingly, anti-Communist hysteria cost Paley money and gave succor to his enemies. Murrow's serious documentary show, *See It Now*, was not highly rated, and its controversial content frightened sponsors, who feared a public backlash from the broadcasts. Paley usually backed Murrow; occasionally, he asked him to compromise. The control of a huge television network by one man was a double-edged sword: on the one hand, a figure like Paley might unduly impose his personal whims or politics through a media outlet that reached up to half of all Americans every single day; on the other, a private owner can stand fast on worthy values in the face of criticism.

In *Good Night, and Good Luck*, as Murrow prepares to go on the air with his exposé of McCarthy's methods, Paley at first urges Murrow to "let it go. . . . McCarthy will self-destruct." In addition, he orders Murrow to conduct what amounts to an internal witch hunt to make sure no one on his staff has Communist ties that can be used by McCarthy. Paley points out that if Murrow gets his facts wrong or fails to move public opinion, he and his reporters will be out of work—and Paley might lose his network. Hundreds of careers are on the line, not just Murrow's. The network, though, is Paley's to lose. He owns it. And when he is ultimately convinced that airing the McCarthy report is the right thing to do, he is free to gamble with it.

Individual or family ownership of large corporations faded during the merger-mad 1980s and 1990s. Today most big media companies are "publicly owned," an ironic misnomer indeed. In a so-called publicly owned company, a group of stockholders, usually dominated by two or three major shareholders, controls the corporation. The "public," to invoke the democratic sense of the word, holds no stake whatsoever in the enterprise. Journalism, with its First Amendment protections, has a pronounced and specific obligation to the democratic public, but the vast majority of media companies that practice, package, and sell what they call journalism are answerable primarily to a shadowy group of megastockholders whose overriding interest is profit.

The recent destruction of the well-regarded Knight Ridder newspaper group illustrates the perils of "public" ownership. When its founding families were the majority owners of Knight Ridder, its newspapers emphasized public service and could choose to take chances that would help the company fulfill its First Amendment duties. If profits lagged in the short term, so be it. Once the company became primarily stockholder owned, its stock just one of many in the portfolios of investors seeking to maximize their return on investment, Knight Ridder's mission began to change.

As stockholders demanded ever-greater financial returns on their investment, Knight Ridder and its papers were measured by only one criterion: profit margins. A Pulitzer Prize–winning series that cost money to produce was considered a fiscal affront. In 2005, Knight Ridder's stockholders forced the company to sell its holdings to a newspaper group with lesser credentials. That group, McClatchy, then put twelve former Knight Ridder papers on the market because they did not meet its profit requirements (on average, newspaper profit margins are right up there with those of the big oil companies). One paper, the award-winning *Times-Leader* in Wilkes-Barre, Pennsylvania, came within days of being sold to, and closed by, its crosstown rival, which sought to eliminate competition in order to increase profits.[5]

In *Good Night, and Good Luck*, Paley is free to support Murrow, but his professional reputation, as well as his financial fate, is on the line each time Murrow produces a controversial show. CBS executive Sig Mickelson (Jeff Daniels) constantly reminds Murrow of this in the film. As Murrow prepares to air a report criticizing the court-martial of U.S. Air Force sergeant Milo Radulovich for Communist views his father and sister once espoused, Mickelson upbraids him for putting the network in fiscal and political jeopardy.

> Mickelson: Do you understand the position you're putting us in? I have to go back to Mr. Paley and Alcoa, who sponsors your show—
> Murrow: And also has some military contracts—
> Mickelson: And I have to tell them that they're going to be in a tough bind because of a beef you had with Joe McCarthy.
> Murrow: We're not going at McCarthy.
> Mickelson: You're starting the goddamn fire.

A License to Print Money

Unlike books, newspapers, and magazines, broadcast stations and networks are regulated by the government. Despite the First Amendment's seemingly ironclad protection of speech from government interference, the federal government asserted the right to regulate broadcasting in the 1920s in the "public interest, convenience and necessity."

The government did more than just regulate broadcast content; it also required those privileged to hold a broadcast license to perform public duty in return for the entrée to profits a government license provided (industry critics called it a "license to print money"). In Murrow's day, the Federal Communications Commission (FCC) took its duties very seriously. Paley hired Murrow in the 1930s as director of education at CBS Radio. He would head a division that would utilize broadcasting's potential for public enlightenment and, not coincidentally, fulfill the network's public service obligations. When television appeared on the scene, Murrow's responsibilities expanded into that medium.

For the public, and for Paley, government regulation had mixed effects. On one level, the FCC's public service requirements acted as a brake on ratings- and profit-mad network executives who would put anything on the air as long as people tuned in.[6] On another level, though, the state could exert leverage on broadcasters critical of the government. In the early 1950s, McCarthy represented the Republican Party, which controlled the executive and legislative branches of government, and thus the FCC.

In the movie, the threat of government interference surfaces as Fred Friendly (George Clooney) prepares the Radulovich report. When he rebuffs two Air Force officers who want CBS to kill the report, one explains that while the Air Force has been a "friend and ally" of Murrow and CBS, airing the report might end that good relationship. Colonel Jenkins does not overtly threaten government action against CBS, but he does warn Friendly to consider carefully the ramifications of running the story. "The story you are going to run tomorrow," Jenkins says, "is without merit. So before you take any steps that cannot be undone, I strongly urge you to reconsider your stand. These are very dangerous waters you are attempting to navigate."

Fear of government reprisal, including the possibility of losing their broadcast licenses, compelled many industry executives to remain passive in the face of McCarthyism or even to abet the senator and his allies in the government, the corporate world, and the military.[7]

A Dubious Interpretation of Objectivity

In *Good Night, and Good Luck*, Murrow's critics and nervous CBS executives constantly try to rein him in by accusing him of "taking sides" and abandoning "neutrality," both violations of what they erroneously construe as the journalistic ethos of objectivity. Objectivity as a value originated in the modern sciences and represented a thorough and free-ranging search for truth, even if that search ended in the demolition of the scientist's carefully constructed hypothesis. The scientist was also expected to document his or her research fully so that others could test it. Journalist and philosopher Walter Lippmann urged journalists to adopt a similar ethos of rigor and transparency. He envisioned journalists as working without political or economic biases to show the public the truth by providing facts and explaining what those facts meant.

Objectivity, as Lippmann conceived of it, however, has been problematic for the profession. How can journalists working for private interests not be influenced by the political leanings of their bosses (let alone their own) or by the fact that those bosses ultimately decide the terms of employment, including compensation? While many journalists rallied around the word "objectivity," they ignored the rigor and fearlessness it implied and reinterpreted it to mean "neutrality," that is, always telling both sides of a story equally, instead of helping their audience determine which side was telling the truth. But Murrow was a Lippmann-esque purist. When CBS executive Mickelson complains to Murrow in the movie that his story on Airman Radulovich seems to take Radulovich's side, Murrow replies, "The other side's been represented rather well for the last years. . . . I've searched my conscience. I can't for the life of me find any justification for this. I simply cannot accept that there are, on every story, two equal and logical sides to an argument. Call it editorializing, if you'd like." Walter Lippmann would have called it "objectivity."

Libertarian visionary John Milton envisioned a "marketplace of ideas" where all would be free to speak, deliberate, and act politically. His metaphor became a rationale for the First Amendment. Murrow, though, recognized that vested interests—the military, the White House, HUAC, gigantic corporations and the like—had undue and instant access to the marketplace of ideas by virtue of their enormous wealth and their control of sophisticated public relations operations. A marketplace of ideas where some can buy box seats and the great many are relegated to peering through a knothole in the fence is inherently undemocratic.

A journalist's job is not to endorse reassuring bromides for elites but to act as a forward scout for readers so they can see what's coming. For instance, near the end of World War II, Murrow was one of the first reporters, and certainly the most compelling, to explain to Americans the realities of the Holocaust in a broadcast from the Buchenwald concentration camp. In even tones, he described bodies stacked like cordwood and emaciated prisoners who appeared barely human. Telling his audience of two liberated inmates crawling toward the latrine, Murrow said, "I saw it. But I will not describe it."

Journalists are not stenographers. The public needs them to sift through conflicting statements and assign some sort of truth or plausibility value to each. The public also needs to understand journalists' affiliations and what they stand to gain or lose from the public policies their coverage inevitably influences. Truly objective journalists do try to acknowledge and put aside personal and political biases, but not in a quest to be "neutral." They do so in the service of seeing facts clearly and fashioning an interpretation that will help the public make sense of the onrush of facts, fictions, and outright lies. Neutrality, as a value, is a pale shadow of real objectivity, a point Murrow's character illustrates vividly in *Good Night, and Good Luck*.

Mass Taste and Ratings

Television is a neutral instrument. It can carry programs that inspire or repulse (or inspire revulsion). It can be a force for education or a "box full of wires." America is a big country with many tastes. Today, niche cable networks can target golfers, epicures, poker junkies, and fans of old television shows. But in the 1950s, each night the American broadcast audience was split three ways between the major networks.[8]

In a capitalist economic system, television's first purpose is the same as any other technology's: to create wealth for those who own it. Everything else is secondary. Early television was a hodgepodge of genres and formats. The technology was new, and no one knew quite how to use it. Converted radio dramas and movies filled many hours of airtime. Inexpensively produced programs like wrestling, boxing, and quiz shows were popular. There was little or no news to speak of. The first regular national newscast, the *Camel Caravan of News*, required its host, John Cameron Swayze, to puff his way through fifteen minutes of information (none of which could remotely touch upon the interests of the tobacco industry).

Into this information vacuum stepped Edward R. Murrow, whose voice and visage had become iconic because of his wartime radio reporting. Murrow's *See It Now* featured interviews with national and international leaders, including, controversially, Communist leaders. Murrow also interviewed artists and scientists and took his crew to the scene of flooding on the Missouri, migrant labor roundups in the South, and the battlegrounds of South Korea. The show was praised and respected, but its ratings were less than robust.

In order to keep *See It Now* on the air, Murrow had to agree to do a lighter and more highly rated show, *Person to Person*, the granddaddy of all infotainment programming today. On this show, he interviewed entertainers and movie stars or took a human-interest approach to political figures.[9] In *Good Night, and Good Luck*, disgust is etched on Murrow's face as he wraps up a vapid visit with the pianist Liberace. But the premise of *Person to Person* went beyond sheer ratings to the issues of demographics and marketing. As the announcer who introduces the show makes clear before the Liberace interview, the sponsor, Kent Cigarettes, was looking for a show that would appeal to an upscale demographic and "chose Mr. Murrow's program to tell you about Kent." That is the real purpose of the show: to create a suitable environment to sell cigarettes, whose health dangers Murrow explored on a lower-rated documentary program.

ETHICS IN ACTION

The key episode in *Good Night, and Good Luck* is, of course, the showdown with McCarthy. It was a showdown that evolved slowly as Murrow counted both the personal and public costs of McCarthy's witch hunts. On a personal level, even Murrow was not immune from persecution. By 1954, McCarthy was powerful, but not quite powerful enough to take on America's most trusted and revered newscaster. So, as he did in Hollywood and elsewhere, he went after lesser lights, men and women whose destruction would serve his symbolic purposes, feed his power, and cause discomfort for their friends and associates, such as Murrow, who were too powerful to confront directly. As Murrow warily circles McCarthy in the years and months before the final showdown, he must make compromises that prevent him from standing on principles he holds sacred. He must also choose not to intercede to save friends lest he damage his long-term prospects of defeating McCarthyism.

In *Good Night, and Good Luck*, Murrow stands by as his colleague Don Hollenbeck is tarred with McCarthy's red brush. Hollenbeck is eventually driven to suicide by newspaper columnists working on behalf of McCarthy's witch hunt. Had he chosen to defend Hollenbeck publicly, Murrow might have been able to save his career, and thus his life. He knew, however, that expending his political capital on Hollenbeck would leave him without resources for bigger fights. In the film, Hollenbeck the individual must suffer so that battles that will benefit the larger public can be fought. The greatest good for the greatest number sounds benign—unless one is not among the greatest number.

The Hollenbeck episode raises vexing questions about ethical strategy: Is it preferable to allow small evils to triumph until we have the leverage to combat the larger evil effectively, or do ethics require us to act the moment we perceive wrongdoing? Are we complicit in whatever unethical acts occur while we marshal our forces for the larger battle? Another of McCarthy's victims did provide Murrow with the opportunity to stage a dress rehearsal for the final showdown. His report on the Air Force's unfair persecution of Airman Milo Radulovich represented a cautious approach to McCarthyism as an investigative target—"poking it with a stick," as Murrow puts it in the film.

Murrow, in real life and as depicted in *Good Night, and Good Luck*, is an excellent model for prospective journalists not simply because his actions are ethical but also because he clearly articulates the reasoning that led him to choose those actions. Ethicist Deni Elliot points out that truly ethical behavior derives from moral reasoning. A beneficial act performed by chance or accident is not really ethical. Murrow's legacy endures long after many of his stories have been forgotten because he created a template for the kind of thoughtful moral reasoning vital not only to journalism but also to citizenship, and he did so with memorable rhetoric. Murrow invokes the Old Testament (Ezekiel 18:20) to explain to his audience why Radulovich should not have been secretly court-martialed: "We believe the son shall not bear the iniquity of the father. Even though that iniquity be proved, and in this case it was not."

Murrow's moral analyses are more than just literate; they are informed. His elocution is the result of a lifetime of immersion in knowledge and ideas. All journalists have an obligation to educate themselves widely, not simply so they can write fluently but so they can reason well. Lifelong learning also has one important practical benefit for journalists and their audiences—it's much harder to lie to a knowledgeable person than to an ignorant one.

The Radulovich story illustrates the maxim that journalists "should comfort the afflicted and afflict the comfortable." Journalists should do much more than inform the public; they should use their skills, knowledge, reasoning, and platform to ameliorate injustice by enlightening the public. A mere airman did not have the political, legal, or financial resources to stand up to a gargantuan government bureaucracy like the Air Force. Once Murrow presented Radulovich's case in the court of opinion, however, the Air Force could no longer justify the obvious unfairness with which it treated him.

For Murrow, the issue was about far more than the fate of one airman. Murrow resonated in his time, and still resonates in ours, because he had a gift for finding and articulating the universal issues embedded in discrete events. His summation in the Radulovich report brims with wisdom: "Whatever happens in this area of the relationship between the individual and the state, we will do it ourselves. It cannot be blamed on Mao Tse-Tung or on Malenkov. And it seems to us, [producer] Fred Friendly and myself, that this is a subject that should be argued about endlessly." (Unlike many other broadcast journalists, Murrow did all he could to demystify his work and acknowledge that while an anchor is the front man, his stories are the result of collaboration with others.)

Although the film barely touches on it, Murrow similarly undertakes the cause of the underdog in his report on migrant workers, *Harvest of Shame*.[10] His goal is not simply to elicit outrage or pity but to explain to his audience that even though migrants are virtually invisible and have no political power, they are still a vital part of the food chain from which most Americans benefit—by buying groceries whose prices are low because those who harvest them live in virtual enslavement. We cannot absolve ourselves of moral responsibility, he suggests, simply by choosing to ignore the relationship between them and us.

While the McCarthy episode provides the dramatic center of *Good Night, and Good Luck*—director George Clooney wisely used actual footage of the senator in the film—McCarthy himself served as an adversary in an ethical dialectic as relevant today as it was then. McCarthy's means-justify-the-ends mentality is vividly expressed in his on-air response to Murrow's report: "The bleeding hearts scream and cry about our methods of trying to drag the truth from those who know or should know [about a Communist conspiracy in the military]. . . . They say, 'Oh, it's all right to uncover them, but don't get rough doing it, McCarthy.'" As our government imprisons alleged enemy combatants without charges and approves torture today, McCarthy's sentiments are as trenchant as are Murrow's, maybe more so.

Corporate and sponsor pressure ultimately led Paley and CBS to force Murrow to tone down his controversial reports, which ultimately led him to resign from the network and accept an appointment by President John F. Kennedy as director of the U.S. Information Service. The words that conclude his exposé on McCarthy, however, echo down through the decades and provide a lesson for journalists and the public we are charged with serving:

> We must not confuse dissent with disloyalty. We must remember always that accusation is not proof and that conviction depends upon evidence and due process of law. We will not walk in fear, one of another. We will not be driven by fear into an age of unreason, if we dig deep in our history and doctrine and remember that we are not descended from fearful men—not from men who feared to write, to associate, to speak and to defend the causes that were for the

moment unpopular. The actions of the junior Senator from Wisconsin have caused alarm and dismay amongst our allies abroad, and given considerable comfort to our enemies. And whose fault is that? Not really his. He didn't create this situation of fear; he merely exploited it—and rather successfully. Cassius was right. "The fault, dear Brutus, is not in our stars, but in ourselves."

Good night, and good luck.

NOTES

1. Murrow delivered a knockout blow to McCarthy only after other critics, including several courageous newspaper columnists and editorial cartoonists, had weakened his public standing. In addition, Joseph Welsh, an attorney for army officers accused of subversion, called McCarthy out during televised hearings prior to Murrow's broadcast. After listening to one of McCarthy's long, irrational personal attacks on one of his clients, a disgusted Welsh replied, "At long last, sir, have you no decency?" Welsh's remark awoke many slumbering consciences to the inherent unreason and malice of McCarthy's anti-Communist crusade.

2. Witch hunters characterized members of the Abraham Lincoln Brigade and their supporters as "premature antifascists." By their twisted logic—since no one knew at the time of the Spanish Civil War how horrible fascists, particularly the Nazis, would eventually become—siding with Communists against them was evidence of disloyal tendencies that would develop later.

3. Legally, the Rosenbergs were railroaded, although decades later evidence emerged lending credence to the charge that they did indeed help the Soviets acquire the secrets of the H-bomb.

4. Steve Schifferes, "Secret McCarthy Papers Released," BBC News Online, http://news.bbc.co.uk/1/hi/world/americas/3002239.stm (accessed 21 June 2006).

5. In a last-minute development, a former publisher of the *Times-Leader* purchased it, preserving Wilkes-Barre's two-newspaper status.

6. Still and all, shortly after Murrow left CBS in 1960, FCC chairman Newton Minnow famously called television a "vast wasteland."

7. The fear of government retribution resurfaced when the *Washington Post* investigated the Watergate scandal twenty years later. As the newspaper exposed corruption in the White House, government officials threatened to disrupt the company's broadcast holdings as punishment for the newspaper's stories.

8. What are considered high ratings today would have seemed like disasters in the 1950s. For instance, for the week of May 23, 2006, CBS led the ratings with an average of twelve million viewers (a 7.8 rating) and a 13 share (13 percent of all televisions turned on were tuned to CBS programs). A ratings point equals 1 percent of all households with television sets. Share equals the number of sets on at a given time. A popular sitcom like *I Love Lucy* in the 1950s might achieve a 30 rating and a 50 share.

9. Prior to the 1960 presidential elections, Murrow interviewed an up-and-coming senator with a lovely new bride named Jackie (hauntingly, John F. Kennedy read for Murrow's cameras a poem called "I Have a Rendezvous with Death").

10. When Murrow died in 1963, CBS produced a one-hour obituary that recounted many of his best stories. Titled "This Is Edward R. Murrow," it is a riveting piece of filmmaking and should be required viewing for anyone who wants to learn more about this broadcast pioneer. The PBS series *American Masters* also produced an excellent program about Murrow; you can find out more about it at http://www.pbs.org/wnet/americanmasters/database/murrow_e.html (accessed 19 June 2006).

10

CRIME REPORTING

Veronica Guerin

Robert Brown

In one of several books he has written on organized crime, British journalist Duncan Campbell observes, "If journalism is the first rough draft of history, then crime journalism has a habit of being rougher than most."[1] Reporters on the crime beat might receive death threats, sometimes on a regular basis, but mercifully few actually get killed or even seriously assaulted in pursuit of their stories. This is because violent criminals have a rather perverse respect for freedom of the press. "Organized crime had certain boundaries beyond which it would not go," an Irish crime journalist explains. "Unwanted publicity was an occupational hazard which success brought. It was a cross the gangster must bear. Calling attention to oneself by shooting the messenger just was not done."[2]

So, the murder of Irish crime journalist Veronica Guerin on a sunny summer day in 1996 not only shook Ireland to its foundations but also sent shock waves around the world. Shootings by motorcycle assassins may be an almost daily occurrence in Colombia, where there is even a term for such hit jobs (*asesino de la moto*),[3] but nothing like this had ever happened before to a reporter on the streets of Dublin in broad daylight. The fact that the victim was not just a committed newshound but also the mother of a young son made this crime even more repellent. In an article published nine months after her death, Mike Sager, a writer-at-large for the glossy men's magazine *GQ*, eulogized, "From the moment of her instant death—two bullets in the head, three in a group near her heart—Veronica has had a profound impact on life in Ireland. She was the first Irish reporter ever killed in the line of duty, and her sainthood was now complete; people can tell you where they were when they heard the news of her martyrdom."[4]

A REAL-LIFE DRAMA

International outrage and revulsion goes some way to explaining why Veronica Guerin has been immortalized in a major Hollywood movie. In the fun factories of Southern California, it's easy to make a heroine out of a fearless young female sleuth who takes a stand against heroin pushers, especially if she is a pretty blonde credibly portrayed by Cate Blanchett. It was the *GQ* profile that first aroused Hollywood's interest in this subject, although several Irish screenwriters had already spotted its cinematic potential. The stories about Ireland's criminal underworld that Veronica Guerin filed for the country's best-selling newspaper, the *Sunday Independent*, had themselves for some time created a Dublin drama every bit as gripping as anything ever staged in that city's famous Abbey Theatre. Ireland has always been a nation of newsaholics, and these addicts were soon lapping up their weekly fix from a cast of colorful and sinister real-life criminals. For legal reasons, Guerin had to conceal their identities behind such nicknames as "The Coach," "The General," and "The Monk," but that did not diminish the drama.

No one was ever left in any doubt about the identity of the lead character: Veronica Guerin placed herself center stage and was always given star billing by her editors. Her murder was just the final climactic scene of a serial drama in which she had repeatedly placed herself in the deepest peril and been beaten, shot, and otherwise discouraged from doing her job. But nothing would stop her from exposing the lives of gangsters and drug lords. Even when she was shot in the leg at point-blank range, she plowed on with her investigations.

UP CLOSE AND PERSONAL

The headline of the *GQ* article, "The Martyrdom of Veronica Guerin," might also have served as the title of the eponymous movie directed seven years later by Joel Schumacher—except it was impossible to cast this journalist in the role of a modern-day Joan of Arc. As soon as they started researching her life and death in any sort of depth, the moviemakers would

have swiftly discovered that Veronica Guerin was no straightforward heroine figure. She wasn't just curious about this criminal underworld. She
didn't just take an interest in this phenomenon. She developed an obsessive
fascination with the dark underbelly of Dublin and decided to penetrate it
by getting up close and personal with its most sinister and ruthless inhabi-
tants. And she wasn't averse to using her sexuality to such ends. The Hollywood version of her life story doesn't avoid this aspect of her character. One
of the early scenes shows the reporter flirting in a bar with one of her underworld contacts, the crime boss John Traynor (nicknamed "The Coach"),
who gently fondles her as he whispers into her ear, "You're a dangerous little bitch, aren't you?" Commenting on this scene, director Schumacher said
of Guerin, "She was a very seductive and manipulative person, as most great
journalists are. She would get what she needed out of people and she was a
very attractive woman and she had great legs, so she would use that."[5]

Veronica Guerin would, in her own words, "do anything and go anywhere
for a story." The only place she didn't go very often was into the newsroom
of whatever paper happened to be employing her at the time. She preferred
to work away from the office, away from all the normal controls and conventions of a major national newspaper. One of Dublin's leading press commentators, Fintan O'Toole, believes there was something quite disturbing
about her newsgathering techniques: "The fact that she was meeting dangerous men, men who used guns, nailed people to floors and approached
her with iron bars, was the sub-text to so many of her crime stories. Had she
not been in that danger, they would not have been such arresting stories. It
was as if there was a tease going on in relation to the whole story. The tease
was very dark and strange, and also sexual . . . this woman out on her own."[6]

DUBIOUS ETHICS

Another almost equally prominent female journalist in Ireland, Emily
O'Reilly, was moved to write not just a magazine feature but a whole book
about the life and death of this crime reporter, and it was anything but a ha-
giography. In its advance publicity, the publisher billed it as "an extraordinary story about a bold but reckless young journalist and about the dubious
ethics of modern journalism." The moviemakers could not have avoided
this unflattering biography of Veronica Guerin as they browsed the book-
shops of Dublin—in fact, they gave its author a small credit at the end of
their film for additional research—but they clearly had great difficulty incorporating into their screenplay the ferocious debate about Veronica

Guerin's journalistic ethics and modus operandi that raged in Ireland's media village in the fevered aftermath of her death. The complex truth about Veronica Guerin doesn't slot easily into the classic Hollywood story structure, which tends to pitch a usually admirable or likable protagonist against dark and sinister forces. Although some screenwriting manuals suggest "deheroicizing" protagonists by making them "vulnerable, driven by demons, drawn to the dark side," few directors would follow this to the point where audiences lose empathy for the lead character.[7]

A previous biopic made a bold attempt to buck this formula. *When the Sky Falls*, produced in 2000 by the satellite channel British Sky Broadcasting, did a fair business at the Irish box office, but nowhere else. The problem wasn't just that lead actress Joan Allen couldn't quite master an Irish accent but also that movie audiences could have found the fictional protagonist (an apparently ruthless and reckless crime reporter called Sinead Hamilton, who was obviously meant to be Veronica Guerin) cold and calculating. The film had a negligible impact in the United Kingdom and failed to secure a cinema release in the United States. Producer Jerry Bruckheimer couldn't risk a similar reaction after plowing $30 million into his retelling of the same tale.

So, just in case the multiplex audiences of Middle America might go cold on the central character, he gave us a film that doesn't completely avoid the Dublin reporter's dubious ethics—Cate Blanchett depicts Veronica Guerin as a dogged and unconventional reporter who is also naive and reckless—but doesn't explore them with any depth of insight. The publicity poster for the film posed one simple question: "Why would anyone want to kill Veronica Guerin?" The answer would have been blindingly obvious to anyone with even a cursory knowledge of her brief and tragic journalistic career. Posing more difficult and searching questions, however, might have caused this movie to bomb at the box office, even in her native Ireland, questions like, Why is Veronica Guerin the only journalist in Ireland who has ever been violently eliminated by Ireland's drug barons? Why did her employers, Ireland's largest newspaper publishing group, allow her to pursue her obsessive campaign against Dublin drug barons to the point where she not only sacrificed her own life but also endangered that of her young son? Why did the proprietor and editor of the *Sunday Independent* fail to protect her not just from these lethal criminals but also from herself?

Emily O'Reilly addresses all of these questions in depth in her book. She accepts that the subject was a brilliant journalist, but she believes her brilliance stemmed from a personality that lacked the normal controls over personal and professional behavior. "Veronica Guerin never discriminated," O'Reilly writes. "To her there was no difference between doorstepping a politician and doorstepping an alleged murderer. To her there was no difference between taunting a businessman in order to secure a story and taunting an individual whom she had claimed to believe had ordered two separate gun attacks on her home and on her person."[8]

FORGETTING THE FAMILY?

In one of the most stomach-churning scenes in the film *Veronica Guerin*, the reporter turns up unannounced to confront face to face the man who would eventually order her execution, crime godfather John Gilligan. Infuriated that she has been snooping around the sprawling equestrian center he built outside Dublin from his ill-gotten gains, he launches a violent assault on her, punching her repeatedly in the face and ripping off her blouse to check if she is concealing a microphone. Later, Gilligan threatens to kill her and sexually assault her young son if she doesn't back off. Guerin staggers out of her bed and vomits in a toilet as she struggles to absorb the enormity of the threat. Earlier in the film, we see a bullet being fired into the family home as she tucks her son into bed—a warning shot from the underworld. Such chilling scenes graphically illustrate the level of intimidation the reporter had to endure. But they might also leave some moviegoers wondering why any mother would expose her child to such appalling danger. That is what Veronica Guerin did do, not least through her disturbing tendency to drag her young son along with her on stories.

When the Sky Falls opens with the reporter's husband angrily retrieving their son from the reporter's sporty red car, which she has been driving around Dublin's docklands at night in pursuit of some elusive criminal source. Her apparent neglect of her child is a recurring theme of that movie, which doesn't make her a very likable lead character. Emily O'Reilly, who herself juggled a successful journalistic career and raising five children, is particularly scathing about this aspect of Guerin's modus operandi, stating in her book, "Any woman who would take her infant son on potentially dangerous assignments with her should have been fired, or at least put into work where her child was not at risk." Even Guerin's filmmaking friend, Michael Sheridan, has difficulty comprehending this conduct, writing in his *Letter to Veronica Guerin* that many people "cannot understand why you could have put the pursuit of the criminals in front of the needs of your family or exposed yourself or them to danger and ultimately death. It is a debate which doesn't allow for easy answers. It borders faith, courage, naivete, foolhardiness, sheer bravery and a number of other imponderables."[9]

Sidestepping this debate, the first act of *Veronica Guerin* suggests that the reporter's unbridled compassion for other, far less fortunate children compelled her to launch her crusade against Ireland's biggest drug barons and pursue it so obsessively. Venturing into the most deprived neighborhoods of Dublin's notorious Northside, she confronts the full human cost of the scourge of drugs when she seeks to interview a group of young drug addicts shooting up on a stairwell with filthy syringes, doubtless already infected with HIV. In a subsequent scene, she encounters a band of drug pushers driving around in a flashy car while plying their lethal trade in the same bleak neighborhood. The film then cuts to the reporter back in her comfortable home in a leafy and affluent suburb. In a kitchen conversation with her husband, she voices her frustration at the press's failure to stir up public outrage about this state of affairs. "No one cares," she tells him.

MODEL MUCKRAKING OR JUDGMENTAL JOURNALISM?

One of London's leading film critics, Philip French, has noted, "The movie cleverly establishes three worlds—the new underworld of fashionably dressed, Mercedes-driving criminals, the working-class north Dublin targeted by the drug dealers, and the cozy, prosperous middle-class exurban milieu of Veronica and her family. By challenging the first of these worlds on behalf of the second one, she is putting her own privileged existence in danger."[10] This casts her in the role of a classic muckraker, comforting the afflicted and afflicting the comfortable. It is the image of the moral crusader, which Veronica Guerin encouraged in real life, explaining her conduct and convictions thus: "I suddenly realized that here in my own backyard exists a world that no one knows anything about, with people making huge amounts of money from drugs, crime, fraud, and I felt that I and the public ought to know more about this world. . . . It's when nobody seems to care that it really bothers me and the reason they don't care is most worrying—the scum are killing each other."

Guerin's conviction that she alone cares is challenged in the film by the Dublin detective who becomes her most reliable source and confidant in the Garda Siochana (Ireland's police force). Exasperated by her relentless probing and pointed criticisms, he tells her, "You're not the only one trying here, Veronica." What must have really got to this detective was that Guerin seemed to be trying to do his job. As O'Reilly writes in her book, "Veronica was no longer just a journalist. She was a reporter, detective and private investigator rolled into one. She now saw her role as nailing the criminals, finding the evidence to convict them—not in the courts, but in the pages of the *Sunday Independent*."[11]

Journalists who set themselves up as judge and jury can jeopardize future convictions in court by allowing defense lawyers to argue that prior media coverage has made it impossible to conduct a fair trial—the main reason why contempt-of-court laws are so rigid in Ireland and the United Kingdom. Judgmental journalism can also make flawed judgments. As the film shows, Veronica Guerin at one point wrote a damning article about a leading Dublin criminal nicknamed "The Monk" on the basis of misleading information fed to her by a rival gangster, information she failed to corroborate. Another leading Dublin journalist, Vincent Browne (who had been editor of the *Sunday Tribune* when Guerin worked there), argued in the aftermath of her death that it is not the function of journalists to investigate crimes and criminals in the way she did. The police, the courts, and the prison system are in place to tackle crime bosses. The main role of the press is to hold these institutions of power accountable for the way they cope with crime and criminals.

Lise Hand, Guerin's best friend at the *Sunday Independent*, believes that her former colleague had her own conception of the system of power and how to shake it: "Veronica always said it was our job as journalists to bring corruption to light, to inspire the people and put pressure on the legislature to make Ireland a better place. I think everyone lost a bit of innocence when Veronica died. Maybe she was a bit naïve. She wasn't as hard-bitten as some of us other hacks. She basically had the same feelings about crime as your ordinary Joe Sober, except the difference was that instead of sitting in a pub with a pint giving out about the state of the nation, Veronica got off her arse and did something about it. That's what it takes to be a hero, a little gem of innocence inside you that makes you want to believe there still exists a right and a wrong, that decency will somehow triumph in the end."[12]

THE BENEFITS OF EXPERIENCE

Such naiveté might have stemmed from the fact that Guerin got into the news industry without any formal training. She had worked as an accountant, a public relations consultant, and an aide to Ireland's most colorful and controversial politician, Charles Haughey, before she started filing her first stories, but she had never set foot in a journalism school. A scene in *Veronica Guerin* just after she gets shot in the leg shows a group of reporters from rival publications gathered in a Dublin pub. One of them suggests that she might use the insurance money to take a course in journalism. It is presented as a bitchy comment by a bunch of jealous peers who resent her growing recognition.

Fintan O'Toole is among the real-life Irish journalists who believe that Veronica Guerin developed naive notions about her role in the fight against crime: "Somebody's who's more experienced as a journalist might have said, 'Look, I don't have so much to prove that I actually have to continue to see myself as some kind of crusader on whom the fight against crime in Ireland depends fundamentally and critically.'" Nevertheless, O'Toole feels her personal characteristics are not the issue. "She should never have been allowed to be in a situation where somebody was not stepping in and saying, 'This is not a burden you have to bear. This is not a question of whether you, as a woman, are letting down women, letting down women in the media, letting down the people of Ireland, letting down the *Sunday Independent*.'"[13] Alan Byrne, a close friend of Guerin's, agrees with this assessment: "You can say that she shouldn't have done what she was doing, she shouldn't have exposed herself to such risks. As a reporter your instincts are to expose yourself to such risks, to take the risks to get the story."[14]

Arguably the greatest achievement of *Veronica Guerin* is to demonstrate, as perhaps only a good feature film can, how Guerin was gradually sucked into a dangerous game in which she soon ceased to be the central player and became a helpless pawn. As the film's director has pointed out, "We had the wisdom of hindsight of knowing what happened to her. She didn't have that; she was simply doing one thing after the other. . . . [T]he circumstances change incrementally and you simply deal with things as they come along. And the circumstances become normal, they just become the environment in which you're working."[15] As the environment in which this crime reporter was working became deeply dangerous, however, the responsibility lay with others to exercise proper judgment on her behalf, Byrne argues. "It wasn't really Veronica's call as to what she should or should not have been doing," he says. "It was somebody else's call and it was somebody else's decision as to whether they were happy with the way she was operating. A reporter is not best placed to make a judgment, because the closer you get to something, the harder you'll work on it."[16] That call, according to Byrne and many others who knew Guerin, should have been made on her behalf by the media company that employed her.

HOW THE *SINDO* SINNED

The reporter's younger brother, Jimmy Guerin, was bitterly angry about the fact that her employer had failed to exercise this duty of care. A month and a day after his sister's murder, he wrote a letter to Dublin's most prestigious daily newspaper, the *Irish Times,* calling on Ireland's biggest newspaper company to reexamine its employment practices. "Proprietors and editors must examine the dangers to which they are exposing staff members. It is ultimately their responsibility to ensure the safety of people in their employ. Veronica was in great danger for close on two years, and I believe that steps could have been taken to prevent her death."[17]

Bolstering her image as a public and conspicuous opponent of dangerous underworld figures was, her brother strongly believed, exactly the opposite of what the *Sunday Independent* should have been doing at the time. He was far from alone in his conviction that the *Sunday Independent* should have insisted upon its crime reporter's remaining more anonymous and undercover. Veronica Guerin's high public profile created a huge problem in terms of her safety. Reflecting upon her death, fellow Dublin crime correspondent John Mooney explains, "If you're involved in that level of investigation, finding out how criminals are running businesses and criminal activities, you cannot have a public profile. . . . Crime reporting is different because people can kill you. It's a cross between police work, journalism and intelligence-gathering. You really operate as an intelligence operative more than anything else—and what defines that is secrecy."[18] Others were even bitterer in the aftermath of her death, pointing a direct finger of blame at her bosses. Paddy Prendiville, the editor of Dublin's leading satirical magazine, had been a close friend of Guerin's and publicly demanded to know why her editor did not rein in his star crime correspondent.

In *When the Sky Falls*, the fictional editor finds himself confronted by a pack of press and broadcast reporters who forcefully put it to him that he has failed to protect one of his staff. There are no such scenes in *Veronica Guerin*. Instead, the editor of the *Sunday Independent*, Aengus Fanning, is portrayed as a kindly, avuncular character who is pained by her exploits and gently urges her to abandon the crime beat. "Write about fashion. Write about football," he says. "What if I told you that I wouldn't publish your stuff?" There is no doubt this did happen. Six days after she was shot in the leg, the *Sunday Independent* ran a front-page story in which Veronica Guerin joked, "My employers have offered me alternatives. . . . [A]ny area I wish to write about seems to be open to me . . . but somehow I cannot see myself reporting from the fashion catwalks or preparing a gardening column."[19]

Yet there is also plenty of evidence that the *Sunday Independent*, also known as the *Sindo,* was guilty of creating a cult of personality around its crime reporter. Guerin was churning out three stories a week and featured prominently in the newspaper's ad campaigns. Her growing profile got her invited onto chat shows and radio phone-ins. Promoting its star writers in this way was very much the *Sindo*'s style. As her friend Paddy

Prendiville puts it, "The *Sindo's* insatiable appetite for more crime sto-ries, the heightened publicity surrounding Guerin's personality as the country's premier crime reporter, and the paper's new tack of outing Dublin criminals combined to render Guerin more vulnerable than ever."[20] This was a real-life drama being played out in the backstreets of Dublin with potentially lethal consequences. The cynical way in which her employers milked this dangerous situation is barely questioned in *Veronica Guerin.* In fact, there is just one fleeting reference to it. If you watch closely, you may catch sight of a double-decker bus emblazoned with an ad for the *Sunday Independent* declaring "Veronica Guerin—a Life under Threat."

Something you won't see in *Veronica Guerin* are scenes that form a sta-ple ingredient of Hollywood films about newspapers—editors and reporters engaged in raucous arguments about the content and direction of the pa-per. This is because in real life the editor of the *Sunday Independent,* rather strangely, didn't ever chair any editorial meetings. The absence of such a regular forum meant that there was no proper debate among the senior staff about the paper's approach to crime coverage—or anything else. It also meant that Guerin ended up even more isolated.

Seeking to defend the *Sunday Independent* in the bitter aftermath of her death, executives on the paper dismissed suggestions that they should have reined in the reporter. Anyone who knew Veronica, they argued, un-derstood that if she hadn't been allowed to carry out her work for the *Sun-day Independent* in the manner she considered necessary, she would sim-ply have gone to another newspaper. It was not *Independent* policy to out criminals. It was Veronica's idea, and one about which she was passion-ate.[21] The then–managing director of Independent Newspapers (Ireland), an Englishman named David Palmer, compared Guerin's campaigning ex-ploits to that of a war correspondent—a comparison also made by Schu-macher. "I know some people think she was foolish and reckless," he ac-knowledged. "But I think you say that about any journalist who goes to the war—in her case, the drug war here, or in the case of the European and American journalists who have been covering Afghanistan."[22] Major me-dia employers, however, are deeply mindful nowadays about both the physical dangers and psychological toll to which they submit their war correspondents. Such reporters usually undergo survival training and are often accompanied into the battlefield by ex-military personnel assigned to protect them and pick up on any early signs of post-traumatic stress dis-order. Veronica Guerin was given no such support while covering Dublin's drug war.

DEEP THROATS IN DUBLIN?

Her friend Michael Sheridan suggests that her detractors should watch *All the President's Men*. "Woodward and Bernstein covered the break-in at Watergate and the subsequent events at the risk of their lives. How often were they warned about the danger by their source, Deep Throat? And yet Ben Bradlee did not put a leash on the reporters while story after story in the *Washington Post* tore down the fabric of the Nixon administration. But they didn't get shot."[23] Since Veronica Guerin's death, Emily O'Reilly has also wondered what former *Post* editor Bradlee might have made of it all. She thinks Bradlee would never have permitted Guerin to assume the high profile she did—one that gravely endangered her life. Indeed, she doubts whether Guerin would have lasted a month on the staff of the *Washington Post*. When Bradlee was editor of that paper, O'Reilly reminds us, he wrote a chapter on standards and ethics for the *Washington Post Deskbook on Style*, a manual of editorial conduct in every area of the newspaper's work. On "The Reporter's Role," Bradlee writes, "Although it has become increasingly difficult for this newspaper and for the press generally to do since Watergate, reporters should make every effort to remain in the audience, to stay off the stage, to report history, not to make history."[24]

O'Reilly believes the *Sunday Independent* broke the Bradlee rule by allowing Veronica Guerin to place herself on center stage. The film *Veronica Guerin* finishes on a triumphant note with a prolonged epilogue telling us how one brave woman's fearless stand against Dublin's drug barons forced Ireland's lawmakers to make sweeping changes to the country's justice system, which washed organized crime and illegal narcotics down the River Liffey. Yet, even as this film was getting its first screening at a glitzy premiere in the Irish capital, the Dublin press was chronicling how the city's drug problem was worse than ever, and the godfathers of organized crime were flouting the laws with more arrogance than before the reporter's death. None of this was mentioned, of course, in the schmaltzy ending. The movie would have bombed at the box office just as swiftly as its heroine perished under a hail of bullets had its final image been a bleak caption that read, "Veronica Guerin died in vain."

NOTES

1. Paul Williams, *Evil Empire: John Gilligan, His Gang and the Execution of Journalist Veronica Guerin* (Dublin: Merlin, 2001), xix.

2. Williams, *Evil Empire,* xvi.

3. Rob Brown, "Death by Deadline," *Financial Times Magazine,* 10 October 2004, 10.

4. Mike Sager, "The Martyrdom of Veronica Guerin," *GQ,* March 1997, 231–37.

5. Public interview with Joel Schumacher and Cate Blanchett at the National Film Theatre, London, posted on the *Guardian Unlimited* website, 15 July 2003, http://film.guardian.co.uk/interview/interviewpages/0,,998670,00.html (accessed 24 January 2007).

6. Emily O'Reilly, *Veronica Guerin: The Life and Death of a Crime Reporter* (London: Vintage, 1998), 180.

7. David Bordwell, *The Way Hollywood Tells It: Story and Style in Modern Movies* (Berkeley: University of California Press, 2006), 29.

8. O'Reilly, *Veronica Guerin,* 187.

9. Michael Sheridan, *A Letter to Veronica Guerin* (Dublin: Poolbeg Press, 1999), 21.

10. Philip French, "Carve Her Name with Pride," *Observer* (London), 3 August 2003, http://observer.guardian.co.uk/review/story/0,,1011170,00.html (accessed 24 January 2007).

11. O'Reilly, *Veronica Guerin,* 117.

12. Sager, "The Martyrdom of Veronica Guerin," 280.

13. O'Reilly, *Veronica Guerin,* 181.

14. O'Reilly, *Veronica Guerin,* 117.

15. Public interview with Joel Schumacher and Cate Blanchett at the National Film Theatre, London, posted on *Guardian Unlimited* website, 15 July 2003, http://film.guardian.co.uk/interview/interviewpages/0,,998670,00.html (accessed 24 January 2007).

16. O'Reilly, *Veronica Guerin,* 117.

17. Jimmy Guerin, letter in the *Irish Times,* 27 July 1997, 15.

18. O'Reilly, *Veronica Guerin,* 118.

19. O'Reilly, *Veronica Guerin,* 105.

20. O'Reilly, *Veronica Guerin,* 162.

21. O'Reilly, *Veronica Guerin,* 163.

22. Michael Dwyer, "Joel's Story," *Irish Times,* 13 April 2002, 14.

23. Sheridan, *A Letter to Veronica Guerin,* 32.

24. O'Reilly, *Veronica Guerin,* 190.

⓫

THE UTOPIAN NATURE
OF JOURNALISTIC TRUTH

The Year of Living Dangerously

Joseph C. Harry

In 1965 Australian Broadcast Service reporter Guy Hamilton (Mel Gibson) arrives in Jakarta, Indonesia, to begin a new assignment covering the dangerously fragile political scene. On the authoritarian center-right are forces loyal to President Sukarno (Mike Emperio). Communist forces, representing the poverty-stricken masses, are challenging Sukarno on the left, while Sukarno also faces a religiously conservative Muslim opposition movement. Hamilton quickly meets a freelance television cameraman, Billy Kwan (Linda Hunt), an Indonesian dwarf with a keen mind and, we soon learn, good political contacts he's willing to make available to the greenhorn Hamilton, whose newness on the scene is made obvious by the jibes he must endure from the callous, hard-drinking, cynical Western reporters in residence.

Billy wants to introduce Guy to the "real" Jakarta and so takes him on a walking tour of the city's slums, where they encounter endless evidence of the severe poverty suffered by the masses. Billy tries to convince Guy that here, amid the squalor of Jakarta, is the real story that must be told. Quoting the Bible (Luke 3:10), Billy asks, "What, then, must we do?" He mentions that Leo Tolstoy wrote an entire book with that title but couldn't quite figure the answer out. "We can't afford to get involved," Guy says cockily in response to the ethical question Billy has posed. "Typical journalist's answer," Billy replies with a sardonic grin, but we soon learn that Billy sees something in Guy, something more than just another Western journalist looking for a quick story to meet a daily deadline. Billy believes Guy is, like most mainstream journalists in the 1960s, "ambitious, self-contained, moderate-to-conservative in politics," but Billy also senses "a possibility."

It is the notion of Guy Hamilton as a metaphor for possibility—the possibility of a more ethical journalism and a more collective or inclusive social ethics—that the 1982 film *The Year of Living Dangerously* explores in a compelling mixture of hard-bitten social realism and beautifully artistic symbolism. Directed by Peter Weir and also starring Sigourney Weaver as Jill Bryant, a British military attaché who's been stationed in Jakarta for five years, the film raises a host of questions regarding the ethically problematic nature of mainstream, "objective" journalism, especially as practiced in an international setting. More than this, however, the film manages to weave cleverly, and to purposely leave entangled, its journalistic-ethical questions within a much broader question: what is the nature of human love, trust, commitment, and loyalty, and how may these conflict with professional journalism's ethical commitment to objective truth telling?

Remarkably, one finishes watching the film convinced that the ethical critique of objectivity and the query about love, trust, commitment, and loyalty are inseparable. This inseparability has to do with the fact that journalism, the faithful portrayal of actual human stories that happen every day, is founded on an enduring trust, commitment, and loyalty between journalist and audience, that the stories are, in fact, honest depictions of real life without the journalist's biases getting in the way. This is the idea underlying professional journalism's code of objectivity. In this respect, objectivity, the idea that a reporter makes the best attempt to present, fairly and comprehensively, any and all relevant sides to an issue, is an act of love, trust, commitment, and loyalty not only to readers, listeners, or viewers but also to humankind. It is an ethics of how to operate, the rendering of the truth "without fear or favor," a mantra of the profession.

Yet objectivity is also a professional norm, an occupational ideology that too often may, especially under deadline pressure, be limited to getting a pro and con side and calling it a day. (This, in fact, is just what most of the mainstream Western reporters depicted in the movie do.) And simply being objective when reporting a story may still mean that some people will be harmed. The Society of Professional Journalists (SPJ) Code of Ethics, for example, advocates as its first-listed principle, "Seek Truth and Report It. Journalists should be honest, fair and courageous in gathering, reporting and interpreting information."[1] The SPJ states as its next principle, "Minimize Harm. Ethical journalists treat sources, subjects and colleagues as human beings deserving of respect."[2] These two principles might come into

conflict; reporting the truth may well at times result in creating more harm for some. This dilemma is made clear with regard to Hamilton's decision to "objectively" report an important story about an incoming arms shipment for Communist forces.

The SPJ sets forth two additional principles: "Act Independently" by respecting "the public's right to know" and "Be Accountable" to both the audience and other journalists.[3] Hamilton, as we see throughout the film, certainly acts independently, but his public accountability is seriously in doubt. His reporting of the hot political story will, he knows, endanger the lives of some, including Jill, the British attaché he has fallen in love with and who trusts him with top-secret information that leads to Guy's tracking down and writing the story against Jill's protests.

Collectively, the SPJ principles provide little more than procedural guideposts for working journalists, ultimately leaving each journalist to determine what *is* the public's right to know. One can easily see how this principle could serve as a cheeky defense by a reporter whose main interest may actually be scoring a juicy scoop to advance his career. This, too, is one of Guy Hamilton's motivations, which, as the film makes clear, he attempts to justify under the guise of professional objectivity. These ethical guidelines, while useful as technical principles, also can be contradictory—since serious truth telling will almost always harm someone, and it could be maximum harm, not the minimum kind the SPJ advises.

This chapter explores a way to understand the contradictions of conventional journalistic ethics depicted in the film by using the concept of *utopia*. Rather than take utopia as the ideal of a perfect state of being,[4] I use the utopia metaphor in a more open-ended sense, as a purposeful, ethically driven striving for a more perfect and inclusive state of social existence, realizing that the striving never ends but that steady human social progress is the goal. The real world is full of social and ethical dilemmas and contradictions, so any notion of utopian thought must recognize the essential imperfectability of actually existing conditions.

This conception of utopianism is clear in the work of Fredric Jameson,[5] who lays out a series of propositions useful for analyzing the intertwined journalistic and human dilemmas portrayed in *The Year of Living Dangerously*. Utopian ethics attempts to base decisions on their perceived impact on the social "collective," rather than considering ethical decision-making within a more traditional, moralistic framework in which the "good" is posed against the "evil," or the "right" against the "wrong." Jameson calls for thinking beyond traditional ethics. He criticizes traditional ethics as, at best limited because it is based on "positional" thinking that poses one kind

"good" ethical view against another—for example, Western Christian ethics against Islamic ethics. Utopian ethical thought attempts to leave aside personal and provisional ethics in favor of a broader, more inclusive realm of collective social justice—regarding what is to be done as what will benefit, ideally, everyone.

I will examine key scenes in the film to show how its depiction of the tangled, contradictory webs of personal, professional, and political relationships and interests, especially as experienced by Guy Hamilton, offers a critique of journalism's traditional strengths and limits. The film suggests that the truth-telling goal of journalism remains the central path to a utopian ethics, but that truth telling restricted by the traditional stance of journalistic objectivity may work against a more collective-utopian ethical stance.

THE NEW KID IN TOWN

Having just arrived in Jakarta and befriended Billy, Hamilton feels the need to prove himself. Billy is looking for a journalistic partner and sees Guy as impressionable, especially when Billy promises Guy an interview with the leader of the Communist Party of Indonesia, the PKI. Billy's role is complex because he respects Sukarno's attempt to mediate between the progressive Left and conservative Muslim forces by staying in the authoritarian, but politically delicate, middle. But Billy's sympathies seem more aligned with the Communist Left, even though, as we soon learn, he may actually be a double agent for both Sukarno and the Left. Here the film leads the viewer to contemplate this reigning contradiction: Billy, an Indonesian native and a working photojournalist, seems able to mediate between all sides—professionally, politically, and even personally in his friendships with Guy and Jill, the attaché who may be a British spy.

Billy reminds Guy that the only way a novice can hope to gain access to vital sources in politically fragmented and dangerous Jakarta is via "personal contacts" and that he can provide such contacts. The more established Western reporters, Billy notes, have "reputations," meaning they "can't be ignored." Here, we are introduced to a central ethical theme, the importance of the personal, which as the film progresses becomes related to both journalistic-professional relationships and to romance and friendship. Guy is happy to use Billy to get to the PKI leader, who during his interview with Guy reveals that President Sukarno will allow the PKI to obtain a weapons shipment. This is a big scoop for Guy and is subsequently, though begrudgingly, reported in other news media. Billy, of course, is also happy be-

cause of the new importance attached to the PKI, which he seems to have the most political sympathy for. So, it's a mutually beneficial relationship; each uses the other for his own reasons.

Guy's professional colleagues are envious, but one of them, *Washington Post* reporter Pete Curtis, is also incredulous. He claims Guy reported the PKI story without adequately sourcing it, meaning Guy, in Curtis's view, is being used as a mouthpiece for the PKI president. Ethically, Guy stands accused of sacrificing professional objectivity just to get a scoop, but Guy's scoop has garnered him credibility among the more seasoned reporters— he's gaining a professional reputation. As the film progresses, we see that to be sustained, this reputation requires the steady production of stories. Just what kind of story qualifies as legitimate will be called into question.

Within the rest of the film, two major contradictions appear. One exists as part of a general theme involving the fragile line between trust and distrust, both personal and professional. Another can be seen in how the film poses legitimate "objective" news reporting against less legitimate "melodramatic," subjective, and potentially biased reporting.

Billy wants Guy to trust him, but this trust potentially turns to distrust when Guy finds a secret file Billy keeps on him, calling into question their friendship and their journalistic relationship. Guy is no longer sure just who Billy may be working for. Still, Billy is gradually opening Guy's eyes to the abject poverty and suffering of the everyday masses. This transformation can be seen in the fact that, early in the film, Guy tells Billy that "nobody wants to hear" stories of the suffering masses, implying that only strictly objective political news merits attention, but after developing a personal and professional relationship with Billy, Guy begins to see the value of doing more feature-oriented, emotion-laden stories.

By eventually deciding to write not only "legitimate, objective" news but also highly emotional stories about poverty and suffering, we see Guy's journalistic practice becoming more utopian in a collective sense. He's using journalism to share with the world the miserable reality of what's beneath the surface, and this corresponds to the question Billy asks throughout the film (usually in voice-over), "What, then, must we do?" Guy's personal and professional willingness to go beyond objective reporting, to write stories exposing the poverty of the masses, provides a "mediation on the destiny of community."[6] Guy has decided what he must do, at least within the realm of his professional ethics. He's giving voice to the voiceless, telling the story "of the diversity and magnitude of the human experience boldly, even when it's unpopular to do so," two SPJ ethical principles that reveal a hint of collective-utopian ethics.[7]

However, an ideological contradiction for Guy, the erstwhile objective journalist, is that while he may be able to write what his colleagues would label a "melodramatic" or "soft-news" piece, the kind that advances a utopian sense of political and social recognition for the unrepresented masses, he cannot intervene in any other way. Journalistic ethics don't allow the practitioner to get personally involved in social issues. For Guy, ethical intervention only exists in his producing both hard news and the occasional feature story. His loyalty is to his profession: he's a journalist, not a savior. Still, the fact that his reporting has expanded to include stories of the suffering masses shows his efforts have moved closer to a collective-utopian ethics because the masses are the largest collective, the least empowered group in Indonesian society, and their story is beginning to be told.

As the film progresses, we continue to witness the thematic tug-of-war between trust and distrust with respect to Guy and Jill's working and personal relations, as well as each's relation to Billy. The trust-distrust theme is revealed not only in what will become, for Jill, a major professional and personal betrayal by Guy but also as an intellectual difference over the legitimacy of Guy's "soft" news features about the poor and suffering.

Jill decides to apologize to Guy for a reference she had made earlier to what she claimed was a "melodramatic" story he'd done about famine in the Lombok area of Indonesia. "I just thought there was one reference too many to children with gaunt rib cages and dull, listless eyes," she tells him. "Well," Guy responds, "the rib cages and the eyes are the real thing." "Perhaps you only needed to mention it once," Jill replies.

In the next scene, Jill reveals to Guy that Billy knows Guy's father died in World War II. This revelation indicates not only that Billy is likely a secret agent (for whom, it's never quite clear) but that Jill may also be a British spy whose sympathies lie with the Sukarno regime. Jill asks if Guy thinks Billy is an agent. Guy admits he's not certain but wonders how Billy gets such good interviews. "People trust him," Jill replies. After Guy reveals to Jill that Billy is keeping a file on him, Jill says nonchalantly that Billy keeps files on "people he cares about," but the exact nature of this "care," whether it's personal or political, remains cloudy. The delicate nature of trust as a central theme is further revealed when Guy asks if Jill is a spy, to which she jauntily replies, "If I were, I wouldn't tell you." Guy drives Jill back to her lodgings at the British Embassy, and she leaves him with the playful admonition, "Watch out for the melodrama."

We then see Billy alone in his darkroom developing photographs of Guy and Jill taken during their afternoon lunch. It's clear at this point that Guy is possibly being used for political purposes by Billy (and, perhaps, by Jill) and that Billy may be using Jill for uncertain ends as well. (Later in the film, we see Billy poring over the secret file he keeps on her.) Guy, now back at his office, listens on his tape recorder to his Lombok famine story, the same story Jill had earlier labeled "melodramatic." The portion of the story offered in this scene goes as follows: "It's the faces you can't forget. Like images in a recurring nightmare, they just keep coming back—haunted faces, staring blankly back from the windows of tumble-down hovels—the hollow, lifeless eyes, skin stretched tight across bones, hands outstretched; dull, listless eyes, imploring. I move as if in a dream, through the agony that is famine."

The emotionally charged imagery reveals, especially following Jill's accusation of melodrama, the contradiction between two notions of news reporting: straitlaced objective reports about surface political events and the below-the-surface kind of reporting Guy's offering. Here, we see how journalism contains its own utopian moment in the form of unvarnished revelations that other journalists denigrate as mere melodrama. Here, too, we understand that it's a matter of differing opinions about what counts as journalistic trust—an automatic trust in surface objectivity or in a deeper, emotional truth that may only be discoverable if one is willing to face a charge of bias and subjectivity. We begin to understand that Guy's professionally focused eyes have been opened wide to the possibilities of a more truthful kind of journalism, one in which the desire for social and political recognition is offered to a downtrodden people via the telling of their "melodramatic" story to the world. This more just reality is possible through the truth-telling lens of journalism itself, through journalism's own utopian potential buried within its reigning ideology of objectivity.

In another key scene, Jill gets a coded, top-secret message: the Communist PKI is getting a secret arms shipment not authorized by Sukarno. Once the arms are in hand, a bloodbath will ensue, Jill tells Guy. "Civil war!" a wide-eyed Guy exclaims, his joy at getting yet another scoop quite evident. "Yes," Jill acknowledges, adding, "I'm not telling you this for some scoop. I just want you to save your life. I can get you out." But Guy is unfazed. "I'm staying," he says, almost in disbelief that Jill would expect otherwise. At this moment, the old Guy returns, the fiercely competitive Guy who'll do anything for a story. And this is no melodrama; it's straight political reporting, even though he assures Jill he will not report it unless it's independently sourced. "Guy, you can't use this," she insists. "Then you shouldn't have told me," he responds, without a hint of doubt about what journalistic ethics dictate.

Just when we thought Guy's ethical moorings might have expanded permanently toward protecting the interests of the collective social scene, we see him lapsing back into the excitable, ego-fueled response of the competitive journalist for whom the story is everything: *this is a hot story that must be told!* The SPJ code's first principle, "Seek Truth and Report It," does offer an unproblematic defense for this kind of reaction, though principle two, "Minimize Harm," might easily contradict it. Guy's reporting the story will, he knows, lead to maximum harm, death, for at least some segments of the population, to the "bloodbath" Jill has warned of. The SPJ call to minimize harm is a subjective call on the reporter's part—minimal is a relative term. We can imagine Guy deciding that some unspecified, unknowable, relatively minimal number of deaths is ethically justifiable if the greater good is determined to be finding the truth and reporting it.

By comparison, the collective-utopian theme that emerges as the ethical heart of the film, an emotional and consequently political affiliation with those least politically empowered, thus subject to suffer the greatest harm if Guy publishes the story, would lead the journalist to see the greater good as not publishing. Guy's growing personal and emotional involvement with the grim poverty and widespread suffering of the Communist-affiliated masses could lead him to conclude that applying the traditional, story-centered journalistic ethics, whereby reporters seek the truth and report it, making on-the-spot, subjective judgments about what qualifies as "minimized" harm, would, in this situation, be ethically wrong. Such an ethical conclusion questions journalism's traditional ethos of "objectivity," newsworthiness, preventing harm to others, and the all-purpose "public's right to know." The journalist could, for example, decide that the public might well have a right to know but decide not to tell them, anyway.

In the next scene, Billy confronts Guy. "[Jill] told you in confidence," he says, adding that everyone will know the tip came from Jill. Guy responds, "If I don't follow up something like this, I might as well go grow watermelons." The subsequent scene shows Billy scouring Guy's secret file, saying in a voice-over, "You are capable of betrayal. Is it possible I was wrong about you?" This is followed by another voice-over from Billy: "You have abused your position as journalist and become addicted to risks. You attempt to rule neat lines around yourself, making a fetish of your career, making all relationships temporary, lest they disturb that career. Why can't you give of yourself? Why can't you learn to love?" Within the realm of objective truth telling, "making all relationships temporary, lest they disturb" one's career, might be good advice, as one's career might be at risk if relationships become too personal or long lasting. From a utopian stance, however, forming more meaningful relationships and even "giv[ing] of yourself" could be warranted. Billy, by wondering why Guy can't "learn to love," seems to be asking not only for Guy to love Jill but the suffering masses as well.

Yet Billy himself has skirted the boundaries of love, trust, commitment, and loyalty by keeping secret files on Guy and Jill. Moreover, his own journalistic ethics are questionable because as a politically committed photojournalist, Billy seems to want to reserve the right to decide which of Guy's stories are legitimate and which aren't. Billy is happy with the "melodramatic" stories because they advanced Billy's own political goals. Now that Guy has returned to objective reporting, he is seen as having violated Billy's trust and, by extension, Jill's, but Guy is simply doing what any good reporter would do, at least from within conventional journalistic ethics—sourcing out a story and getting it published, even though he understands that such a revelation will lead to a crackdown by Sukarno and to civil war.

Guy has been forced to make a choice. As Kumar (Bembol Roco), his personal assistant and, we find out, a PKI member, asks in a later scene, "Is it wrong to kill to save your country?" and then himself answers, "Sometimes you have to make a choice." Guy has chosen: he will break apart his personal relations and his trust with Jill and Billy for the sake of a story. Yet we can't avoid empathizing with him because throughout the film he's shown, via his "melodramatic" pieces, that he's capable of more than the usual output—he's lived up to Billy's early insight about him, when Billy sensed "a possibility," his utopian promise.

At this point we might ask, to whom do journalists owe loyalty? To the story? To the collective? Conventional ethics would seem to favor the story, provided it's true, fair, accurate, and objective. Utopian ethics would look to the broadest social good, the collective, which would mean that getting the story might not be the highest goal. The SPJ code's third major principle, "Act Independently," which admonishes journalists to remain free of "any interest other than the public's right to know," seems exclusively focused on getting the story. Utopian ethics, with an eye toward collective social progress, would not necessarily hold that goal as central. The "public's right to know," for all its high-minded democratic spirit, still leaves it up to the reporter to determine the public interest and may allow a reporter's ego to overwhelm any larger sense of the collective good.

Guy eventually gains independent sources, some through bribes, to be able to run the PKI arms shipment story. He meets up with Billy, who's livid that Guy has violated Jill's trust and his own. "How far are my loyalties supposed to go?" Guy asks. "I would've given up the world for her," Billy replies, but we can't help but wonder if this is true, considering that Billy has kept a secret file on Jill. "It's not just a story," Guy says. "It's *the* bloody story!" Billy, however, replies, "Don't you understand? You've lost Jill. I gave her to you, and now I'm taking her back. I believed in you. I thought you were a man of light. When I gave you those stories, I made you see things. I made you feel something about what you write. I gave you my trust. So did Jill. I created you!"

A coup is now in full swing, the streets in a murderous panic. Guy tells Jill that he hadn't wanted to hurt or lose her over this. "I got it straight from the PKI," he says, defending his reporting but not mentioning his bribes to get some of the information. "I made a decision to tell you," Jill says, as if she, too, has finally acknowledged the ethical contradiction between personal and professional loyalty, love, and trust. "You're a journalist," she adds with resignation.

Amid the panic and violence following Guy's publication of the PKI arms story, with the Sukarno regime cracking down in a last gasp to retain power, Billy takes a hotel room overlooking the chaotic streets. He opens his hotel window and displays a big, hand-inscribed banner declaring, "Sukarno—feed your people!" We then see him thrown out of his hotel window. The camera pans close, revealing a beatific smile on Billy's dying face, a symbol of the utopian moment realized at the ultimate cost.

That Guy's most recent scoop may have led to this change of regime and to the bloodshed in its wake is yet another contradiction, but Guy believes he did what he had to do professionally. His story also evidently allows him safe exit from Jakarta. Having been beaten with the end of a rifle in an earlier scene, Guy has a seriously injured eye, now bandaged and bloody. He convinces his assistant Kumar to drive him to the airport. "I hope catching the plane is worth losing your eye," Kumar remarks. The literal and figurative references throughout the film to Guy's having his eyes opened to the true misery of Indonesia's masses are driven home here: Guy has lost sight in a real eye in the ethical service of gaining a new, clearer kind of vision. Still, it may not be the clearest possible vision because we also know that Guy remains torn between his conventional and his emergent utopian journalistic ethics.

On the way to the airport Guy and Kumar are stopped by the new Muslim forces who've just taken over. When a soldier recognizes Guy as the reporter who broke the PKI story, which led to a beneficial turn of events for the Muslim forces, he happily lets Guy pass. Guy apologizes to Kumar for all that's happened, knowing Kumar's unlikely to survive. Kumar replies, "We will win because we believe in something." Though it's obvious what Kumar believes in, it's not so apparent what Guy believes in. Billy saw in him a utopian "possibility" that never quite came to fruition. In the final scene, Guy's tape recorder is confiscated and destroyed before he's allowed to board a plane where Jill awaits. He's made a personal choice to stay with her, but we're left to ponder how he may ultimately resolve his journalistic ethics.

WHERE NO FINAL CONCLUSIONS EXIST

The "political" in *The Year of Living Dangerously* resides front and center as the "dangerous" social space where contradictory and inseparable personal, social, and professional interests and impulses do battle. The political "unconscious" within a collectivist ethical stance is the always somewhat hidden, never thoroughly understood or completely attainable desire for a more integrated, humane social world. Utopia is a positive, but ideologically fraught, search for the collective good life. Therefore, a utopian ethos cannot lead to a describable, fully formed social world because it is always emerging, in the initial sense as an intellectual practice, a "form of thinking—the collective—which has been effectively shoved to the nether side of our [political] unconscious."[8]

The SPJ code appears to be based in what we might call a more conventional utopian vision, which finds faith in the individual journalist, relying on him or her to make story decisions by justifying them within "the public interest." It's a story-centered ethical vision with publication as the superlative goal, an end in itself. By comparison, the utopian collective would, as its primary objective, look to actual social conditions, located by assessing, recognizing, and thus giving voice to a powerless, underrepresented mass. Here the story is a vehicle or means, not an end in itself.

Collective-utopian ethics is not objective in the conventional journalistic sense because it might lead the journalist to let love guide decisions concerning those least able to communicate their struggles to the rest of the world. So, the difference is between trusting in the story, an individually focused ethics, and trusting in recognizing and relating to the interests and struggles of the disenfranchised, the collective utopian, which is always in the making.

At one point in the film, Billy shares with Guy a philosophical insight about the country's Wayang culture, the native traditional mode of thought. Billy says that in the West, clear answers and a distinct division between right and wrong are rational expectations in ethical decision-making. In Indonesian culture, however, contradiction rules—there's no expectation of clear light, distinct right or wrong, anything firmly good or evil. "No such final conclusions exist," Billy announces. Guy experiences an ongoing sense of ethical contradiction during his time in Indonesia—that no "final conclusions exist." Within this ambiguous social context, he struggles to come to ethical terms with his own contradictory human and professional pressures. *The Year of Living Dangerously* purposely avoids ethical closure, trusting viewers to ponder how Guy might act in the future. Guy himself remains, to the end, an ethical contradiction, caught between his emerging sense of the utopian promise buried within the truth-telling lens of journalism and the everyday competitive pressure to get the story, at *almost* any cost.

NOTES

1. Society of Professional Journalists Code of Ethics, http://www.spj.org.ethicscode .asp (accessed 28 November 2006).

2. Society of Professional Journalists Code of Ethics.

3. Society of Professional Journalists Code of Ethics.

4. For a good overview of different notions of utopia as a concept, see William T. Conlon, "Five-fold Crisis in Utopia: A Foreshadow of Major Modern Utopian Narrative Strategies," *Utopian Studies* 14 (Spring 2003): 41–69.

5. Fredric Jameson, *The Political Unconscious: Narrative as a Socially Symbolic Act* (Ithaca, NY: Cornell University Press, 1981).

6. Jameson, *Political Unconscious*, 70.

7. Society of Professional Journalists Code of Ethics.

8. Staci L. von Boeckmann, "Marxism, Morality, and the Politics of Desire: Utopianism in Fredric Jameson's *The Political Unconscious*," *Utopian Studies* 9 (Spring 1998): 32.

12

JOURNALISM AND THE VICTIMS OF WAR

Welcome to Sarajevo

Howard Good

I'd been scanning the index of one of the leading media-ethics textbooks, looking for the entry for "empathy." There was none. So, I took down another media-ethics textbook from the shelf, this one well over four hundred pages long, and tried again—nothing there either. I repeated the search with two more media-ethics textbooks I'd somehow crammed into my over-full office bookcase. I found "embedded journalists" and "Eminem" listed in one and "e-mail" listed in another, but I didn't find "empathy" anywhere.[1]

That's strange, I thought. How can these books not mention empathy when philosophers, psychologists, and even biologists consider it so important? They have described empathy, the ability to feel with and/or for others, as "the bedrock of our moral systems," "the very foundation of morality," "the essential preparation for moral interaction."[2] Burton L. Visotzky goes so far as to say, "It is the whole point of moral education to be able to imagine being in another's position."[3]

Not that this kind of conjecture is common or easy. Poet W. H. Auden writes, "About suffering they were never wrong,/The Old Masters: how well they understood/Its human position; how it takes place/While someone else is eating or opening a window or just walking dully along."[4] The poem describes *Landscape with the Fall of Icarus*, a painting by Peter Brueghel the Elder, in which Icarus, burning from having flown too near the sun, plunges to his death while villagers go on about their lives, oblivious to his plight.

Seventeenth-century English philosopher Thomas Hobbes believed that human nature itself worked against the arousal of empathy. In his magnum opus, *Leviathan*, he claims, "Such gentle virtues as justice, equity, mercy, and, in sum, *doing to others as we would have done to*, without terror of some power to cause them to be observed, are contrary to our natural passions."[5] More recently, Sandy McFarlane, head of psychiatry at the University of Adelaide in Australia and a world expert on trauma, has pointed out, "Empathy is a challenge that defeats most people. If we haven't lived through the distressing, disturbing experience of another, then the more removed we are from understanding or relating to it."[6]

The obstacles to empathy are many. Psychologist C. Daniel Batson has said they "include anything and everything that makes it difficult for us to attend to or value another person's welfare," for example, "self-preoccupation or absorption in an ongoing task; seeing the other as an object or 'thing,' as a statistic and not a person who cares about his or her own welfare; seeing the other as a person but as different from ourselves, as one of 'them' not 'us,' as Black not White, a man not a woman, Arab not Jew, Catholic not Protestant."[7] To complicate matters further, researchers don't always agree on what exactly empathy entails. Some use the term to refer to "pity or commiseration for another's condition."[8] Others call this "sympathy" and distinguish it from empathy, which they define as a kind of role taking, "the cognitive act of adopting another's perspective."[9] Still others use the terms interchangeably.

Whether the ability to feel with and/or for others is called "empathy" or "sympathy," most journalists strive to suppress it. Journalistic norms require them to keep their personal preferences and opinions out of news stories. As one of the media-ethics textbooks back in my office puts it, ". . . the ethics of newswriting is concerned with facts and impartiality in the presentation of those facts,"[10] which more or less explains why you won't find "empathy" listed in the book's index if you look.

Yet ethics isn't only about following norms, rules, and traditions; it can also be about challenging them. There's something questionable about remaining impartial or objective in the face of large-scale suffering. In his memoirs, Vincent Sheean, a brilliant foreign correspondent in the years leading up to World War II, disdains the typical reporter as "a professional observer at the peep-show of misery."[11]

It certainly seems possible that there are times and places—Iraqi Kurdistan in the 1980s, Bosnia and Kosovo in the 1990s, Darfur in the 2000s—in which rigid adherence to the principle of objectivity would be morally wrong. At such moments, the horrors may be too great, the victims too innocent and helpless, for journalists to continue business as usual. *Newsday* reporter Roy Gutman, who won a Pulitzer Prize for his coverage of the Bosnian War, insists, "We can't watch passively while people are being killed in front of us. There are higher requirements."[12]

An anecdote from Bosnia suggests the terrible price of failing to recognize this: A journalist visits a sniper nest in or around the besieged capital of Sarajevo. The sniper tells the journalist that he has two civilians in his sights. "Which one of them do you want me to shoot?" he asks. The journalist turns to leave, and the sniper fires twice. "That's a pity," he calls after the journalist. "You could have saved one of their lives."[13]

"WELCOME TO HELL"

So announced the graffiti scrawled on the walls of bombed-out buildings in Sarajevo. It was no exaggeration. "Something was always burning there," a journalist who covered the Bosnian War for British television recalls, "and someone was always dying."[14]

The two-and-a-half-year siege of Sarajevo was "the longest and most destructive siege of any major city" since that of Leningrad during World War II.[15] Almost no part of Sarajevo was out of reach of Serb artillery or snipers. When the siege finally ended in February 1994, shelling and gunfire had killed more than nine thousand Sarajevans, fifteen hundred of them children, and 60 percent of the city's buildings had been destroyed or severely damaged.[16] Sarajevo had once been "the most civilized and tolerant place in the Balkans, one of the great homes of European cosmopolitan culture."[17] Under bombardment, however, the city was reduced to "something like a postmodern Stone Age."[18] First, the public transportation system went, then the telephones, water, gas, and electricity. People who used to pride themselves on their sophistication now scrounged in lots and alleys for firewood and depended on United Nations handouts for food.

The Bosnian War, set off by the breakup of Yugoslavia into Serb, Croat, and Muslim nations, was exceptionally brutal. Prodded by local demagogues and old ethnic rivalries, the Serbs pursued a program of ethnic cleansing: Bosnian Muslims were massacred, raped, and forced out of their homes, acts proscribed by the rules of war and international humanitarian conventions. David Rieff claims that even referring to this kind of behavior as "war" is "to distort and, more gravely, dignify" the real nature of what occurred. He simply calls it "slaughter."[19]

Most of the journalists who lived through the siege of Sarajevo were moved by the suffering of the Sarajevans and outraged by the cruelty of the Serbs. Many soon gave up any pretense of neutrality. Tom Gjelten of National Public Radio did "little favors" for people, "carrying letters in and out, contacting family members outside, or bringing them candles, vitamins, and batteries."[20] Other journalists advocated between the lines of their stories for Western governments to intervene. To those who thought the press should have remained more dispassionate, Rieff had a ready answer: "It is hard to be dispassionate about ethnic cleansing and mass murder."[21]

Michael Nicholson, much to his own surprise, was among the journalists who felt compelled to do something more about the situation in Bosnia than just objectively report it. Although he'd covered fourteen wars during thirty years as a correspondent for Britain's Independent Television News, had seen "blood, sweat, and tears flow in abundance," he wasn't prepared for what Bosnia held in store for him.[22] "One of the things about Sarajevo," he later told an interviewer, "was that it was one of the few instances . . . in which you were very much part of the scene because you couldn't get out of the place. You were under siege yourself. You weren't on a hill watching a town under siege being shelled; you were in that city being shelled, sharing the anguish and despair of the people, and therefore . . . how could you be objective."[23] Nicholson was especially affected by the suffering and death of children in the war. Children were "machine-gunned as they played under the cherry trees, blown to pieces with a mortar shell as they fetched water for their mothers, killed by a sniper's bullet as they queued for bread." He found it impossible to stay on the sidelines, the professional observer keeping suffering at arm's length, when "it was the children who were suffering the most."[24]

The writings of social psychologist Mark H. Davis can provide a clinical explanation for why Nicholson and other journalists came to empathize with the victims of ethnic cleansing, despite the journalistic taboo against getting personally involved. "Situations vary tremendously in terms of their power to evoke a response from observers," Davis writes. "Strong displays of negative emotion, especially by weak or helpless targets, are particularly able to engender powerful observer responses. In fact, faced with such extremely strong situations, other variables, both situational and dispositional, may recede in importance."[25] Or, to put this in plain language, the cumulative weight of the horrors Nicholson witnessed in Bosnia—burning houses, refugees trudging down highways, children crying for their lost parents— pushed him over a line that, as a veteran journalist, he had been conditioned to respect.

One day Nicholson visited an orphanage on the outskirts of Sarajevo. The sight of two hundred children in danger from the relentless Serb shelling filled him with a mixture of anger and despair. He was so troubled by their situation that he helped organize a rescue mission and even took one of the children, nine-year-old Natasha, home to England and adopted her.

Nicholson recounts his awakening to empathy in his book, *Natasha's Story*, which became the basis for the 1997 movie *Welcome to Sarajevo*, written by Frank Cottrell Boyce and directed by Michael Winterbottom. The movie applauds his transformation from observer to participant, but, of course, in the real world, not everyone agreed with his actions. Some journalists just don't believe that wounded and dying children are an adequate reason to abandon objectivity.

"WE'RE NOT HERE TO HELP"

One of these journalists, at least for a while, is Michael Henderson (Stephen Dillane), as Nicholson is renamed for the movie. In an early scene, a fast-talking, hard-drinking American television reporter, Flynn (Woody Harrelson), helps a priest drag a wounded woman out of the street under sniper fire. Flynn's display of coolness and courage wins the admiration of his fellow journalists, with the notable exception of Henderson. He finds Flynn unprofessional, a lightweight preening for the cameras. When Henderson's own cameraman, Greg (James Nesbitt), defends Flynn by saying, "He was just trying to help," Henderson invokes the principle of objectivity. "We're not here to help," he snaps. "We're here to report."[26]

The difference between helping and reporting is soon glaringly obvious. Shells hurled from Serb guns in the hills around Sarajevo crash into a bread line. The press races to the scene. Dozens of people lie dead or horribly wounded all over the street. Greg starts filming. A woman sitting on the curb bleeding shouts at his camera in Bosnian. He just keeps filming. Henderson asks their local driver and translator, Risto (Goran Visnjic), what the woman is saying. "She's saying . . . she's upset, and she's saying . . . she doesn't know what she's saying," Risto explains. "She has lost her control. You shouldn't film her."[27] With that, Risto moves off to help load bodies into civilian cars for transport to the hospital. It's a silent rebuke to Henderson, Greg, and the rest of the press for forgetting, as they too often seem to do in their pell-mell pursuit of the best story or footage, that these are real people, real as themselves, who are suffering and dying.

"The more you see," Nicholson writes in *Natasha's Story*, "the more it hurts and the greater the difficulty to be objective."[28] As the movie cuts from the slaughter in the street to the chaos at the hospital, we sense the hurt gathering behind Henderson's eyes. A little girl who lost her parents in the attack starts talking to him in the corridor. "She just keeps saying, help me. Can you help me?" Risto translates. Henderson tells Risto to ask the girl if she has any other family, adding, "We can give her a lift." The girl doesn't answer, just looks Henderson in the face, then walks away. Watching her go, Henderson says, "The best way we can help is by getting the news out."[29] Although this may not seem like much under the circumstances, it actually represents a sizable shift in Henderson's perspective. Where he previously considered reporting and helping as distinct, he now describes reporting itself as a form of helping.

But is it? The attack isn't even the lead story on the news back in England. "And would you care to tell me what is the lead story?" a furious Henderson asks his field producer, Jane (Kerry Fox). "The Second Coming?" Hardly. "The Duke and Duchess of York are getting divorced," Jane says. "Or separated. Not sure which."[30] The American networks are just as trivial minded and parochial. Their lead story is the Super Bowl.

Henderson's mounting frustration and guilt are manifested in the nightmares that increasingly plague his sleep. In a typical one, a child comes running out of a burning house. It lifts its arms to Henderson. Just as he's about to pick the child up, it gets shot and screams.[31]

Philosopher William Frankena notes that "we usually go our own busy and self-concerned ways, with only an external awareness of the presence of others, much as if they were things, and without any realization of their inner and peculiar worlds of personal experience." Henderson is gradually emerging from that kind of blindness. He's developing a sensitivity or insight we would all do well to develop, "an ability," in Frankena's words, "to be aware of others as persons, as important to themselves as we are to ourselves, and to have a lively and sympathetic representation in imagination of their interests and of the effects of our actions on their lives."[32] It's the start of his break with the long-held principle of objectivity.

The break deepens when he discovers the children living in filthy, crowded conditions at the Ljubica Ivezic orphanage. He becomes obsessed with alerting Western governments and aid agencies to their plight, even though Jane insists that there are other, more important stories for him to report. "As long as the UN are here, we're keeping the kids on screen," he says. "Every night a different kid, the same message: 'Get me out of here.' I am going to make it impossible for them to leave those kids behind." Jane reacts to this with the same disdain Henderson himself once would have. "That's not news," she scoffs. "That's a campaign." Henderson doesn't care what it is. He just repeats, "I'm going to get those kids out."[33]

And he does, including a girl, called Emira (Emira Nusevic) in the movie, whom he takes home with him to England. It isn't his reporting that accomplishes the task, however. In fact, as the shells fall closer to the orphanage and the world continues to ignore the children, he gives in to despair. "Whatever we do," he bitterly tells Jane, "it makes no difference."[34] The power of the press has become yet another casualty of the war. Only a chance encounter with an aid worker, Nina (Marisa Tomei), who has brought food in and is taking children out, allows Henderson to make good on his vow. He and Greg accompany her and the children on the long, harrowing journey over the mountains. At the end of the trip, Nina assures him, "You did a good thing. You did the right thing." Nonetheless, when he returns some months later to Sarajevo to tie up the loose ends of Emira's adoption, he's nervous about the kind of welcome he'll receive from his old colleagues. He shouldn't have been. "If we ever get out of here," Jane says in greeting, "we're all taking a kid back."[35]

The movie clearly intends us to see Henderson's struggle to rescue the children as moving and admirable, "a humanitarian gesture in an inhumane situation," and it is.[36] But that raises a larger question: what does it have to do with journalism?

"THE JOURNALISM OF EMPATHY"

Unlike his movie counterpart, Nicholson wasn't universally admired for his humanitarian impulses. "I was accused of violating a sacrosanct rule of journalism," he writes, "viz.: Never get involved. I read that I had 'ignited fervent debate in the news rooms of Europe'. . . . Some journalists were apparently 'appalled that Nicholson sacrificed forever his ability to report impartially.' All of which was codswallop,"[37] that is, nonsense. But it wasn't all nonsense. The question of whether journalists should ever become emotionally involved in the stories they cover was well worth raising. As journalism professor Philip Seib warns, "With much of the public already skeptical about the news media's practices and intentions, any modification of the standard of objectivity must be undertaken with great care."[38]

One of the fiercest critics of Nicholson and other journalists who sided with the beleaguered Bosnian Muslims was Mick Hume, editor of the now-defunct magazine *LM*. Hume has criticized news coverage of the war for presenting "a titanic battle between good and evil in which journalists adopted a sustained anti-Serb narrative." Worse, he claims, "journalists who stake out the moral high ground in this way do it not for the sake of innocent victims . . . but to fill a vacuum of moral certainty in their own life, their work, or in the society in which they originate." War reporting becomes for them "a twisted sort of therapy."[39]

Those journalists who chose to respond to such criticisms never denied that they had lost faith in objectivity; they did deny that losing it compromised or devalued their reporting. "You can still report the facts," Nicholson says. "You can still be close to the truth as any person can be and still show a commitment, an emotional anguish. I don't see them to be contradictory."[40] He, like most of the press corps in Bosnia, had emerged from the war with an enlarged sense of journalistic responsibility toward the weak and persecuted. They thought the press should, of course, be fair, but fairness didn't mean treating the victimizers on an equal basis with the victims. "I believe that there are moments in history," explains Ed Vulliamy, who covered the Bosnian War for a British newspaper, *The Guardian*, "when neutrality is not neutral, but complicit in the crime."[41] David Rieff justifies the press's partisanship in Bosnia by comparing what was happening there to the Holocaust. Journalists came to sympathize with the Bosnian cause, he says, "in exactly the same way one hopes that if representatives of the foreign press had been stationed in the Warsaw ghetto in 1943, they would have sympathized with the Jews."[42]

The Bosnian War produced "the most horrific human rights abuses seen in Europe since the end of World War II."[43] Even veteran war correspondents found it hard to recover from wading through so much horror.[44] Several years later, Tom Gjelten, who had reported on war and revolution in Central America before going to Sarajevo, was still trying to sort out the lessons Bosnia held for the press. In a 1998 study funded by the Carnegie Commission on Preventing Deadly Conflict, he suggested that journalists may need to reflect more deeply on the meaning of objectivity:

> Although we must report impartially, without being swayed by the people or events we are covering, this obligation is not met simply by according each party in a conflict equal weight in the representation of its views. If we had reported that the Serbs and Croats were responsible for all the wartime atrocities in Bosnia and that the Muslims were innocent, we would have been incorrect. But we would have misled our readers and listeners just as grievously if we had portrayed all sides as being equally responsible for the war and equally culpable of war crimes.[45]

This statement closely reflects the definition of impartiality Richard Gold-stone, chief prosecutor of the international war crimes tribunal, gave in a 1995 interview. "Being evenhanded in my opinion doesn't mean 'one for you' and 'one for you' and 'one for you,'" Goldstone said. "Being even-handed means treating similar atrocities in a similar way."[46] Impartiality or objectivity or fairness isn't about finding a kind of middle ground; it's about finding the truth.

If the truth seems too grandiose a goal for mere journalists, then consider the alternatives. Should they just stand around and watch while innocent civilians are being slaughtered? Should they only report exactly what offi-cials tell them and leave evaluation to the public? Or maybe they should act like the British war correspondent in the old joke who arrives on some hor-rific scene and asks, "Anyone here been raped and speak English?"[47]

The Bosnian War wasn't the first war to engage the sympathies of the re-porters covering it, though they were criticized as if it were. During the Spanish Civil War, a number of distinguished writers and journalists— Arthur Koestler, Martha Gellhorn, Ernest Hemingway, George Orwell, Herbert Matthews, Vincent Sheean—also agitated for Western interven-tion. There is, in fact, an underground or alternative tradition of British and American war correspondents practicing what historian Greg McLaughlin has called, not a little sardonically, "'something must be done' journalism."[48] The tradition extends from Richard Harding Davis's bewailing "The Death of Rodriquez" by a firing squad on the eve of the Spanish-American War, to John Reed's celebrating *Insurgent Mexico* and *Ten Days That Shook the World*, to John Hersey's re-creating the nightmarish effects of the A-bomb in *Hiroshima* and Michael Herr sending back hallucinatory, stream-of-con-sciousness *Dispatches* from Vietnam.

Is this a bad model for today's journalists to embrace? Conventional wis-dom would say so.[49] As a general rule, journalists are trained to distrust emotion and avoid getting wrought up over the people and events they cover. The assumption is that emotion, like doing shots, disorders the brain and interferes with seeing clearly. The more emotional or attached journal-ists become, the more unreliable their reporting is believed to be. Accord-ing to conventional wisdom, the ideal position for journalists is to stand somewhat apart, pad and pen in hand and feelings under tight control.

Now, if anything is nonsense—or "codswallop"—it may be that. "A re-porter's first duty," Nicholson contends, "is to get as close as he can to a story. Standing safely as a spectator on the sideline, he only sees things at a distance."[50] For more and more journalists, getting as close as they can to a story means having empathy for the people involved in it. Empathy, in their opinion, doesn't distort perception—just the opposite. Feeling with and/or for others serves as a clue to reality, a door to understanding.

"I believe empathy and good journalism are co-dependent," *New York Times* reporter Isabel Wilkerson told the audience at her 2002 lecture, "The Journalism of Empathy: How to Be Caring and Factual at the Same Time." Wilkerson, who won a Pulitzer Prize for a story about a ten-year-old boy struggling to survive in inner-city Chicago, practically lived with his family for a month, coming early, staying late, offering to drive them whenever they wanted to go somewhere. "I was a participant observer," she said, "breathing the air of my subject, doing the things that they would normally do."[51]

Another Pulitzer Prize–winning journalist, Anna Quindlen, has noted that though "reporters are often asked about their obligation to readers, perhaps the most important obligation is the one we owe the subjects of our stories, whose lives are limned by our words, for better or for worse." It's an obligation she rarely sees honored today by the press, which is too busy turning everyone into a celebrity, a commodity, something for the public's delectation. Because of that, she has wondered if journalism schools should teach not only accuracy but also empathy, the skill of "imagining yourself in the place of the people you interview."[52]

There's a theory that journalists who show concern for the subjects of their stories will trigger like concern in their audiences. It's this theory the press corps in Bosnia largely followed. "All along," David Rieff says, "it had been the task many of the journalists set themselves . . . to change the sentiments of their readers and viewers about the slaughter."[53] There was only one problem—the theory didn't work.

"A VERY SAD EPITAPH"

In 1999, looking back on his many years as a war correspondent in hells like Vietnam, Biafra, and Bangladesh, Nicholson expressed terrible disappointment and regret. "One begins one's career as a young man," he recalled,

> really in a kind of cavalier fashion but underlying all that is a belief that your pen, camera, . . . your writing can help change the way the world is. By making it public, by showing suffering, by showing war, by showing corruption, . . . you're going to help change it. But when the time comes to hang up your boots as I'm just about doing, you realize that you've done very little to change the world. All you've done is to advertise its ills. It's a very sad epitaph.[54]

Bosnia simply added another heartbreaking line to that epitaph. The Western press had hoped that an informed citizenry back home would prod their governments to intervene in the mass murder of Bosnian Muslims. "Instead," David Rieff says, "the sound bites and 'visual bites' culled from the fighting bred casuistry and indifference far more regularly than it succeeded in mobilizing people to act or even to be indignant."[55]

Just because we live in the Information Age, with the news media rock 'n' rolling 24/7, that doesn't mean we let the information seep in. The more images of suffering people see, the less they seem to respond. Much of the blame for this has been attributed to the formulaic way in which war, natural disasters, famine, and other calamities get covered. Fast, fragmentary, sensational, the news often leaves audiences feeling overstimulated and burned out all at once. The paradoxical response is so widespread that scholars have actually given it a name, "compassion fatigue."[56]

Bosnians became embittered against the press when the West continued to ignore their plight. They resented the exploitation of their suffering in pictures and headlines that titillated people far away but did zero for them. Soon, it wasn't unusual to hear, in the middle of a bombardment, a Sarajevan cynically yelling at photojournalists, "Are you waiting for a shell to go off so you can photograph some corpses?"[57]

Susan Sontag, in her 2003 book *Regarding the Pain of Others*, wonders how any of us who work for or use the news media can justify tripping like sun-lotioned tourists through a vast, hellish landscape of suffering and death, pausing here and there to gape at the most horrific sights. There's "shame as well as shock in looking at the close-up of a real horror," she writes. "Perhaps the only people with the right to look at images of suffering of this extreme order are those who could do something to alleviate it— say, surgeons at the military hospital where the photographs were taken— or those who could learn from it. The rest of us are voyeurs, whether or not we mean to be."[58]

Is it part of the journalist's job, then, to alleviate suffering? How exactly would a journalist do that—by taking sides or by watching and explaining from the sidelines? And what's the responsibility of readers and viewers in all this? Can they just choose to remain indifferent? These aren't idle questions, not today when state disintegration is increasingly common and the Yugoslav pattern of ethnic violence, sieges, destruction of historical monuments, and atrocities against civilians prevails in conflicts around the world.

In a documentary made in the 1980s titled *War Reporters*, an off-screen interviewer asks a now old and gray Martha Gellhorn, "How effective can [war reporting] be? Are you going to change minds, attitudes, governments?"

Gellhorn, who'd been to every major war of her generation, hesitates before answering, but when she does answer, her voice is surprisingly young and defiant. "I think," she says, "anything is better than silence. If nobody puts it down on the record anywhere, then the monsters win totally."[59] Maybe she's right. Maybe journalism can make a difference. Maybe like a stake through the heart or a silver bullet, the right words and pictures can defeat monsters.

NOTES

1. The books I consulted included Clifford Christians, Mark B. Fackler, Kim B. Rotzoll, and Kathy Brittain McKee, *Media Ethics: Cases and Moral Reasoning*, 6th ed. (New York: Longman, 2001); Philip Patterson and Lee Wilkins, *Media Ethics: Issues and Cases*, 5th ed. (Boston: McGraw-Hill, 2005); Louis Alvin Day, *Ethics in Media Communications: Cases and Controversies*, 4th ed. (Belmont, CA: Thompson Wadsworth, 2003).

2. Frans de Waal, *Good Natured* (Cambridge, MA: Harvard University Press, 1996), 88; Sisella Bok, *Mayhem* (Reading, MA: Addison-Wesley, 1998), 38; Martha Nussbaum, quoted in Susan Verducci, "A Conceptual History of Empathy and a Question It Raises for Moral Education," *Educational Theory* 50 (Winter 2000): 63.

3. Burton L. Visotzky, *The Genesis of Ethics* (New York: Random House, 1996), 87.

4. W. H. Auden, "Musée des Beaux Arts," in *The Major Poets, English and American*, ed. Charles M. Coffin (New York: Harcourt, Brace & World, 1969), 529.

5. Quoted in Morton Hunt, *The Compassionate Beast* (New York: William Morrow, 1990), 43.

6. Quoted in Margie Smithhurst, "Reporting Trauma Triggers Empathy: A Report from the Inaugural Dart Center Australasia Conference in Melbourne, 26 October 2004," Dart Center for Journalism & Trauma, www.dartcenter.org/australasia/articles/symposium_report_01.html (accessed 18 October 2005).

7. C. Daniel Batson, "How Social an Animal? The Human Capacity for Caring," *American Psychologist* 45 (March 1990): 344.

8. Pearl M. Oliner and Samuel P. Oliner, *Toward a Caring Society* (Westport, CT: Praeger, 1995), 32.

9. Mark H. Davis, *Empathy: A Social Psychological Approach* (Boulder, CO: Westerview Press, 1996), 11.

10. Day, *Ethics in Media Communications*, 36.

11. Vincent Sheean, *Personal History* (New York: Literary Guild, 1934), 25.

12. Quoted in Philip Seib, *The Global Journalist: News and Conscience in a World of Conflict* (Lanham, MD: Rowman & Littlefield, 2002), 57.

13. Greg McLaughlin, *The War Correspondent* (London: Pluto Press, 2002), 178.

14. Michael Nicholson, *Welcome to Sarajevo* (New York: Hyperion, 1993), 42. Hereafter the book is referred to as *Natasha's Story*, its original title.

15. Tom Gjelten, *Sarajevo Daily: A City and Its Newspaper under Siege* (New York: HarperCollins, 1995), 240.

16. David Rieff, *Slaughterhouse: Bosnia and the Failure of the West* (New York: Simon & Schuster, 1995), 215; Gjelten, *Sarajevo Daily*, 3–4.

17. Nicholson, *Natasha's Story*, 23.

18. Gjelten, *Sarajevo Daily*, 14.

19. Rieff, *Slaughterhouse*, 17.

20. Gjelten, *Sarajevo Daily*, 187.

21. Rieff, *Slaughterhouse*, 9.

22. Nicholson, *Natasha's Story*, xiii, 8.

23. Quoted in McLaughlin, *War Correspondent*, 154.

24. Nicholson, *Natasha's Story*, xvi, 32.

25. Davis, *Empathy*, 15.

26. Frank Cottrell Boyce, *Welcome to Sarajevo* (London: Faber & Faber, 1997), 15.

27. Boyce, *Welcome to Sarajevo*, 38.

28. Nicholson, *Natasha's Story*, 32.

29. Boyce, *Welcome to Sarajevo*, 40–41.

30. Boyce, *Welcome to Sarajevo*, 41.

31. Boyce, *Welcome to Sarajevo*, 125.

32. William Frankena, "A Critique of Virtue-Based Ethics," in *Moral Philosophy: A Reader*, ed. Louis Pojman, 2nd ed. (Indianapolis: Hackett Publishing, 1998), 268–69.

33. Boyce, *Welcome to Sarajevo*, 65.

34. Boyce, *Welcome to Sarajevo*, 83.

35. Boyce, *Welcome to Sarajevo*, 122, 140.

36. Boyce, *Welcome to Sarajevo*, viii.

37. Nicholson, *Natasha's Story*, 86.

38. Seib, *Global Journalist*, 54.

39. McLaughlin, *War Correspondent*, 167, 169–70.

40. Quoted in McLaughlin, *War Correspondent*, 154.

41. Quoted in Seib, *Global Journalist*, 85.

42. Rieff, *Slaughterhouse*, 218.

43. Tom Gjelten, "Professionalism in War Reporting: A Correspondent's View," Hamline University, www.hamline.edu/world/gjelten/war.html (accessed 14 December 2005).

44. Rieff, *Slaughterhouse*, 25.

45. Gjelten, "Professionalism in War Reporting."

46. Quoted in Gjelten, "Professionalism in War Reporting."

47. Rieff, *Slaughterhouse*, 51.

48. McLaughlin, *War Correspondent*, 9.

49. The supposed negative effects of emotion on reasoned judgment are summarized in Delores Gallo, "Educating for Empathy, Reason and Imagination," *The Journal of Creative Behavior* 23, no. 2 (1989): 98–115.

50. Nicholson, *Natasha's Story*, xiii.

51. Quoted in Laurie Toupin, "Being a Journalist Means Being Human," Poynteronline, www.poynter.org/content/content_print.asp?id+10646&custom+ (accessed 18 October 2005).

52. Anna Quindlen, "The Great Obligation," MSNBC, www.msnbc.msn.com/id/4710298/site/newsweek (accessed 17 October 2005).

53. Rieff, *Slaughterhouse*, 257.

54. Quoted in McLaughlin, *War Correspondent*, 14.

55. Rieff, *Slaughterhouse*, 216.

56. Susan D. Moeller, *Compassion Fatigue: How the Media Sell Disease, Famine, War, and Death* (New York: Routledge, 1999), 9.

57. Susan Sontag, *Regarding the Pain of Others* (New York: Picador, 2003), 112.

58. Sontag, *Regarding the Pain of Others*, 42.

59. *War Reporters*, Films for the Humanities and Sciences (Princeton, NJ: 1996).

AFTERWORD

Left Hanging

I take down the hanging plant to water it—oh, no, there's a nest inside. It happened last summer, too, and almost killed the fuchsia, but I can't just lift the nest out. The bird has woven it around the stems, intricately incorporating the plant, a cunning design, like a cathedral built of astonishment and mortar. I'm wearing work gloves—thick fingered, stiff, not really suitable for gardening. I tug experimentally at the nest, then more firmly. It's already coming apart, twigs and dry moss, when I notice the eggs, tiny as the eyes of a baby and pale blue, and am immediately sorry. I look up, half-expecting to be attacked from the sky, but the sky is empty. Empty.

This is a kind of parable about how ethics works. Even when you try to do what's right, the results can be problematic. I wanted to save the plant, but, in the process, I ended up destroying the eggs. I didn't mean to destroy them. I was only trying to remove the nest so the roots could get water. I figured the bird could always build another nest elsewhere. It wasn't like I hadn't thought about what might become of the bird—I had—but the results were the same as if I hadn't. That's because of the incompleteness of my knowledge. If I'd known about the eggs, maybe I wouldn't have tried to remove the nest. I certainly would've removed it a lot more carefully.

The outcome of our actions rarely coincides exactly with our intentions, even when our intentions are honorable and just.

You might think I would have realized that where there's a nest, there could be eggs—but I didn't. I was so absorbed in my immediate task and so conditioned by my past experience (I hadn't found any eggs in last year's nest), I overlooked the obvious.

Sometimes we confront an ethical problem without realizing we're confronting one, which only compounds the problem.

Another thing: had I been wearing gardening gloves to garden, not those thick, clumsy work gloves, my touch might've been subtler. Instead, the nest was pretty much demolished by the time I saw the eggs, robin's eggs from their color.

The process we use to make decisions inevitably affects the quality of the decisions we make.

I felt bad about it. In winter, I hang a bird feeder from the hook where the plant was hanging. Perhaps one of the birds I'd fed had built the nest. The possibility bothered me. I got this uneasy feeling that I'd betrayed a trust.

To choose one good is often to lose another, or two others.

Of course, I never meant to do harm, and compared to governments and corporations, the harm I did was negligible. I didn't tyrannize or bomb anyone or enrich myself at the expense of others or the environment, but I was filled with guilt all the same. Deep down, I kind of expected to be punished.

If we don' t do good, at least we shouldn't do bad.

How superstitious was that! The only punishment I suffered was self-inflicted. It came from having violated my own values, my sense of what's important, my image of who I am. For a moment, I stood there fretting. Then I tossed the broken remnants of the nest onto the brush pile and hung the plant back up.

Failure is usually assumed to be cause for despair, but, actually, it's cause for hope—hope because we can emerge from failure wiser, less arrogant, more human.

The plant has been growing well ever since. It has many new blooms, frilly pink flowers that remind me of tutus. If a plant can be said to look happy, then this one looks happy.

We may never know for sure whether we've made the right choice or the wrong one, but it's good in and of itself, like truth or beauty, to reflect on the terrible responsibility that comes with choosing.

DISCUSSION QUESTIONS

THE PAPER

1. Practice writing a more responsible headline than "Gotcha!" assuming you have the "perp walk" shot but not the "cop quote." Keep in mind it has to be short (no more than five words) and grab readers' attention. What are the ethical and practical challenges involved in writing such a headline?
2. The note that tipped Henry Hackett off to the mob story angle was actually lying on the desk of the *Sentinel*'s editor. In effect, Hackett stole the information from a rival. Does this make the information morally off limits for the *Sun*? Why or why not?
3. Is Alicia correct when she implies that the *Sun* doesn't have to be as accurate as other papers because it's a tabloid? Are there different standards of truthfulness and accuracy for different news media? Or are print, TV, and Web journalists all bound by the same ethical standards? Explain your reasoning.

SHATTERED GLASS

1. Who or what was to blame for Stephen Glass's deceptions making it into print, and what needed to happen to prevent it?

2. Suppose that everything Glass wrote was true. Would his stories then have met the criteria of ethical reporting? Is there anything wrong with journalism that is entertaining or "snarky," or does it depend on what kind of news outlet you work for and who your intended audience is?

3. How do you balance trust in your colleagues and loyalty to your friends with careful verification and fact-checking?

4. Glass talks about the pressure his family's expectations have put on him. To what extent does that explain or excuse his actions?

WAG THE DOG

1. Although *Wag the Dog* is fictional, can you find parallels between the movie and recent real-life instances of politicians using the media to manipulate the public's perception of reality?

2. If you were Mr. Fix It, meaning a media image consultant brought in to fix the president's public relations crisis, how would you handle the press regarding the president's alleged behavior with the Firefly girl? What would you encourage the president to say and do? Which press outlets would you contact to get out your side of the story and why? Would you create a fake war to distract Americans from the Firefly story? Why or why not?

3. One of the key moments in *Wag the Dog* occurs in the opening scene when Winifred Ames asks Conrad Brean if he wants to know whether the president's alleged behavior with the Firefly girl is true, and he responds, "What difference does it make if it's true?" If you worked on the president's press staff, how would you answer Brean's question to Ames? Would it make a difference to you if the allegations were true before you began dealing with the press? Would you need to know if they were true, even if you didn't want to know? Why or why not? Would knowing the truth affect whether you would take the job of "fixing" the situation for him? What if you were the reporter covering the story? How would you go about verifying the Firefly girl's claims? What sources would you need to interview? What documents could you use as sources of information?

4. If you were a reporter assigned to cover the White House when stories of the B-3 bomber and war with Albania began to surface, how would you go about verifying the facts of the stories? Which sources would you interview and why? What kinds of documents could you re-

quest from the White House to verify facts? What law requires the government to comply with your request?

ABSENCE OF MALICE

1. After getting your first job in journalism, what if you work with colleagues and superiors who don't appear to know or care about the professed ideals of journalism? Would you worry, then, about the ethics of your actions? If you didn't worry about ethics, could there be negative consequences? Likewise, if you did concern yourself with ethics in such a newsroom, could you experience difficulties at work?
2. Is it realistic to expect professionals in the heat of meeting deadlines to engage in formal moral reasoning? Why or why not?
3. In your own experience in work and at school, what tends to get the most attention—technical excellence or moral excellence? What, if anything, does this say about the relative importance of these two dimensions of "good work"? For yourself, is one more important than the other? If not, why not? If so, which one and why?
4. If your colleagues or peers encourage you to do something that violates your own sense of right and wrong, is there anything you can do? What if the colleague is, like Mac in the movie, your immediate superior?

MR. DEEDS GOES TO TOWN AND MR. DEEDS

1. A journalist's greatest obligation is to try to tell the truth as the facts dictate. Is deception or lying, then, ever acceptable in pursuing a story? Why or why not?
2. Make two lists of stories, one that you believe would justify undercover reporting and a second that you believe would not justify undercover reporting. Defend your answers.
3. Describe how you would report on the following stories:
   a. Restaurants: How would you find out about the cleanliness of the food preparation, the condition of the kitchen, and any health hazards involved? What reporting techniques would be justified, and what techniques wouldn't be?
   b. Celebrities: How would you find out if your favorite female celebrity was an alcoholic or pregnant or involved with another celebrity? What reporting techniques would be justified, and what techniques wouldn't be?

    c. Corruption: How would you find out if the mayor is getting kick-backs from the city's top construction firm, which is constantly getting the city's business? What reporting techniques would be justified, and what techniques wouldn't be?

THE PRIDE OF THE YANKEES

1. How would you respond if a well-known athlete you cover and with whom you have developed a friendship confided a personal situation to you, then asked you for suggestions about ways to conceal it? Are there any such situations where you might consider doing such a favor? How would you respond, for example, if the athlete asked you to hide the fact that he or she had been diagnosed with a serious illness?

2. How would you feel about interviewing your favorite athlete: nervous, excited, calm, or professional? How might you prepare for this interview?

3. Agree or disagree with the following statement: "Being friends with pro athletes compromises the professionalism of a sports journalist." Defend your choice.

DIE HARD

1. When an emergency situation arises, what public services do you believe journalists should fulfill in the first hours, then in the days that follow?

2. Most emergency responders have access to some counseling services to help them deal with the trauma of witnessing death and destruction. What services are available to journalists, and how should a news organization go about providing such services?

3. Journalists often are accused of "getting in the way" in emergency situations. In what ways do you think journalists who respond to such emergencies could be of help, not just to the public, but also to the police, firefighters, medics, and other first responders?

4. If you could "rewrite" the Richard Thornburg character in *Die Hard* to be a sympathetic character, but still keep his scenes more or less the same, what kinds of dialogue and behaviors do you think would make him appear more ethical?

BROADCAST NEWS

1. Twenty years ago, reviewer Peter Travers wrote that the movie *Broadcast News* is "sounding an alarm to a nation that wants it news delivered sitcom style." Do you agree with this statement today? Why or why not?
2. Since Hurricane Katrina and the "Anderson Cooperization" of the news, "Network anchors often behave as if they are the nation's grief counselors," writes "TV Watch" columnist Alessandra Stanley in an April 19, 2007, *New York Times* article. "One reason that [ABC's Charles Gibson] has been gaining in the ratings could be that he acts like the nation's newsman." Stanley is referring to the coverage by network news anchors of the Virginia Tech shootings. Do you believe it is ever appropriate for news anchors to show emotion when reporting? Why or why not?
3. What kind of credibility is projected by news anchors at your local major TV stations? Which anchor (or team) do you prefer watching and why? What does the anchor (or the team) do right? What do other stations' anchors do wrong?

GOOD NIGHT, AND GOOD LUCK

1. How would you define "objectivity?" Is objectivity an appropriate standard for journalism? Does it help or hinder the search for truth? In light of the film, how would you distinguish among these terms: *objectivity, fairness, balance*, and *truth*?
2. How would you compare Murrow's style of journalism with the television journalism of today? Has TV journalism improved or devolved?
3. Would you let a friend and coworker be unfairly maligned and harassed—as Murrow does when his colleague Don Hollenbeck is tarred by McCarthy's red brush—if inaction would allow you to pursue a larger moral goal (in Murrow's case, a measured attack on McCarthy)? Why or why not?
4. Ethicist Deni Elliot says that just actions can only arise from moral reasoning based on sound principles. How would you describe Murrow's core ethical principles? Is he consistent in applying those principles?
5. What is the public's role and responsibility in the rise of demagogues like McCarthy?

VERONICA GUERIN

1. Is any journalistic campaign worth sacrificing your life for? Why or why not?

2. Should a journalist abandon an investigation if it is endangering not just his or her own life but also the lives of others? Why or why not?

3. Aristotle said that virtue lies at the mean between two extremes. Apply this moral principle, generally known as the "golden mean," to the case of Veronica Guerin. If one extreme is cowardice, what might the other be? What trait could be the golden mean in this case? How would you rank Veronica Guerin's professional conduct on the scale you've described? How would you rank her if she had followed the advice of her mother, husband, and editor to back off her investigation?

THE YEAR OF LIVING DANGEROUSLY

1. A central theme in *The Year of Living Dangerously* is the tension between "straight," objective reporting, favored by Western journalists in the film, and the "soft," or even "melodramatic," style of reporting that Guy sometimes produces as a means of documenting the plight of the suffering, voiceless Indonesian masses. What are the potential strengths, as well as some possible ethical problems, with either kind of reporting?

2. Objectivity, the notion that the reporter is detached from the events he or she covers, has been standard operating procedure in American journalism since at least the 1920s. Do you think journalistic objectivity has outlived its usefulness, in an age of around-the-clock news, electronic blogging, and a growing number of television commentators, many of whom report from their own perspectives and still manage to break legitimate news? Defend your answer.

3. Guy became romantically involved with Jill, whose personal trust he violated by using confidential information she gave him. Guy was also a friend and working partner of Billy, whose trust Guy also broke by reporting the same information. Guy's defense was that the information was legitimate and important and that he was only following his professional journalistic principles. Do you think Guy acted properly or not? Defend your answer.

WELCOME TO SARAJEVO

1. Assume that empathy is no less important a quality for journalists to possess than a nose for news or writing ability. What exercises or activities would you recommend to develop empathy in working journalists? In journalism students?

2. In her book *Regarding the Pain of Others*, Susan Sontag asserts, "Perhaps the only people with the right to look at images of suffering . . . are those who could do something to alleviate it—say, surgeons at the military hospital where the photographs were taken—or those who could learn from it. The rest of us are voyeurs, whether or not we mean to be." Do you agree or disagree? Explain how implementing your answer would affect news content.

3. Which, in your opinion, is more important for journalists to be, empathetic or objective? Why?

FOR FURTHER READING

THE PAPER

Bird, S. E., and R. W. Dardenne. "Myth, Chronicle and Story: Exploring the Narrative Qualities of News." In *Social Meaning of News: A Text-Reader*, 333–50. Thousand Oaks, CA: Sage, 1997.

Cooper, T. "Lorraine Code's 'Epistemic Responsibility,' Journalism, and the Charles Stuart Case." *Business and Professional Ethics Journal* 12, no. 3 (1993): 83–106.

Schlesinger, P. "Newsmen and Their Time-Machine." *British Journal of Sociology* 28 (1997): 336–50.

SHATTERED GLASS

Bissinger, Buzz. "*Shattered Glass.*" *Vanity Fair*, September 1998, 176–90.

Bok, Sissela. *Lying: Moral Choice in Public and Private Life*. New York: Vintage, 1999.

Callahan, David. *The Cheating Culture*. Orlando, FL: Harcourt, 2004.

WAG THE DOG

Bagdikian, Ben. *The Media Monopoly*. 6th ed. Boston: Beacon Press, 2000.

Chomsky, Noam. *Necessary Illusions*. Boston: Southend Press, 1989.

Kovach, Bill, and Tom Rosenstiel. *The Elements of Journalism.* New York: Crown Publishers, 2001.

Protess, David L., Fay Lomax Cook, Jack. C. Doppelt, James S. Etterna, Margaret T. Gordon, Donna R. Leff, and Peter Miller. *The Journalism of Outrage: Investigative Reporting and Agenda Building in America.* New York: Guilford Press, 1991.

ABSENCE OF MALICE

Gardner, Howard. "Good Work Well Done: A Psychological Study." *The Chronicle of Higher Education,* 22 February 2002, B7.

Gardner, Howard, Mihaly Csikszentmihalyi, and William Damon. *Good Work: When Excellence and Ethics Meet.* New York: Basic Books, 2001.

Gardner, Howard, Wendy Fischman, Becca Solomon, and Deborah Greenspan. *Making Good: How Young People Cope with Moral Dilemmas at Work.* Cambridge, MA: Harvard University Press, 2004.

MR. DEEDS GOES TO TOWN AND MR. DEEDS

Black, Jay, Bob Steele, and Ralph Barney. *Doing Ethics in Journalism.* Greencastle, IN: Sigma Delta Chi Foundation, 1993.

Koeger, Brooke. *Nellie Bly: Daredevil, Reporter, Feminist.* New York: Crown Press, 1994.

Saltzman, Joe. *Frank Capra and the Image of the Journalist in American Film.* Los Angeles: University of Southern California, Norman Lear Center, Annenberg School for Communication, 2002.

Shapiro, Bruce. *Shaking the Foundations: 200 Years of Investigative Journalism in America.* New York: Nation Books, 2003.

Smith, Ron F. *Groping for Ethics in Journalism.* 4th ed. Ames: Iowa State University Press, 1999.

THE PRIDE OF THE YANKEES

Strupp, Joe. "Caught Not Looking." *Editor & Publisher* (October 2006): 42–47.

Henry, Neil. "Toy Department Deserves More Respect." *Quill* (August 2005): 39–41.

Waxman, Shari. "When Heroes Go Bad." *Columbia Journalism Review* (March–April 2004): 61–62.

DIE HARD

Caeti, Tory, John Liederbach, and Steven S. Bellew. "Police-Media Relations at Critical Incidents: Interviews from Oklahoma City." *International Journal of Police Science & Management* 7, no. 2 (2005): 86–97.

Chermak, Steven, and Alexander Weiss. "Maintaining Legitimacy Using External Communication Strategies: An Analysis of Police-Media Relations." *Journal of Criminal Justice* 33, no. 5 (September–October 2005): 501–12.

Freedman, Tovia G. "Voices of 9/11 First Responders: Patterns of Collective Resilience." *Clinical Social Work Journal* 32, no. 4 (Winter 2004): 377–93.

Garner, Gerald W. *The Police Meet the Press.* Springfield, IL: C. C. Thomas, 1984.

Selke, William L., and G. Marshall Bartoszek. "Police and Media Relations: The Seeds of Conflict." *Criminal Justice Review* 9, no. 2 (1984): 25–30.

Simpson, Richard A., and James A. Boggs. "An Exploratory Study of Traumatic Stress among Newspaper Journalists." *Journalism & Mass Communication Monographs* 1, no. 1 (Spring 1999): 1–26.

BROADCAST NEWS

Anderson, Bonnie M. *News Flash: Journalism, Infotainment, and the Bottom-Line Business of Broadcast News.* San Francisco: Jossey-Bass, 2004.

Auletta, Ken. *Three Blind Mice: How the Networks Lost Their Way.* New York: Random House, 1991.

Friendly, Fred W. *Due to Circumstances Beyond Our Control.* New York: Random House, 1967.

GOOD NIGHT, AND GOOD LUCK

Bayley, Edwin R. *Joe McCarthy and the Press.* Madison: University of Wisconsin Press, 1981.

Navasky, Victor S. *Naming Names.* New York: Penguin, 1981.

Olson, Lynne, and Stanley S. Cloud. *The Murrow Boys: Pioneers on the Frontlines of Broadcast Journalism.* Boston: Mariner Books, 1997.

VERONICA GUERIN

Bordwell, David. *The Way Hollywood Tells It: Story and Style in Modern Movies.* Berkeley: University of California Press, 2006.

O'Reilly, Emily. *Veronica Guerin: The Life and Death of a Crime Reporter.* London: Vintage, 1998.

Sager, Mike. "The Martyrdom of Veronica Guerin." *GQ*, March 1997, 231–37.

THE YEAR OF LIVING DANGEROUSLY

Good, Howard. *The Image of War Correspondents in Anglo-American Fiction.* Journalism Monographs 97. Columbia, SC: University of South Carolina, Association for Education in Journalism and Mass Communication, College of Journalism, July 1986.

Jameson, Frederic. *The Political Unconscious: Narrative as a Socially Symbolic Act.* Ithaca, NY: Cornell University Press, 1981.

Kalb, Bernard. "Cinematic Art vs. Reality in Indonesia." *New York Times*, 23 January 1983, sec. 2, 17, 22.

WELCOME TO SARAJEVO

McLaughlin, Greg. *The War Correspondent.* London: Pluto Press, 2002.

Moeller, Susan D. *Compassion Fatigue: How the Media Sell Disease, Famine, War, and Death.* New York: Routledge, 1999.

Rieff, David. *Slaughterhouse: Bosnia and the Failure of the West.* New York: Simon & Schuster, 1995.

Seib, Philip. *The Global Journalist: News and Conscience in a World of Conflict.* Lanham, MD: Rowman & Littlefield, 2002.

Sontag, Susan. *Regarding the Pain of Others.* New York: Picador, 2003.

SELECTED JOURNALISM
MOVIES FOR FURTHER VIEWING

Note: Movie titles are listed in chronological order.

Nothing Sacred (1937). In this screwball comedy, a newspaper cashes in on the fake story of a young woman (Carole Lombard) supposedly dying of radium poisoning. The movie is an ironic celebration of phoniness.

Nancy Drew, Reporter (1939). Nancy Drew (Bonita Granville) often pretends that she is not a reporter but an innocent girl trying to get information, photographs, or both. She is involved in both active and passive deception, as well as masquerading.

Meet John Doe (1941). Frank Capra's film depicts a newspaper columnist (Barbara Stanwyck) fabricating the story of a man (Gary Cooper) who says he will kill himself to protest social conditions. The deception triggers a national movement celebrating neighborliness and self-sufficiency, whereupon the newspaper publisher seeks to harness the movement to serve his own evil ends.

Call Northside 777 (1948). Chicago Reporter P. J. McNeal (James Stewart) reopens a ten-year-old murder case involving a man convicted of killing a policeman. In one key scene, he demonstrates passive deception by letting others assume he is a policeman so he can get access to public record documents that have been unfairly denied to him as a reporter.

Deadline U.S.A. (1952). Made at a time when bankruptcies and mergers were decimating the ranks of big-city dailies, this movie chronicles the death spasms of the *Day*, a venerable newspaper about to be sold to a competitor by its founder's heirs and killed. The movie portrays the cutthroat newspaper business as a kind of counterpart to the crime syndicate that the *Day's* editor, Ed Hutcheson, takes on in one last glorious burst of crusading. Hutcheson, played with abrasive integrity by Hollywood tough guy Humphrey Bogart, passes through the movie spouting aphorisms on the importance of a free and responsible press. "An honest, fearless press," he intones at one point, "is the public's first protection from gangsterism, local or international." Nonetheless, there are scenes that can leave the attentive viewer wondering at Hutcheson's own ethics. What's he doing, for example, giving that washed-up boxer a cash-filled envelope in exchange for information? And how come he's using the resources of the newspaper to investigate a romantic rival?

A Face in the Crowd (1957). Directed by Elia Kazan and starring Andy Griffith in a role vastly different from his Sheriff Andy Taylor persona, *A Face in the Crowd* tells the story of a small-town criminal (Griffith) who builds his radio-industry fame and fortune on the gullibility of the American public through simple media manipulation and con artistry. Contemptuous of the very audience that idolizes him, Griffith's character's true personality is revealed via television in a moment of betrayal by the very woman who discovered him.

Medium Cool (1969). The title refers to communications theorist Marshall McLuhan's description of TV as a "cool medium." John Cassellis (Robert Forster), the movie's main character, is a TV cameraman-reporter who travels across a violently fractured America in the tumultuous spring and summer of 1968. He records Robert Kennedy's funeral, antiriot training at a National Guard camp, and the street battles between police and protesters outside the Democratic convention in Chicago. "Jesus, I love to shoot film," he says, seemingly indifferent to the viciousness of what he's shooting. In this, the movie, though rooted in some of the defining moments of the sixties, anticipates with surprising accuracy today's image-riddled, media-driven culture of passive spectators and unblinking voyeurs.

All the President's Men (1976). Two young *Washington Post* reporters, Bob Woodward (Robert Redford) and Carl Bernstein (Dustin Hoffman), known collectively as "Woodstein," grope their way through the maze of the worst political scandal in modern U.S. history, Watergate. With epic persistence, they work the phones, knock on doors, sift through documents, and argue and plead with editors on behalf of their stories. But they also harass and trick sources, browbeat colleagues, and exhibit other disturbing signs of vanity, ambition, and monomania. As it follows the reporters' furious pursuit of the truth, the movie raises the all-important

question whether the ends justify the means, a question further complicated by the fact that no one at the *Post* knows yet what the ends will turn
out to be.

Network (1976). Paddy Chayefsky wrote this satire about the pressures
and madness of television ratings, especially in TV news divisions. Howard
Beale (Peter Finch) is the highly rated anchor who slowly loses his audience
and his job; he quickly swirls into personal decline, asking his viewers to re-
peat after him, "I'm as mad as hell, and I'm not gonna take it anymore!"
This satire is too close to the truth today.

The Adventures of Nellie Bly (1981). Nineteenth-century pioneer female
journalist Nellie Bly (Linda Purl) exposes corruption in New York City, including substandard conditions in New York City's notorious Blackwell's Island Insane Asylum.

Under Fire (1983). This war correspondent movie shows a photojournalist (Nick Nolte) staging a picture to further the revolutionary cause during
the 1979 Nicaraguan civil war. The film raises questions concerning when a
moral cause trumps journalistic ethics.

The Natural (1984). Sportswriter Max Mercy (Robert Duvall) follows the
progress of Roy Hobbs (Robert Redford) throughout the film. Presented as
a sinister force out to thwart the hero, Mercy is working closely with gamblers betting against Hobbs's team, the New York Knights.

Fletch (1985). Irwin "Fletch" Fletcher (Chevy Chase) goes undercover
for most of the movie to expose a drug ring, risking his life in the process.
He uses active deception and masquerading through most of the film.

News at 11 (1986). A made-for-TV movie, but available on video, this
movie features an anchor faced with a bevy of ethical issues; the main
dilemma, however, is the news coverage of an alleged sexual assault by a
teacher on a student. The news director pressures him to take advantage of
the situation and sensationalize the accusations.

Street Smart (1987). A magazine writer (Christopher Reeve) makes up
the story of a Times Square pimp and parlays it into a TV news job. The fictional pimp bears an uncanny resemblance to a real-life one (Morgan Free-
man), and complications ensue.

Eight Men Out (1988). When sportswriters Ring Lardner (John Sayles,
who also wrote and directed the movie) and Hugh Fullerton (Studs Terkel)
begin to probe whether the Chicago White Sox threw the 1919 World Series, they face opposition from players, fans, team owners, and even their
own colleagues. Very few movies show the work of sportswriters in any detail (two others are 1942's *The Pride of the Yankees* and 1984's *The Natural*).
This one provides a fairly comprehensive overview of the various and often

conflicting roles—cheerleader, mythmaker, truth seeker, custodian of rules and records—that sportswriters must somehow negotiate.

Die Hard 2 (1990). In this sequel, John McClane (Bruce Willis) battles a team of American Special Forces mercenaries trying to liberate a war criminal from U.S. custody. William Atherton reprises his role as the sleazy reporter Richard Thornburg, and the film presents other working journalists in various negative lights.

Canadian Bacon (1995). Written and directed by Michael Moore, this satire provides a comic take on the situations that arise after the U.S. president (Alan Alda), faced with a stalled domestic economy and low approval ratings, decides to declare war on Canada to distract Americans from problems at home. The president's main tool for building public support for the war is media manipulation.

Godzilla (1998). In this Hollywood remake of the classic Japanese monster film, a band of humans from various walks of life team up to outsmart and defeat a giant mutated lizard on the rampage in Manhattan. Central characters include a plucky young TV journalist, her heroic cameraman, and the sleazy senior news anchor who steals her story.

The Insider (1999). *60 Minutes* producer Lowell Bergman (Al Pacino) and whistle-blower Jeff Wigand (Russell Crowe) risk their reputations and safety as they battle the corrupt tobacco and broadcast-news industries to bring the truth to light. The movie illustrates how organizational constraints and source relationships can pose hazards to responsible journalistic inquiry, verification, and reporting.

Never Been Kissed (1999). A *Chicago Sun-Times* copy editor, Josie Geller (Drew Barrymore), goes undercover as a high school student to find out what teenagers are like today. She becomes a popular student and falls in love with one of the teachers before she is exposed.

Seabiscuit (2003). For a take on sports broadcasters during the 1930s, check out William H. Macy's portrayal of Tick Tock McGlaughlin, complete with creative sound effects. Also notice how the print journalists tend to stick together in the same pack while covering Seabiscuit's races.

CLASS PROJECTS FOR INSTRUCTORS

THE PAPER

Assign the following research project to students or groups.

Find several newspaper stories written about the 2006 mining accident in West Virginia and complete these activities:

1. Circle all factual information that could have been verified. Next, check the sourcing for these facts. How do the reporters know what they report? Do they include any qualifiers or disclaimers to indicate that information has not been confirmed or is otherwise doubtful?
2. What seems to be the storyline implied in the stories you reviewed? Can you think of recent news stories with a similar "cast of characters" and "plot"? What alternative storyline could have been used to frame the mining accident?
3. What kinds of details could the reporters have included had they had more time? Compare the newspaper stories you found about the mining accident, if possible, with stories shown on television or posted online. How do you think the production cycles for these different news platforms affected the truthfulness of the stories you examined?

WAG THE DOG

Assign the following research project to students or groups.

When *Wag the Dog* debuted, some Americans compared the Bush administration's reasons for beginning the 1990–1991 Gulf War with the situation of Conrad Brean's fake war with Albania: as a way to distract the American public from the president's problems or agenda at home. Find out for yourself whether the comparisons are correct. Start by researching the basics surrounding the start of the Gulf War. Newspaper stories, news magazine articles, and transcripts from television and radio news from the time make great places to begin your research.

While doing your research, make sure to ask the following questions: What were the administration's reasons for going to war? Did Congress support the administration. Why or why not? What was the president's approval rating before the war, after its start, and by its end? Did American citizens support the war? Why or why not? How long was the war? Why did it end? What did the war accomplish?

After you've completed your research, list all similarities and differences you found between the circumstances surrounding the real war and the fake war. Consider what you've discovered, then decide whether the accusations that Bush started the Gulf War to distract Americans from his problems or his agenda at home is accurate. Finally, write a two-page essay on whether the comparisons are warranted, using the evidence you uncovered to support your position.

ABSENCE OF MALICE

Require each student to write a paper on a media professional's work. Ask the students to analyze the work's technical and moral dimensions, then consider the factors that helped or hindered the professional to do "good work."

In class, break into groups to compare and contrast the work of the various professionals, especially the factors that appear to have affected the professionals' abilities to do work of high technical and moral quality. Ask each group to present its findings, focusing on how the group identified "good work" and the conditions that support (or undermine) it. Allow time for others to ask questions. Do they agree with the analysis? Do you? Why or why not?

THE PRIDE OF THE YANKEES

1. If applicable, invite a few members of one of your school's athletic teams to visit the class and talk about their experiences working with sports journalists.
2. Ask class members to bring in videos or DVDs of their favorite sports journalism broadcasts (*SportsCenter*, local broadcasters) or the sports page from the college newspaper and from area dailies to show in class. Critique both the topics of coverage and the content. Do the journalists show too much favoritism toward the athletes, or are they objective?

DIE HARD

Invite local police, firefighters, medics, and emergency-management officials to class to watch scenes from *Die Hard* with the students. Follow the viewing with an open discussion about what journalists should and should not do in such situations.

BROADCAST NEWS

Invite a local television news journalist to watch scenes from *Broadcast News* with the class and talk about what he or she believes about the business of TV news today. Can he or she relate to scenes in the movie? Ask relevant questions concerning anchor image, financial pressures, ratings pressures, and ethical dilemmas the visiting journalist has encountered.

THE YEAR OF LIVING DANGEROUSLY

Identify a controversial issue on your campus or community. Break the class into two groups; each group should gather all possible facts on the issue and locate sources on different sides of it. Some sources may be professional experts, academics, or government officials. Others may be local citizens and members of civic or activist organizations.

Assign one group to write a story collectively on the controversy from a detached, traditionally objective stance, using all sources from all sides but giving prominence to experts and officials. The second group should write the same story by focusing on the negative or potentially harmful impacts of the issue on people and give prominence to the sources with highly emotional views, even though they may not have "expert" status. The focus and tone, especially in the story leads, should be different for each story. After both are written, compare and contrast each kind of story as a class. Discuss whether one type of story is superior to the other and why or why not.

INDEX

ABOUT THE CONTRIBUTORS

Berrin A. Beasley is associate professor of communication at the University of North Florida and a senior fellow with the Blue Cross Blue Shield Center for Ethics, Public Policy and the Professions. She is a former daily newspaper reporter and television news anchor/producer, whose research interests include journalism ethics and the portrayal of women in the media.

Sandra L. Borden is associate professor of communication at Western Michigan University, where she also codirects the Center for the Study of Ethics in Society. She teaches ethics, freedom of expression, and media criticism. Her research has been published in several books and journals, including the *Journal of Mass Media Ethics* and *Communication Monographs*. She is the author of *Journalism as Practice* (2007).

Robert Brown is subject leader for journalism, advertising, and communication in the School of Creative Industries at Napier University, Edinburgh, Scotland, where he has been pioneering the study of representations of journalism in British and Irish popular culture. Having been a visiting professor at the Asian College of Journalism in Chennai (Madras, India), he also recently contributed a chapter to *21st Century Journalism in India*, edited by Nalini Rajan (2007)

John Carvalho, who earned his Ph.D. from the University of North Carolina, Chapel Hill, is assistant professor of journalism and director of the journalism program at Auburn University in Alabama. A former newspaper sportswriter and Associated Press staff member, he now studies sports media history, particularly of the 1920s and 1930s.

Michael Dillon teaches in the Department of Journalism and Multimedia Arts at Duquesne University in Pittsburgh, Pennsylvania. He is the author of *The Life and Times of E. H. Butler: A Crusading Journalist Navigates the Gilded Age* (2003) and coauthor of *Media Ethics Goes to the Movies* with Howard Good (2002). He has published numerous scholarly articles and book chapters. Prior to earning his Ph.D. at Pennsylvania State University and embarking on an academic career, Dillon was a newspaper reporter and won fifteen awards for journalistic excellence. His recent essays have appeared in *New York Newsday*, the *Philadelphia Inquirer*, the *Pittsburgh Post-Gazette*, and the *Dallas Morning News*.

Matthew C. Ehrlich is professor of journalism at the University of Illinois, Urbana-Champaign. He is the author of *Journalism in the Movies* (2004). His research on movies and journalism has also appeared in *Journalism: Theory, Practice and Criticism*, *Journal of Communication Inquiry*, *Notre Dame Journal of Law, Ethics & Public Policy*, and *Critical Studies in Media Communication*.

Howard Good, who received his Ph.D. from the University of Michigan, is professor of journalism at the State University of New York, New Paltz, where he originated and teaches the course in media ethics. Good has written eleven books, including *Acquainted with the Night*, *Outcasts*, *The Journalist as Autobiographer*, *Girl Reporter*, and *The Drunken Journalist*, all of which deal with the portrayal of journalists in novels, movies, or memoirs. He is also the author of a series of books on public education: *Educated Guess*, *The Theory of Oz*, *Inside the Board Room*, and *Mis-Education in Schools*. He cowrote *Media Ethics Goes to the Movies* with Michael Dillon and edited *Desperately Seeking Ethics: A Guide to Media Conduct*. He has published two chapbooks of poetry, *Death of the Frog Prince* and *Heartland*, and was nominated for a Pushcart Prize in poetry in 2006. He can be reached at goodh@newpaltz.edu.

Joseph C. Harry, who has a Ph.D. from Ohio State University, teaches mass media and journalism courses at Slippery Rock University of Pennsylvania. His research is in media ethics, the sociology of journalism, and critical-textual analysis of various media. Prior to his academic career, he worked for more than a decade as a reporter for daily newspapers in Florida and California.

Lee Anne Peck, who received her Ph.D. from Ohio University, is assistant professor of journalism and mass communications at the University of Northern Colorado. A former editor and writer at several publications, Peck teaches public relations, magazine writing, and media ethics, which is her research area. She can be reached at Leeanne.peck@unco.edu.

Bill Reader is an assistant professor at the E. W. Scripps School of Journalism at Ohio University, where he teaches courses in reporting, editing, and journalism ethics. He worked as a newspaper reporter, copy editor, and editorial page editor in central Pennsylvania throughout the 1990s and covered his share of critical incidents—murder-suicides, fires, train accidents, and weather emergencies.

Joe Saltzman, an award-winning broadcast journalist, is professor of journalism at the University of Southern California's Annenberg School for Communication and director of the Image of the Journalist in Popular Culture (www.ijpc.org), a project of the Norman Lear Center. He is the author of *Frank Capra and the Image of the Journalist in American Film* (2002).

S. Holly Stocking teaches media ethics in the School of Journalism at Indiana University, Bloomington. She studied journalism at Northwestern University's Medill School of Journalism and worked as a reporter for the *Los Angeles Times*, the *Minneapolis Tribune*, and the Associated Press. She earned her Ph.D. at Indiana University, Bloomington, and has coauthored or coedited four books, including *How Do Journalists Think?* with Paget Gross. She can be reached at stocking@indiana.edu.